HOW TO BUILD A
GLOBAL CITY

HOW TO BUILD A GLOBAL CITY

Recognizing the Symbolic Power of a
Global Urban Imagination

Michele Acuto

CORNELL UNIVERSITY PRESS   ITHACA AND LONDON

First published 2021 by Cornell University Press

Library of Congress Cataloging-in-Publication Data

Names: Acuto, Michele, 1984– author.
Title: How to build a global city : recognizing the symbolic power of a
    global urban imagination / Michele Acuto.
Description: Ithaca [New York] : Cornell University Press, 2021. | Includes
    bibliographical references and index.
Identifiers: LCCN 2021021957 (print) | LCCN 2021021958 (ebook) |
    ISBN 9781501759703 (hardcover) | ISBN 9781501761300 (paperback) |
    ISBN 9781501759710 (pdf) | ISBN 9781501759727 (epub)
Subjects: LCSH: Cities and towns. | Globalization—Social aspects. |
    Globalization—Political aspects. | Globalization—Singapore. |
    Globalization—Australia—Sydney (N.S.W.) | Globalization—United Arab
    Emirates—Dubai.
Classification: LCC HT119 .A28 2021 (print) | LCC HT119 (ebook) |
    DDC 307.76—dc23
LC record available at https://lccn.loc.gov/2021021957
LC ebook record available at https://lccn.loc.gov/2021021958

To Luigi Tomba
per tutti i caffè che ti devo,
Peter Hall
for a pizza I never got to return,
and Steve Rayner
for the tips over tuna sandwiches—
unique scholars, inspiring mentors, gentlemen, and, most of all, friends

Contents

INTRODUCTION

World Urban Forum: Medellin, Colombia, noon.

"So, how do you build it?" My interlocutor, at the time of the interview, is a well-known mayor of an equally well-known city. He is quite honestly and not too sarcastically asking me about the "recipe" for "building a *global city*." Of course, he has his own practice-based opinions and I have my scholarly skepticisms. Can we really determine which "ingredients" make an urban settlement "global" by some measure? Can we combine them according to some written or spoken advice as if they were a ready-made recipe? Can they be put on a "menu" of sorts for city leaders the world over to choose from according to context? Such an attempt would be neither the first nor the last. The answer to "how to build a global city" might make it into a newspaper article, a well-paid speaking engagement at a major international forum, and gather a few retweets on social media. It might even get a book deal like this one, strategically placed on a corner shelf of an airport bookstore, for the jet-setting business-class entrepreneur to summarily skim through on a hop between Hong Kong and Toronto. My interlocutor and I speculate about this over a cold drink at a mass gathering of "urbanists" of all sorts who have flocked to the Colombian city from all corners of the globe. "Powerful stuff," admits my interlocutor. I could have dismissed the query (or perhaps rhetorical question) by my interviewee, but I sensed the question held much truth in its intent—at least for those in a position to shape the direction of urban development in countries around the world. The power of that "stuff" is what drove me to write not a recipe book but an account of the ingredients and the chefs that attempt to make cities "global"—a global urban elite, so to speak.

The *global city* is not a new subject in academia. In fact, some early peer reviewers of material for this book amply questioned the need for yet another lengthy tome about a possibly tired concept such as that of the global city more than three decades after it was widely popularized by the homonymous book by Dutch-American political economist Saskia Sassen. While one could even contend the modern scholarship about global cities has nearly a century's worth of lineage, we could also argue that the role of cities as turnstiles of global connections goes deep into the history of civilization. Some of the notions that I will discuss—and go in search of in three cities—have in fact accompanied humanity for as long as we have built stable marketplaces surrounded by dwellings and allowed them to link with each other in the exchange of goods, people, and ideas. Some have even argued that it is in fact dangerous to continue portraying a concept that has contributed to ever-greater inequality in an unevenly urbanizing world prey to capitalist ebbs and flows. So why should we continue to seek more knowledge about an old subject? The idea of the global city seems anything but tired, even when confronted by a sudden halt in global flows as at the outset of 2020 or indeed the deep economic recessions throughout the past century. In a moment of crisis, and in the wake of continuing deep inequality, understanding the way we build cities to be globally intertwined might matter fundamentally as much as for those that do so as for those that seek to redress their inequalities. The goal of this book, then, is to point out the complexity of the ideas (plural not singular) that underpin the continued success of the global city and of those who put them into practice. These are powerful ideas, often wielded by powerful people, and thus I would contend they still merit a discussion of how their power works. In the tradition of political science, as Rod Rhodes put it, we might still need to get "up close and personal" with the global urban elite and its global urban imagination.

In particular, I went in search of the ways in which twenty concepts underpinning the way we speak of and imagine the global city in academia are used and connected in the urban development of three places with distinct global aspirations. These are the stories of Singapore in Southeast Asia, Sydney in Australia, and Dubai in the United Arab Emirates (UAE). In recounting these stories I aim not to dismiss the importance of dwelling and the lived experiences of those that inhabit each city, often with little voice and capacity to shape its form. Rather, it is explicitly with an eye toward the impact of ideas on the lives of these "cityzens" that I unpack the (symbolic) power and politics of the global city and the elites that underpin it. The result is a somewhat systematic collection, with some degree of correlation analysis, of 170 semistructured interviews conducted between 2009 and 2018 and also a large number of ethnographic vignettes, document and policy analysis, as well as accounts of some events which have shaped the global orientation of these three places in the last half century.

This is not a work of just structured conversations but also of quiet observation, opportunist querying, and lots of note taking on ideas about the globalization of urban governance that I have scribbled on the side of my own participation in the "symbolic system" of global urbanism. Sydney, Singapore, and Dubai are by all means not apolitical places. From the strongly articulated political feelings that I encountered in the Australian metropolis, to the art of reading in between the lines in the Southeast Asian "Lion City," to the carefulness of critique and quick glances over one's shoulders that characterize these conversations in the Emirate, the debates and contrasts about how and why these cities should globalize are not always free from retaliation, stigmas, and professional implications. Some level of discretion is advisable. Because of these and other practical fieldwork necessities, behind the glossy data and the charts that pepper this book are scribbled pages in a notebook, not neat field reports or a library of tape recordings. This approach leaves much to the author's own interpretation and near on-the-spot filing (as each interview was then directly coded anonymously in a spreadsheet right after most conversations), which requires much contextual knowledge but is also subject to my own inevitable biases as a scholar and practitioner of urban governance. For this I assume all of the blame and ask for a degree of trust from the reader. Throughout the book, data are represented by narratives or are visualized either through graphs or infographics for the sake of readability and accessibility of the discussion to a wider-than-academic public, with perhaps some apologies for the more methodologically minded readers, and of course offer an open solicitation for more technical engagement beyond the confines of the book.

To be clear, the goal here is not to test how much impact academic-speak about the global city has in practice. Nor is it about tallying the most popular ideas, finding the most well-known scholars, or drawing a strict line between the urban researcher as thinker and the urban practitioner as doer. Practically, in fact, I account for many scholars as part of that very global urban elite in some ways at least. Rather, the main aim of this book is very much one of capturing the complexity of what it means to be (and become) "global" for a city beyond a trope, that of *the* "global city," and into its subtleties, toward a more refined understanding of the (global) urban imagination that drives the development of places like Singapore, Sydney, and Dubai. I take a selection of the key ideas supporting global city research and juxtapose them in a disaggregated way against the ways key elites are shaping urban development, from planners and architects to government officers and corporate managers or, indeed, local academics, to guide the investigation of the way we speak of and imagine global cities. The aim of this approach is to encourage a greater appreciation for what unites practice and theory and academic tradition, and to encourage the circulation of ideas as to the globalization of urban settlements, as I advocate for a progressive and yet engaged agenda for global city thinking. In that, this is a book of conversations and about conversations, sprinkled with snapshots of viewpoints about the urban development, and indeed the global urban imagination, of a trio of cities few would dispute are now relatively global presences onto the world atlas.

My inquiry started with curiosity as to the ways elites speak of global cities, as my influential interlocutor did, and their alignment (or not) with the scholarship behind this concept. It eventually evolved, as several chapters of the book seek to illustrate, into an inquiry into the imagination that stands behind this global city-speak and diverse urban aspirations that bolster it. Imagination, the (symbolic) power to cast and recast its orientation, and the future (of cities as well as of globalization) are key themes of the book. They emerge jointly, in my view, as that field of the possible where a more progressive and cosmopolitan way of thinking about the "global" in the "global city" can be found, fought, and socialized not just by rejecting the elites altogether but by taking a proactive stance in driving their focus by speaking a common language and promoting a different kind of urban aspirations. This is, I am sure, likely a minority view of action research and scholarly activism. Yet it is also, as I stress across the book, no critique or dismissal of the power of other forms of activism. Rather, perhaps owing to my bias toward diplomacy and negotiation as forms of interventions into politics, my proposal for a cosmopolitan, progressive, and engaged scholarship of the global city should be read as but a viable alternative to these at the very least.

Undoubtedly, the events of 2020 and the global health crisis that ground to a halt many of the globalizing connections spotlighted in this book pose a fundamental question as to whether the "recipes" I discussed in Singapore, Sydney, and Dubai could really work in the long run. Dubai's viability as a global hub is yet again into question, while Sydney and Singapore confront hard locked-down economic downturns and deep questions about their dependence on global circuits of capital. This work, fortunately or unfortunately, was completed between the last few months of 2019 and the very outset of the crisis. To that extent, I chose neither to alter the heart of the study, the subject of the vignettes and experiences narrated here, nor to hazard far-fetched predictions on the future of cities as we know it in a now so often invoked "post-COVID world." I hope this exercise in understanding global city-speak and imagination, and in accounting for the symbolic power of an idea that charted much of the trajectory of urban development in the twentieth and early twenty-first centuries, will serve as both a lesson as to how we got here and a more nuanced guide for where we might go next. In that spirit, I invite you to jump in with feet on the ground in Singapore, on an evening in the early 2000s.

SPEAKING OF GLOBAL CITIES

World Cities Summit: Singapore, 6:00 p.m.

Every other year since 2010, the World Cities Summit has taken place in Singapore's iconic Marina Bay Le Sands, where an international plethora of urban development dignitaries gather to celebrate and share ideas about the prosperity of cities. Awarding a "world city prize" in the name of Singapore's founder, Lee Kuan Yew, the event embodies a now well-established way of looking at a fast-urbanizing planet via the lens of "world" or "global" cities: places that are highly connected across national boundaries, turnstiles of global logistics, and home to cosmopolitan societies. The summit is an apt chance to meet these cities in person. This year the awardee is the Colombian city of Medellin, represented by characteristic shots of its overbuilt hilly *barrios* and the Metrocable gondola lift system towering above the city's suburbs. The Colombian metropolis is joined at the summit by a number of honorable mentions including Toronto and Sydney, recognized as "facilitat[ing] the sharing of best practices in urban solutions that are easily replicable across cities."[1] These are widely recognized as "global" cities: focal points of globalization in an age where our planet is increasingly urbanized.

Of course, having researched the term "global city" and its characteristics for quite some time in my career, I remain healthily skeptical of what this global city-speak conveys. Yet I am also captured by the grip this idea has had on the built environment profession at large over the past few decades.[2] Perhaps most famously depicted in British geographer Sir Peter Hall's *The World Cities* (1966) and in Saskia Sassen's *The Global City* (1991), it is in a way scholarly jargon that has gone mainstream—or at least it is a clear bridge between the dusty pages of academic volumes and the shiny leaflets of elite urbanist gatherings. In chatting with some of the summit participants, I am assured this is not just branding. "We take these urban theories very seriously," one of three Singaporean ministers present at the ceremony tells me during the event's reception. There is a complex relation between the way the academe conceives of these concepts and the shape they take in the words, deeds, and aspirations of those who build these very cities. "University-speak may be quite incomprehensible, but the ideas of global city making, of a global form of urban practice . . . , well those are there to be seen all over the world," continues an Australian development specialist contracted to the City of Sydney who is enjoying a glass of wine with us. What we are talking about here is the sense that the global city, as an idea, conveys more than a simple slogan. Embedded in it are numerous assumptions about the way cities ought to be and, in fact, *are* built in the twenty-first century. This is, in short, a "global urban" imagination.[3]

A few minutes later, I am in a quiet corner of the hotel, scribbling some of these thoughts in my small field notepad, only to notice a colleague nearby who is intent on the same act and subtly giving away her academic identity, as only scholars do when they see each other in the field. Later identifying herself as a fellow doctoral researcher hailing from an Ivy League institution, she introduces herself and admits to overhearing part of my earlier conversation. In an act of academic comradery, she dismissingly whispers to me, "Oh these people." The summit, like many other now-well-established events in what is perhaps a regular conference-based marketplace of global city ideas, is ripe with citable quotes and signifiers for an urban researcher trying to make sense of cities in a time when the lives of urban dwellers all over the planet are not just interconnected by globalization but often decided by elites. It is a prime representation of the political economy of a powerful idea such as that of the global city and its grip on the way major contemporary hubs of globalization like Singapore are being developed and governed.

Except that the global city is not just an idea. Perhaps more correctly it is a field of urban imagination that gazes globally rather than locally. In a sense, as Donald McNeill fittingly put it, it is a more of a "genre writing" represented by the likes of Hall, Sassen, and many others, and one that can demonstrate more than a century of scholarly lineage.[4] To many in urban studies (across planning, geography, and architecture, for instance), it is directly associated with the social and spatial reconfiguring of internationally connected places, and of course their inequalities. It evokes a sense not just of turnstiles of the world's economy, as Hall put it in his 1966 book, but also of the socioeconomic implication of globalization on cities, with its polarization between the haves and the have-nots—the crux of Sassen's 1991 *The Global City*. From this point of view, the global city is a portmanteau that blends into an easily graspable signifier, a multiplicity of meanings and concepts about the logics and implications of globalization on places around the world. It is a shorthand for a complex global urban imagination that spurs not only a global sense of place but also its underlying debates about the desirability and complication of cities becoming globalized. This is not just theory or popular writing: its implications and, I wonder in Singapore, teachings are continually translated in the tangible practices that politicians, developers, planners, and many others perform to quite literally build the urban hubs of our planet. If we take this beyond the often-inscrutable parlance of the academe, the global city might in a larger sense stand as one of the most successful urbanist genre writings of our recent times. It is an umbrella concept for a body of meaning transformed and transferred by the political economy of global urbanism, which becomes tangible buildings and everyday habits for millions of people living in these cities. In this sense, the global imagination of the global city is very practically intertwined with life on its streets.

Of course, from a more critical scholarly viewpoint, one could easily shrug off the value of this event in particular, and of the whole circuit of global city-speak in general, as many have repeatedly done for at least the past two decades. Yet the facts at hand might eventually force us to engage with this business and its elites if we want to bridge beyond the walls of research and academic debate. This does not necessarily mean buying into those elites. Rather, it is about understanding the imagination and aspirations that underpin their operation so that we may better advocate for progressive reforms.

The imprint of global urbanism has a distinct infrastructural presence across continents and a sizable reality in global markets. Millions of people traverse continents to and from these cities, trillions of dollars are rerouted via their financial and logistic hubs, and their presence plays a central role in how we imagine places far across the globe. "We build global cities," my above-mentioned Singaporean interlocutor tells me at the summit, "so how could you possibly do away with the concept? Just look outside!" In this sense, the words of my developer friend are not too different from something that Peter Hall himself told me at the beginning of my research journey. While I was sitting among the piles of books and scribbled manuscripts in his Ealing studio in 2009, he stressed: "the point is to take this thing of the world city seriously," because one cannot ignore its existence in that, he reminded me, it is "made of money, bricks, and aspirations." I henceforth ventured in those three directions on the world cities map, to get a grasp on the political economy of global city-speaking more specifically, and in search of the money, bricks, and aspirations embedded in the politics of global urbanism more generally. The Singaporean episode that I recount above, as well as many others I report in the pages of the book, is perhaps not statistically significant or universally binding in its theoretical implications. What it represents quite fittingly, however, is a set of three interconnected features of this global urban imagination I aim to illustrate here.

First, that we should not ditch the global city altogether but rather take it as less of a monolithic concept and more of a stand in for a body of meaning of global urban thinking (and research)—a shorthand, as I have defined it above, for that field of urban imagination that gazes globally from a specific place. Albeit contested in scholarly debates, as I note below, this idea holds a powerful status in urban practice and offers a unique gateway into the powers that are shaping the so-called "urban age," whose aspirations shape much of the urban development the world over.[5] In times like these, it becomes paramount, for both the academic and the practitioner involved in shaping globally connected urban centers, to better understand how the global city presents us with a "tactical battleground," as McNeill pointed out in his work on Paris, Sydney, San Francisco, and many other global hubs, where the politics of urbanization take place.[6] Second, that when speaking of global urban practices, whether to advance or criticize them, we must understand this idiom as part of a broader political economy of global urbanism constituted by a system of ideas, gateways, and experts that shape the way our built environment is made the world over. Conversely, and third, that both the scholars that theorize these ideas and the practitioners that use them need to confront the responsibility implied in these ideas: there is an inherent politics of imagining global cities (as concepts and as real lived places) where the translation between research and practice, text and everyday life, author and object, needs much closer attention.

As I argue, the global city and those who are complicit in the construction of global urban imaginations can wield substantial power over the trajectory of urban development. The global city exists objectively, embodied in the globally oriented and internationally influenced infrastructure of these cities, as well as subjectively, in the gestures, habits, and ways of thinking of both urban practitioners and urban dwellers. In this sense, the power of the idea(s) of the global city in modern times is, as I illustrate by borrowing from French political sociologist Pierre Bourdieu's work, a "symbolic" form of power. It wields the capacity to control the social production of distinction, connecting and dividing our imagination of a globalized world and shaping our understanding of the nature of cities. I do so by building on the work of two British urban geographers, Donald McNeill and Tim Bunnell, who, respectively, have been calling for greater attention to the practice of global urbanism and to the importance of urban imaginations and aspirations in shaping the lives of billions of city dwellers the world over.

Global Successes and
Scholarly Backlashes

In November 2013, after a period of relative anonymity, Dubai captured the front pages of major newspapers after it was chosen by the Bureau of International Expositions to host the 2020 Expo. "We renew our promise to astonish the world," pledged Dubai's ruler Sheikh Mohammed bin Rashid al Maktoum.[7] Commentators discussed whether Dubai might be "back" on the global scene and ready to "wow the world" once again through its futuristic urbanist plans to host the event under the "biggest souk in history."[8] The announcement—and the grandiose plans for a 438-hectare *souk* (market) structure joining Dubai, its key regional port of Jebel Ali, the new Al Maktoum International Airport, and neighboring Abu Dhabi—sparked renewed interest in the global "return" of Dubai after the crisis of the past years. Until then, anyone who had listened to the predominant narrative on the subject could have easily assumed that Dubai had sunk into the sands of the Emirates like a modern-day Atlantis, crumbled into its ambitious project and vexed by the never-ending aftershocks of the 2008 global financial crisis.[9]

At the same time, Sydney was making headlines as it reasserted its primacy among global city success stories. For a decade now, the Australian city had consistently been in the spotlight of the global media, which regularly report it at the top of a variety of livability, quality of life, and cultural rankings. In November 2013, Sydney was once again named as one of the best city "brands," where it ranked behind only London on a proclaimed "best city" pedestal, while also making its traditional appearance at the top of widely read annual lists like those of the *Economist* Intelligence Unit, *Monocle*, Conde Nast, and the *Financial Times*. Despite the Australian metropolis's troubles, from coping with the Global Financial Crisis (GFC) to soaring housing prices to challenging social polarization, Sydney seemed to have emerged as a successful and desirable paradigm of the contemporary global city. Even the serious riots of December 2005 in the suburb of Cronulla and the blazing bush fires that threatened its vast suburbs in the very same weeks of shining media successes in November 2013 seemed to have been quickly forgotten as Sydney stood in the global imaginaries as a livable and hospitable "Harbor City."

Parallels to the Singapore story echoed repeatedly in the halls of the World City Summit are blatant here. Growing evidence testifies that a new generation of cities are seen as rising to global renown. Yet scholars, perhaps more than most public commentaries, have yet to accept the seductions of this global city rhetoric. On the one hand, crushed under its entrepreneurial ambitions, the apparent demise of Dubai after the 2008 GFC was for many a memento of the volatility of the global city aspirations of planners and scholars alike.[10] On the other hand, the often unquestioned global success of Sydney and Singapore seems to many a risky smoke screen in front of growing polarization concerns in destinations often desirably thought of as modern and livable. Throughout the first decade of the 2000s, the hype and excitement around the global city paradigm sustained the sprawl of a globalizing rhetoric across both urban academia and practice. Many now assert this focus has engendered a problematic worldview of the global city where "categorizing, ranking and labelling cities has become so prominent and so damaging to the future prospects of cities everywhere."[11] Urban studies has witnessed in the past decade at least a pervasive emergence of a strong critique of the global city scholarship of the 1990s and early 2000s. Mostly driven by critical geographers, postcolonial studies, and Global South planners, this backlash against the commercialized popularity and categorizing imperative of the early days of the global city scholarship has made a notable dent in the credibility of the global city as a sound theoretical and practical framing. The debate, at the turn of the 2020s, still echoes in many parts of academia. For instance, some in geographical forums pointed alternatively at the unfair straw-man treatment of the global city tradition, whereas others noted it might be time to put the concept to rest and move on.[12] As Jenny Robinson noted in her plea to ditch the term and focus instead on the "ordinary" realities of cities big and small, the term might be meaningless for the study of wider processes of urbanization and might in fact be politically dangerous for scholars to reiterate a "synecdoche" that perpetuates inequality in the built environment. It plays into the hands of the rich and weakens the space for the voiceless. Rather, scholars should throw their intellectual and political energies behind alternative formulations that can support a very different type of urban politics. Global city scholars are, in short, accomplices to the socioeconomic divisions their scholarship might help uphold. These critiques have echoed regular calls for a shift in focus from the "globalist" bias of the global city to an "ordinary city" research orientation where all cities are seen as "global" or "global(izing)" to some extent, and the "global city" should be discredited as a dangerous "master category."[13] Should we then jettison the global city altogether? Or would this disenfranchise academics even further away from the elites that are driving urban development globally? Can we even distill academia from some of the (local or global) circuits of these elites when scholars themselves occupy positions of privilege and often engage in these very activities? As even anecdotal evidence from the stories above reveals, the global city certainly remains a pervasive presence in urban practice: what, then, are we to make of this scholarly crisis, in which the practical orientation in metropolises the world over seems to have been seduced and taken over by this concept? Are academic concepts in (or against) global city research too exoteric to be graspable or implementable on the ground? Or are academia and built-environment professions fundamentally at odds with each other? As I suggest here, we need to step beyond the assumption that the global city is but a brand.

More Than a Brand

The global city is perhaps one the most apt instantiation of our globalized, unequal, and often dissonant times. It connects the momentum of urbanization that has been driving more and more people to cities with the planetary connections of globalization that have been recast socioeconomic relations across the globe. If this intersection of global flows and urban processes has historically been embedded even in the rise of premodern metropolises in the East and West such as Carthage, Jerusalem, or Chang'an, the impact of modern-day globalization on cities has but added to such a complex nature and expanded its contradictions. This is made even more disorienting once we realize that today many of these globalizing processes, networks, and ideas are actually made and recast in these very cities, which become at the same time engines and subjects of the global reconfigurations defining the twenty-first century. In the eyes of many, some cities in particular appear to many to be more central than others in articulating these processes. London, Paris, New Delhi, and Hong Kong, to name just a few, are so intertwined with the global imaginary and the networks that shape international affairs that it seems almost futile to name them in addition to their countries of origin. Rather, these cities have emerged as interconnected parts of a global urban geography that has transcended national borders and local specificities. They have become, as Sassen's famed expression summed it up, "global" cities. As Sassen puts it in *The Global City*, if globalization is often characterized by abstract and ephemeral dynamics where time and space are frequently recast, resulting in contradictory effects, we can attempt to "filter" them, she says, through the specifics (e.g., culture, political structures, economic functions, history, and buildings) of those places where they are mainly articulated. And we can identify a specificity of some more prominent or "central" places, if not a hierarchy of cities. The processes they articulate are not free from power and power relations and are hierarchical in themselves in today's economic-centric globalization. I firmly believe that theoretical tenet is as true today as it was in 1991—even though we face a global urban condition that is perhaps drastically different from that of the late 1980s. Intra- and inter-urban inequality, particular articulation of flows, and agglomerating characteristics of place still ring true in the twenty-first century.

Certainly, as the Singaporean anecdote above suggests, the global city is no longer, if in fact it ever was just, a scholarly phenomenon. A global urban imagination pervades the conversations and aspirations of international and local elites the world over. It has now catalyzed mounting popular and policy engagements characterized by exponential growth in global city reports, plans, campaigns, and documentaries. Moving beyond academia in the late 1990s and setting itself as a widely employed expression in much of the mass media and local government conversations, the global city has become a central protagonist of the discussions surrounding the popularized rise of the "urban age" at a time when cities are at the center of global attention.[14] Global city-speak, and its underpinning imagination and aspirations, has progressively surfaced as an explicit growth and internationalization strategy by local authorities and city leaders. This is, of course, not limited to the three cities analyzed in this book (Dubai, Sydney, and Singapore), and parallels worldwide are easy to find beyond the obvious models of London and New York. In fact, as the ideas upholding the global city gain traction and global urbanism is practiced far and wide across built-environment professions (and more), a new generation of global hubs is fast affirming itself beyond our traditional international reference points.

It is the case, for example, of Hong Kong and its Brand Hong Kong initiative, launched in 2001 to promote the Chinese Special Administrative Region as "Asia's World City."[15] Coupled with the finance initiative Invest Hong Kong, which is aimed at attracting larger quantities of inward capital and the development of a new art and leisure district in West Kowloon, Hong Kong's approach has to date managed to position the metropolis as not solely a core hub of East Asia but a top-ranking competitor at a global level. In this case, the city government took the lead in recasting the global image of the metropolis and promoting it through a "globalizing" strategic plan and a new global city narrative for the emerging Asian center. A plethora of growing international centers like Hong Kong have been pursuing a rhetoric of globalization by invoking the global city in campaigns, strategic plans, urban renewal policies, and media statements. It is this widely accepted popularity, then, that forms much of the thrust of my inquiry in this book. On the one hand, the urban studies scholarship is now split between being well accustomed to global-speak and, in many instances, rejecting it. On the other, the global city has also progressed as a luring focus for emerging cities seeking worldwide fame, as well as for established economic, commercial, and political capitals concerned with maintaining their grip on global publics and flows. In this rise to everyday fame, some of the ideas supporting the notion of the global city change, move away from each other, and find new meaning as they are filtered through the specifics of places like Singapore, Dubai, and Sydney.

To capture these processes in this book, I mix systematic discourse analysis with ethnographic and participant observation of urban development elites in Singapore, Dubai, and Sydney. Data collection for the study involved 170 one-on-one qualitative semi-structured interviews (for roughly thirty to forty-five minutes each), conducted with these elites. Interviewees were thus selected via snowball sampling for their role in shaping, or commenting on, the urban development trajectories of the three cities. Of the total number of inter-

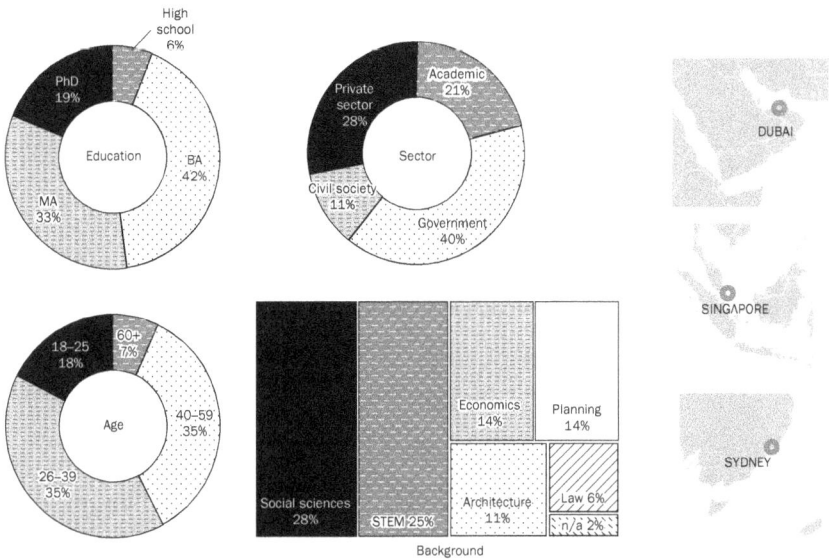

FIGURE 1. Outline of interviews (education, sector, age, and background profiles).

views, fifty-four of these conversations focused on, and were carried out in, Dubai, fifty-eight in Singapore, and fifty-eight in Sydney.

Qualitative data from the interviews were coded to identify explicit or implicit mentions of twenty core concepts that underpin the global city literature (see chapter 2) and its key contemporary debates (see chapter 3), ranging from the idea that global cities are sites of "command and control" of globalization (often attributed to Saskia Sassen) or that they perform "gateway" functions in world affairs (e.g., Peter Hall), to questions of how these cities are broken apart socioeconomically through "splintering urbanism" (e.g., Steve Graham and Simon Marvin) and how a "metrocentric" bias affects urban thinking (e.g., Tim Bunnell and Anant Maringanti). This allows me to paint a picture of what kind of "global city-speak" (as Donald McNeill put it in 2017) is at play between major urban governance stakeholders in these cities, and to discuss the politics of the global city in a more nuanced fashion than simply using it as a single concept.

The Symbolic Power of the Global City

The ways in which we build global cities today are very much intertwined with the creation of difference and distinctiveness. We aim to put a place on the map while also engaging in a market for similarity that attracts and is familiar to those

TABLE 1 The study's twenty concepts

CONCEPT	SAMPLE ACADEMIC LITERATURE	OVERALL SALIENCE	MOST CLOSELY CORRELATED CONCEPT
Rescaling of urban governance	Brenner, *New State Spaces* (2004); Keil, "Globalisation Makes States" (1998)	0.088	Cosmopolitanism*
Metrocentricity	Bunnell and Maringanti, "Practicing Urban and Regional Research" (2010)	0.088	Off the map**
Relationality between cities	Sassen, *Cities in a World Economy* (1994); Söderström, *Cities in Relations* (2014)	0.100	Off the map**
Command and control functions	Sassen, *The Global City* (1991); Taylor and Derudder, *World City Network* (2004)	0.103	Opportunity*
Network ghettoes	Marvin and Graham, *Splintering Urbanism* (2001)	0.118	Elite*
Capturing a "global" opportunity	Clark, *Global Cities* (2016); Glaeser, *Triumph of the City* (2011)	0.126	Entrepreneurship**
Cities "off the map"	Robinson, "Global and World Cities" (2002); Yeoh, "Global/Globalising Cities" (1999)	0.138	Metrocentric**
Worlding	Ong and Roy, *Worlding Cities* (2011)	0.138	Premium connections*
Hierarchy of global cities (and hierarchical relations)	McKenzie, "The Concept of Dominance" (1927); Taylor, "Hierarchical Tendencies" (1997)	0.141	Off the map*
Materiality of globalization	McNeill, "In Search of the Global Architect" (2005); Amin, "Spatialities of Globalisation" (2002)	0.147	Placing**
Urban cosmopolitanism	Sennett, "The Social Experience of Cities" (2002); Price and Benton-Short, *Migrants to the Metropolis* (2008)	0.147	Premium connections*
History embedded in urban order	Peter Hall, *Cities in Civilization* (1998); Rimmer and Dick, "The Historical Dimension" (2013)	0.159	Rescaling^

Urban innovation	Florida, *The Rise of the Creative Class* (2002);	0.162	Materiality~
Urban entrepreneurship	Harvey, "From Managerialism to Entrepreneurialism" (1989); Hall and Hubbard, "The Entrepreneurial City" (1998)	0.168	Opportunity**
Placing globalization	Sassen, *The Global City* (1991)	0.171	Materiality**
City/urban leadership	McNeill, "Barcelona as Imagined Community" (2001); Rapoport et al., *Leading Cities* (2019)	0.176	Off the map**
Polarized or "dual city"	Mollekopf and Castells, *Dual City* (1989) Massey, *World City* (2007)	0.180	Worlding*
Premium connections	Marvin and Graham, *Splintering Urbanism* (2001)	0.250	Materiality*
Gateway functions	Peter Hall, *The World Cities* (1966); John Friedmann, *World City Hypothesis* (1982)	0.250	Relationality*
Urban/transnational elites	Beaverstock, "Transnational Elites in Global Cities" (2001); Sklair, "The Transnational Capitalist Class" (2005)	0.265	Off the map*

^Weak correlation
*Moderate correlation
**Strong correlation
~Negative correlation

we want to draw to our cities. Cities coexist, as Jenny Robinson reminds us, "in a world of cities."[16] They seek to be a bit like each other while also being a bit different. In this business, logics of group-making, as cities compare themselves with selected others, are commonplace. Likewise, a rich cadre of what we could tag as "symbolic entrepreneurs," who drive people's perceptions by presenting diversity and similarity across this world of cities, is thriving in an increasingly professionalized work of global urbanism. From consultants to major built-environment firms, and from academics to public commentators, these all play a part in shaping the politics and power of the global city, both generally as a concept and more specifically as situated places. This is the highly power-laden and quintessentially global world of the political economy of the global city.

These dynamics are well captured in the notion of "symbolic power": the power of distinction. According to Bourdieu, who originally described it in the social theory of the 1970s and 1980s, symbolic power is a form of influence that does not take hold in isolation from other powers—be they economic, social, or cultural.[17] Rather, symbolic power represents the capacity to control the social production of distinction by relying on and deploying other forms of power, such as money, cultural and religious constructs, or social class. The influence of symbolism rests on one's capacity of "constituting the given by stating it."[18] Symbolic power allows people and institutions to "structure" the "reality" around those who are subject to it.[19] It is a practice of mediating social experiences and imposing socially accepted meanings, which in turn affect the actions of others. This form of influence can be exercised only with the complicity of those who are subject to it.[20] Appreciating the ways in which symbolic power operates requires understanding the processes and dynamics that underpin the social world's "symbolic systems,"[21] the intertwined dispositions of symbols (such as languages, images, and built spaces) that form the subtext of human interaction. Symbols and symbolic systems allow for differences in similarity, and consequently for the coexistence and continual creation of individual as well as group identities. Mastering symbolic power in this sense means "pursuing distinction" and voluntarily producing separations and social worlds that affect others' identities and freedom for action. Symbolic power is thus exerted by socializing others into a certain representation of the environment we live in, therefore getting them to act accordingly.[22] Typically, it is exerted by either communicative or physical means, though hybrid forms abound in the digital age. For example, a group sitting in a lecture hall can be "coerced" into exiting the room through its windows if the speaker's rhetoric is so compelling that it convinces the audience that this is the only way out. However, our cold-blooded orator can achieve a similar result through more material means such as a set of "exit" signs on the windows, or even by erecting a wall in front of the room's only door. Distinction is so produced thanks to the speaker's symbolic "capital," a potential constituted by mediating other forms of power such as the speaker's oratory and social status in the first instance, or economic and material capabilities in the second example. From this point of view, I unveil the symbolic power of the notions that support the idea of the global city, and more generally of today's global urban imagination, as well as the politics (as in power relations) that those people and institutions that use these ideas are embedded in.

Why do these aspiring global cities need to emphasize diversity and uniqueness in addition to those functions that traditionally portray them as global? Why look for specificity beyond those more common command and control features that, the literature tells us, are core in defining global cities? The reasoning is twofold. First, these cities have sought to differentiate themselves from their national rivals by achieving primacy at the national level. Second, they have repeatedly claimed their uniqueness on a worldwide stage. Take Sydney, for instance. At the domestic level, the Harbor City represents itself as "Australia's iconic face to the world, its international visitor flag-bearer."[23] However, this flagship role is coupled with frequent rhetoric on the particularity of the Harbor City in the crowded ranks of global city pretenders. As the popular slogan for the See Sydney campaign that flourished in 2009 summarized it: "There's no place in the world like Sydney." The global city is seen to be unique, yet it exists in a commonly globalized urban world. The world and the city are imagined, and spoken of, in a common-but-different way of casting the "global." The campaign, much like several others since at least the 2000 Olympics, was built on recognizable images of iconic buildings like the Opera House or Sydney Harbor, stunning shots of the coastal richness of Sydney's beaches, and dynamic representations of a vibrant, cultural, tourist-friendly city. This representation is not unique to the Australian city, of course: much of Dubai's public relations, let alone those of Singapore, have been built on a mix of those unique-but-global features described thus far. Yet these representations, and the ways elites cast and recast cities, beg not just for criticism of their often-predictable global urban imagination, but also for a more refined way to understand how this imagination operates, even how scholars and researchers are embedded in it. Nuance in the "global urban-speak" and the imagination underpinning the global city is what follows in the next chapters. I map the global city ingredients my affluent and powerful interlocutor had asked me about in Medellin in 2014, as dictionary of global city-speak, or maybe as inventory of the things that make up the global city. Upon this we might construct a more effective way to drive the global urban attention at least partly away from competition and success and a little more toward the needs of urban dwellers and more progressive urban futures.

THE IDEA(S)

Art Gallery NSW: Sydney, 8:00 p.m.

We are at the Art Gallery of New South Wales (NSW) for the exclusive MySydney soiree hosted by the Committee for Sydney, a group of the city's major corporate interests that seeks to address the internationalization of the Harbor City from a "whole of Sydney" perspective. The attraction of the evening is Westfield Corporation property development group CEO Steven Lowy and media tycoon James Packer, both sons of the Harbor City and members of families that have already made a substantial imprint on the urbanization of Sydney. Here, Lowy and Packer have just unveiled their vision for a 275-meter-high Crown Resort hotel with 350 rooms and 60 super-luxury apartments facing Sydney Harbor, to complement what is soon to become the centerpiece of the city's long-awaited and much-troubled Barangaroo development. The height of the building is noteworthy: 275 meters, argue the developers, is essential to make the Crown Resort the kind of global landmark that Sydney needs. Amid cutting-edge features and self-professed iconic skylines, echoes of Dubai begin to pervade the room. Reminded of his travels through the Emirates, Mark, a former academic colleague now transplanted into the planning office of a major city council neighboring Sydney, shrugs his shoulders and cynically asks me, "Seen this before?" Discourse, form, and aspiration of this self-professed global city urbanism leave little doubt that his question is rhetorical. Mark has effectively sneaked me into the event to undertake some covert fieldwork among some of Sydney's "global urban elite," and the soiree is living up to its quote-worthy potential. Packer and

Lowy, as the local *Daily Telegraph* would report the following day, continue by pointing out that this is "how you put Sydney on the map" and make it a "truly global city."[1] The resort is a fundamental centerpiece, one of Packer and Lowy's accolades tells us, to reconfirm Sydney's positioning on the atlas of global flows, making sure the Harbor City does not "fall off the map." Mark and I, by virtue of a common scholarly upbringing, are perhaps the only ones to catch the unintended reference to what has now become one of the canons of the critique of the global city—namely, Jennifer Robinson's much-cited 2002 article "Global and World Cities: A View from off the Map." As Robinson points out, rhetoric and commercialization of the global city ideal have had the perverse effect of constructing a map of global centers of command and control where little space is left for "ordinary" cities, postcolonial sensibilities, and cosmopolitan views of urbanism beyond the Londons and New Yorks of the world. Australian developers have, as the soiree testifies, long been working to prevent Sydney from falling off this imaginary map.

In the meantime, the unveiling continues: the resort is not the only global attraction. The hosts and promotional material explain at length how the development will help create a "breath-taking" and "world-class" but still public walkway from the harbor-side areas of Potts Point and Woolloomooloo, east of Sydney's Central Business District, all the way through to Barangaroo and Darling Harbor on the west side of the city. Livability, the trademark of the Harbor City, has to be represented front and center in the new landmark, and it is a livability of, as the hosts point out, "premium connections" offering easy access to the cultural, retail, and financial heart of the Australian city, linking global networks, tourist pathways, and elite business and world-class natural amenities. Once again, Mark and I agree we are likely the only ones in the room who suspect an unintended referral to Simon Marvin and Stephen Graham's 2001 *Splintering Urbanism*, a critical text in the development of our academic understanding of the inequality pervading the built environment of the global city. As Marvin and Graham persuasively (at least for scholars) demonstrate, the texture of the global city is often, if not increasingly, characterized by a separation of networked infrastructures, polarizing and separating experiences, and lives and trajectories on the basis of premium access and privileged costs.

Yet, as the evening moves from presentations to networking over cocktails, our cynical academic selves are thrown back into the reality of the global city. Experts, developers, and local authorities continually point at the financial and political quarrels that underpin the development and characterize contemporary Sydney. Our interlocutors repeatedly recast the city as a terrain of global challenges, local problems, and, critically, very complex politics that shape the development of "global Sydney." One developer reminds us of the "wars" over the long-abandoned site of Barangaroo. Another architect remarks how all the beautiful sights of the promised walkway leave unanswered the critical challenge of Sydney: mobility, at least in his view. A couple of media commentators even quip how the "charade" of new developments is really leaving behind the socioeconomic "drama" of the polarized Western suburbs. Indisputably, the *politics* of the global city pervades much of the room. And politics continues to dominate the scene as the billionaire hosts make their rounds among industry personalities and millionaire friends. I'm trying to look inconspicuous, standing pressed in a corner next to iced buckets of Brut bottles. Someone from the giant property group Lendlease assures me in a heavy Scottish accent that this is the "new champagne." He does not know of my Italian wine county origins or likely not much about wine either as he vigorously swirls his bubbly wine in pretend connoisseur fashion to boast his fine-wine, elite credentials. Urban elite status is often more about performance than just actual knowledge.

Packer, meanwhile, is gesticulating wildly in his address to the group I am awkwardly standing with. He offers yet another book-worthy citation on topic (which I frantically scribble down later when leaving the event) by plagiarizing more or less intentionally from Raymond Carver's classic quote about love. "You need to get what we talk about when we talk about global cities," he says to an unidentified glamorous woman who challenges him on the actual "global" nature of the Crown Resort. Mark and I are confronted with the realization that, while perhaps not knowing urban theory centerpieces like Robinson or Graham and Marvin, the (elite) crowd of the soiree is not ignorant about the dynamics of global city making. Mark has squarely made his point, and likely changed my research plans. After all, these are the city makers. Even in the very midst of an environment much removed from academic conventions and peer-reviewed journals, we encounter the global city not just in its rhetorical reiteration but also in its very real power politics, social exclusions, and economic troubles. At a glance, far away from the often-removed debates of urban studies, the soiree reminds us that what academics can contribute is neither just technical expertise nor a presumptuous assertion of being the principal custodians of the right kind of knowledge about cities. Rather, the global city scholar can, as some of the core texts above have done, offer a reflection that is systematic, normative, and well informed and goes beyond "cocktail talk" about global cities, but at the same time is humble enough to admit that much of the expertise about global city making is overall a quite applied affair we can participate in, not dominate, for the sake of reminding practitioners of the challenges, limitations, and dangers of global urbanism. Quite evidently, we can still regularly encounter the global city in the field, whether in the words of planners and dwellers, in the plans of local authorities, or even just on billboards along our sidewalks. The pages of what is, then, an academic book should be dedicated not only to critique but also, more importantly, to reflection on the dynamics and challenges of the practice "out there" beyond the front and back covers.

Paying closer attention to the politics of building global cities, I argue that in the cases of Singapore, Dubai, and Sydney, this does not mean discarding "global city" as a vague and inconsistent buzzword, as critiques of this phenomenon might suggest. It is important to spur the discussions like those of the MySydney soiree toward considering systematically the politics of building global cities, the responsibilities of those who partake in them, and the often-absent voices of those who will, after all, live their ordinary lives within the confines that global city makers are setting today. Global city-speak remains central in urban development and holds much symbolic power that we are perhaps quick to dismiss. But what is in an idea? There is a century of discussion and debate surrounding the ingredients of the causes and consequences of globalization in cities.

Studying the Global City

Despite its fashionable place in magazines and news outlets, the idea of the global city is anything but a new phenomenon, and its imagination runs deep into the history of the twentieth century at the very least. Rather, global cities are a well-established theoretical presence in the urban studies literature. As we have seen, this is a genre of predominantly scholarly writing that is well established and generally recognizable across geography, planning, sociology, and several other fields of study. In addition to its presence in academia, however, the idea has become increasingly pervasive in the general public and in practitioner-speak, to a degree that perhaps makes it the preeminent phrase in urbanism and places it above many popular comparable ideas, like that of the "smart" city or "livable" cities. While the early part of the 1900s was peppered with mentions of the "world city," the idea of this city rose steadily in popularity in the early 1960s, with Peter Hall's *The World Cities* (1966) as centerpiece of that ascent, and after a small decline in the early 1980s, rose again rapidly (with John Friedmann's "world city hypothesis" in 1986 as the poster child of this success) until today, demonstrating a growing presence in urban studies and the general "urban" discourse in academia and beyond. The "global city," on the other hand, had a moderate presence from the mid-1960s and then more markedly in the early 1980s as Saskia Sassen refined and then popularized it in *The Global City* (1991). Here, the success of this idea was vertiginous, and in the late 1990s it fast surpassed its twin—the "world city"—achieving a substantial international presence and still holding clout in the global urbanist discourse today, well above concepts like the "smart city" or the "resilient city."

The global city's original role as "analytical device," first brought to worldwide attention by Sassen's homonymous research in the 1990s and Peter Hall's study of world cities in the 1970s, has evolved in a complex and often tacit relation with the work of other urban, economic, and social studies scholars that deals with the globalization of cities. Recognizing this role is important in understanding the depth of the global city idea as a rich tradition of research that speaks to an eclectic pool of authors. This could be metaphorically grouped within what John Friedmann, one of the founding authors of this strand of thinking, described as an "invisible college of world city researchers": an academic congregation that has been constantly expanding from a small analytical hypothesis to a fully fledged research paradigm dominating many of the urban studies discourses at the turn of the century.[2] If the college has a "resident" faculty that explicitly engages in what we might call global city research, many are the visiting scholars and external associates who contribute to it, rendering this narrative one of the most long-lived among the social sciences—a "genre" of writing and thinking that sees cities as embedded in, but at the same time driving, globalization.

The Idea of a World City

We could trace the legacy of the global city to its first direct appearances, as with Saskia Sassen in the 1990s and David Heenan (the first scholar conventionally said to have used the term) in the 1970s, but the roots of this idea go way back to the start of the twentieth century. One for instance could start with the so-called Chicago School at the beginning of the 1900s and its important recognition of the city as a social space that transcends a simply "aggregate" understanding of urban relations.[3] Via the city social interactions are not solely summed up, but also changed and recast in dialogue with a wider society than those who live in that specific place. The global city, in this light, becomes a socially transformative site in the geography of human affairs. Yet the term is not a novel one in either urban planning or policy practice. In the Anglophone world, for instance, we can note the case of the city of Liverpool as early as 1886 aiming to globalize its profile by banking on an *Illustrated London News* article defining it as a wondrous "world city" alongside London. Of course, we could make an analogous argument for understandings of this notion that are as old as classical European depictions of Rome as *caput mundi* (capital of the world), as the Roman empire extended across continents, and of many other ancient, classical, and premodern settlements networked across borders, like Athens, Xian, or Tikal. Similarly, colonial empires, such as those of the British, French, and Spanish, could be considered precursors of present-day global cities.

The global city-speak of today, then, echoes some of the ideas of world cities developed in the first decades of the twentieth century. Walter Christaller, for instance, identified "central places" in his dissertation on the South German system of cities and its hierarchical alignment, published (and perhaps problematically applied) during the expansion of the German Reich.[4] Christaller focused his attention on cities as drivers of the demand/supply chains sustaining the economy, thus describing the emergence of localized systems of centers of various sizes organized around functional hierarchies. This theme also figured in Patrick Geddes's introduction to British town planning titled *Cities in Evolution*—a study that became crucial to the genesis of "world" city research a few years later.[5] The attention Geddes and Christaller paid to the diverse geographical, if not geopolitical, centrality of some cities was a theme capable of sowing productive seeds for today's global city genre of writing and speaking. Key here is also the idea that cities occupy different places in the flows that connect them, some more centrally linked to movements of goods and people than others. These are features of "differential centrality" and "hierarchical unevenness," which are now well understood tenets of global city theorizing. In research terms, this centrality was then further unpacked by Peter Hall's specification of Geddes's work: not all cities are the same, and some cities have tighter ties with (and stronger influence on) the rest of the globe. These strategic places might represent in the eyes of many the echelon of cities—the strategic sites of globalization. The seeds of this thinking have now blossomed in the growing popularity of global urban thinking we will encounter repeatedly throughout the pages of this book. Yet the global geography of cities is not still and immutable. As Roderick McKenzie intuitively described as early as 1927 in his study of a "global network" of cities, the "world's centers of gravity are always in process of change" owing to shifting service bases and underlying global conditions.[6] The global city is then an inherently transitory phenomenon, a status of connectedness to the global that is attained by world cities and rests the positioning of these metropolises as strategic to, but also precariously placed in, globalization. Peter Hall was once again central, in the 1960s and 1970s, to the development of an even closer attention to the importance of cities in civilization, as one of his most famous works was titled, stressing the necessity to see cities in relation to their, and the wider global, histories and the historical trajectories that brought them to where they are. Fundamentally, Hall also noted the worldly character of these cities is determined by what cities do in the distribution of goods, people, and activities on the planet. Borrowing Geddes's terminology, Hall spoke of the centrality of "world cities" as gateways for global and regional flows and sources of specialized services for a wider public, beyond their own local constituencies, a theme that grew strong in the literature on cities and globalization. This role is ascribed by cities, Hall noted, owing to their "functions" as ports to the world.

One must understand "gateway functions," in Hall's sense of what a "world" city does, in order to understand that these cities are sites where a disproportionate part of the world's business is not only conducted but more precisely "gathered and disseminated." Hall noted how these central nodes of manifold planetary networks come to occupy a privileged ("strategic" as Sassen would put it later in the 1990s) position in the unfolding of daily relations across the globe. As I have argued elsewhere, in an epoch dominated by capitalism and growing interconnectedness, the global city becomes more generally a strategic hinge of globalization networks. This function includes roles as centers of political power, gateways for trade and commerce (with seaports, airports, railways, commercial routes, etc.), gathering and dissemination focal points for information and culture (with major academic institutions, museums, internet servers and providers, mass media with global reach, etc.), primary sites of religious organizations, and hubs for global mobility and/or tourism. Although top-tier performances in these criteria are presently regarded as key indicators of global city status, their relevance and order, like the urban hierarchies they support, are in constant flux—as McKenzie had already noted in 1927.

As a direct consequence of the gateway functions line of thinking, it is possible to identify an order of urban settlements within such a system, since world cities carry out different functions and have different degrees of relations, thus aligning in a world "urban hierarchy" that, because of its mobile basis, is in constant flux. Functions as defined by Hall should not be considered as a definitive checklist for global city status, nor should their relative importance be treated as spatially and historically fixed. Yet a key point to be driven home here is that this type of thinking is no historical novelty: we have been thinking, not least scholarly, about cities and their globalization for a long time and these discussions matter.

The Global City Genre

If Hall's work in *The World Cities* progressively gained popularity in academia and practice, with several reprints and editions until the early 1990s, it was John Friedmann in the mid-1980s who provided a further crucial analytical formulation for the study of the global city in academia. Recalling an initial research project designed in 1982 with Goetz Wolff and destined to become "an instant classic," the urban planner conceptualized the "world city hypothesis" in a 1986 article targeted to inspire a systematic study of this phenomenon.[7] The essay, intended as a framework of research, followed the above tradition concerned with the spatial organization of the new division of labor set in motion by the rise of the capitalist class and sustained by the underlying forces of globalization. Friedmann listed several interrelated theses on the nature and role of world cities, reiterating some of Hall's features and merging them with more social considerations of the geography of world economy.

Friedmann's interpretation was rooted in an understanding of the city as defined in economic terms: key cities are "used by global capital as 'basing points' in the spatial organization and articulation of production and markets," making it possible to arrange world cities in a "complex spatial hierarchy" based on such organization.[8] Relations and structure were described as flexible, depicting a dynamic hierarchy that further prompts us toward a particular attention to the variable power geometries of the system. This formulation made extensive use of the terminology developed by world-system theorists, classifying metropolises in core and peripheral countries, underlying how the scales of spatial polarization (global, regional, metropolitan) all inevitably rested on class polarization, and describing their position as organizing nodes of global economics. In this view, Friedmann laid out a map of the system arranged around three distinct geographical subsystems—Asian, American, and West European—linked together on an East–West axis by the relation of the primary cities within: Tokyo, Los Angeles, Chicago, London, and Paris.

At this time, Manuel Castells's *Network Society* trilogy of books is possibly the most influential text for providing a spatial framework for world city studies. This view sees cities and the localization of people, goods, and ideas not at odds with the cross-border pulls of globalization but rather in symbiosis with each other. As Castells famously put it, the "spaces of flows" charting the globalization of society and the world economy still needed "spaces of places" from and through which these flows could be articulated. This approach, read in conjunction with the increasingly popular concept of Immanuel Wallerstein's "world system theory" in the 1980s, gave further justification for the establishment of the Globalization and World Cities (GaWC) Research Network by scholars such as Peter J. Taylor, Jon Beaverstock, and Richard G. Smith in the late 1990s, shortly after launching a related pilot project at the Global Observatory of Loughborough University. Underscoring that this field seemed "to have drawn the short straw when it comes to rigorous research," Taylor and colleagues endeavored in establishing a monitoring group devoted to the study of "hierarchical tendencies among world cities."[9]

The GaWC project rapidly evolved into what is now a well-recognized methodology for producing large-scale quantitative relational data and a conceptual basis upon which to probe intercity relations quantitatively. Using Sassen's identification of advanced producer services as critical to identifying the global city, GaWC researchers selected London-located service firms and used their websites to record other cities in which they had offices. To date, GaWC has probably produced the most impressive collection of data on the global city phenomenon at large, maintaining updated rankings of urban hierarchies and an impressive database of world city resources. Here, as we will see throughout the book, the importance of London as central to the story of what counts as a global city, academically as well as professionally, echoes once again. Building on the idea of some degree of "specialized agglomeration" of world city functions as the driver of global city formation, this approach further reinforced the idea that proximity (of people as well as firms) is key to create centrality of cities in the world economy, and that this centrality (as Christaller had already discussed) is uneven. Yet, perhaps often dismissed by critics or superficial users of GaWC studies, this scholarly approach also stressed the fundamental interconnection that cities are based on. This sense of a city's "relationality" with other cities, conveyed in GaWC's quantitative "interlocking model" for analyzing intercity relations, was centered on a logical premise of "mutuality" that, as Ben Derudder and colleagues later put it, assumes that "cities in networks need each other."[10] While GaWC's application of this approach remains academically (and in some cases ethically) controversial to many, it is important to acknowledge that world city network analysis has come a long way in underscoring and socializing this relational characteristic of what makes a global city.

Going Beyond the Global City

The world city approach of the 1980s soon faced a comparable but contrasting formulation: the global city as elaborated by Saskia Sassen at the outset of the 1990s. With a multicultural education strongly tied to Latin America and Europe, the Dutch sociologist developed her landmark book *The Global City* on the basis set by her previous studies on social stratification and mobility of capitals. Notably, these approaches even featured in the early stages of Friedmann's hypothesis, as he referenced Sassen's theories on the role of the management elite as a privileged class within the restructuring of core world cities. These links notwithstanding, Sassen's thesis diverged from the mainstream hypothesis, and not just in semantics. As she recalled much later, the choice of "global" rather than "world" as an epithet for today's most fundamental cities was meant to "capture the specific articulation of the world economy today, . . . thereby allowing for the possibility that cities that are not historically world cities could nonetheless be global."[11]

According to Sassen, not all world cities necessarily represent global cities, and not all global cities should be seen as global in the same way. In her view we are witnessing a "new [global] socio-spatial order" in which certain places represent a "nexus for new politico-economic alignments."[12] As such, the global city is a heuristic vantage point into the reconfigurations of the late twentieth century. Global city *status* is attained through the capacity of controlling and rearticulating global networks and flows. Importantly, the latter can originate in the city, or "traverse" it, as the urban becomes a facilitator for other entities to reach global significance. Global cities, in this view, become key gateways in a complex web of planetary networks, thus occupying a privileged (or "strategic" as Sassen would put it) position in the unfolding of daily relations across the globe. Yet, the global city's centrality remains a precarious and contingent effect of this globalized positioning. This view has, in this sense, sought to underline the necessary interconnectedness of global (or, more often, world) cities.

Two key ideas emerge in this work and chart today's understanding of a global city. One the one hand, global cities agglomerate not just any function but those that accrue them centrality, as global cities anchor those forms of "command and control" of the world economy that make them so central. As noted above, this consideration is at the heart of the founding of GaWC's approach and the subsequent quantitative analysis of cities' differential centrality. Yet on the other hand, Sassen's work is also highly grounded on the streets of these cities. In fact, in Sassen's view, a necessary socio-spatial transformation accompanies globalization. Consequently, "*global city* is not a descriptive term [but] an analytic construct that allows one to detect the global as it is filtered through the specifics of a place, its institutional orders, and its socio-spatial fragmentations."[13] Global cities are built as global cities, and their population is affected by this orientation toward globalization. Key in this line of thinking is the appreciation that the global city is not a reality firmed in a single theorem, but rather something cast and recast in its practice beyond academia. As scholars of Singapore's story tell us, this underscores the need to understand global urbanism in the processes of "global city formation" rather than "continuing to construct static, synchronic models of global city hierarchies" and the political economy underpinning it.[14] Picking up from Roger Keil's friendly criticism that too little politics is discussed when it comes to theorizing global cities, I propose to pay greater attention to the politics of the ideas underpinning the global city and the governance of how these ideas are put into practice.[15] I want, even for just the brief and limiting space of an unlikely comparison like that of Dubai, Singapore, and Sydney, to take the global city seriously in its visceral urban politics, its long-lived developmental pathways, and the ways in which ideas as to what a global city is and should be are articulated in global urbanism, to step beyond the ebbs and fortunes of the international renown of this portmanteau. I aim, in short, to discuss the symbolic power of the global city.

In doing so, perhaps paradoxically, I suggest taking the ordinary city critique of global urbanism as a starting point and useful complement to the works of those who, like Sassen and Hall, have sought to unpack the socioeconomic and material implications of globalization in cities—seeking to highlight the political dimension of this encounter. This, in my view, can go hand in hand with an appreciation, even a celebration, of the everyday dimension of these cities and their grounded processes of urban life. Indian urbanist Anant Maringanti has rightly pointed out that, as a new archetype of urban theory, the ordinary city is not at odds with the global city.[16] Rather, it stands as a complement to this tradition as a call for an embedded engagement with the texture of the urban within and beyond globalist models that view, like too many summit catalogues and real estate presentations, the city from above far removed from the messiness of its streets and the lives of its many low- and middle-classes who keep the cities functioning. Simply, we should not take the global city at face value, but rather unpack it and experience it in the ordinary consequences that its ideas construct in practice. The street matters as much as the globe when it comes to thinking of global cities. This stance offers a productive starting point to valorize the plurality of urban experiences in these cities while acknowledging their global interconnectivity. It can allow us to pay closer attention to the processes of global city making, while not discounting how the global city, in practice, is a lively political terrain and can, as I argue in this book, become a space for progressive political advocacy. Dubai, Sydney, and Singapore offer us a triad of very diverse political and geographical conditions and rich analytical ground to unpack the relation between "global" and "city" but also between global city ideas and global urban practices. In choosing these sites I encourage the reader to meet a new generation of the hinges of globalization, perhaps signifying the shifting contours of the political economy underpinning global urbanism. In particular, throughout the book I emphasize the symbolic "system" and the "symbolic entrepreneurs" that chart the ground(s) on which these practices, ideas, and markets take place.

Into the Translation Zone

Ultimately, this is a book about the politics of the global urban imagination and of what we might call global city-speak and their instantiation on the ground of these emerging metropolises. I take up the challenge set by McNeill in his *Global Cities and Urban Theory*, where he investigates the practices of global city making as grounded in the cultural economy of urban development. As he concludes, the global city is more than a specific idea.[17] It represents, as I noted earlier and as McNeill puts it poignantly, a form of genre writing whose poetics and "representational devices" confront us with a plethora of symbolic forms tangibly researchable, from strategic development plans to PowerPoints and narratives, and are characterized by certain global city-speak that chronicles the emergence of these metropolises.[18] By taking the global city seriously, but not reifying it into one single thing, the ultimate aim of this approach has been to, to paraphrase Sassen's own original purpose in *The Global City*, encounter the global city (idea, process, and material reality) where it "hits the ground" and becomes everyday urban imagination, and ultimately life.

The urban imagination underpinning the global city, then, becomes a "translation zone" between how we conceive a global city and how it takes shape. This imagination is a "zone" that, as Emily Apter described it, is an inherently political space, even a "contested space," not free from confrontation and negotiations.[19] This means appreciating the politics of how ideas about the how, why, and where of globalization in cities are mobilized, negotiated, combined, and exchanged in the process of global city formation. It plays out in the book by means of mapping the ways urban elites in Singapore, Sydney, and Dubai speak of urban development against the complex tapestry of concepts that make up the global urban thinking described here. As I noted in the previous chapter, this book is underpinned by a series of 170 expert interviews conducted between August 2008 and January 2017, predominantly on site in, and exclusively about, these cities. These discussions focused on the cities' development of their global city status. Academics are counted as *part of* the elites, as I did not want to shy away from interviews with colleagues (several more senior than I was at the time) when they emerged from my snowball sampling and elite identification as key voices of the global development of Singapore, Sydney, or Dubai. Thus, the voices of 32 academics are included in the 170 experts represented in the study. As I return to more extensively in the last chapter, this is also a nod to the participation of scholars to the creation of the global urban imagination discussed here, their elite status in society, and their responsibility toward these very places. Overall, interview conversations were all of comparable length (between thirty and forty-five minutes) and followed a similar semi-structured format designed to unpack the core ideas underpinning the global city. Interlocutors for these conversations were chosen to represent a sample of academics, business and private sector operators, government (local, state, and federal) employees, and civil society advocates. While the selection of the interviewees is biased toward my own judgment of key "authoritative voices" on Dubai, Singapore, and Sydney, a core determinant of all those involved in this study has been some form of participation in the key debates on the globalization of these cities at the time of the interview, whether by writing or speaking in favor of or against, investing in developments, or planning core developments and strategic policies that took place at the time in the Emirate, Singaporean, and Australian metropolises and that explicitly involved the use of the term "global city."[20] Some degree of snowball sampling also played a role in seeking to balance the size of the sample across the various categories of experts. To even out access and frank conversation about the politics of a more outspoken citizenry in Sydney, and possibly more complex sociopolitical realities such as those of Dubai and Singapore, interviewees have been anonymized and, when quoted verbatim or in ethnographic vignettes throughout the book, all identified by a pseudonym for consistency.

The question of who speaks of globalization and cities matters a lot for these considerations. The goal of my approach here has been, as per this book's introduction and Rhodes's famed political science expression, to get "up close and personal" with the elites driving the global city discourse—recognizing that in many cases academia is complicit in this.[21] This is not to silence the voice of the everyday dweller, which I seek to understand more explicitly in chapter 10. The data gathered in the interviews have been cataloged not only by city and by degree of mention (explicit or use of a synonym) of a set of twenty core concepts underpinning the global city, but also by the backgrounds of my interlocutors. Basic personal information that will allow some considerations throughout the book includes age and professional background of each interviewee, respectively identified in brackets (eighteen to twenty-five, twenty-six to thirty-nine, forty to fifty-nine, and sixty and older), or primary occupation (academia/research, government, private sector, and civil society). Interviewees were also identified by level of education (high school, college education, master or equivalent professional degree, and doctorate) as well as the primary specialization of this course of studies (in social sciences and humanities, planning, architecture, business

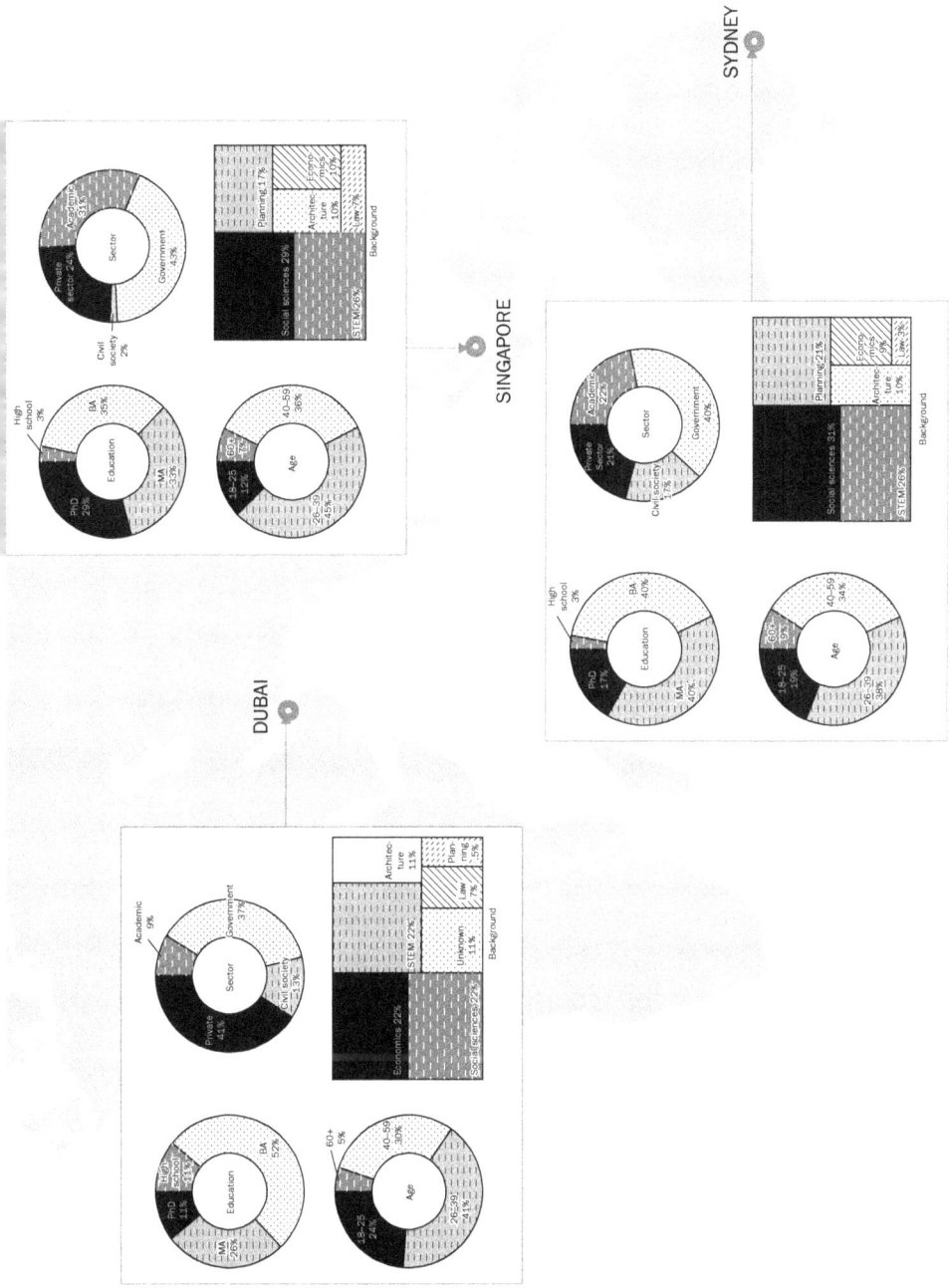

FIGURE 2. Detail of interview profile in each city.

and economics, STEM [science, technology, engineering, and mathematics], and law), at the time of our conversation. These are, of course, only broad categories, which need to be seen as departure points for comparative assumptions, not absolutely inflexible categorizations.

Interviews were designed to elicit whether an interviewee had mentioned (either explicitly or through the use of a synonym) any one of twenty key notions underpinning the contemporary use of the term "global city" (described in this chapter and the following) and were drawn from the present literature on this idea. Explicit and literal mention was scored 1 (e.g., the interviewee mentioned directly "premium connections" as used by Graham and Marvin in their 2001 work), implicit mention by synonym was scored 0.5 (e.g., the interviewee alluded to the concept of elites by discussing "the richer strata of society"), and no mention was scored 0. An important statistical meter at hand here is what I tag as "salience" of a concept: the average mention across all the interviews related to that issue—for instance, how salient the idea of entrepreneurship is among eighteen-to-twenty-five-year-olds in the three cities, or how salient the notion of the "dual city" might be in Dubai. A salience of 1 means the concept appears in all interviews in question, and 0 means it does not appear at all, with intermediate values expressed in decimals (to the thousandths), and accounting for both explicit mentions (valued at 1) and implicit ones (valued at 0.5). So, for instance, "premium connections" would score 1 if mentioned explicitly in all the interviews with architects, 0 if it was not mentioned in any of them, and a salience value of 0.201 would mean it appears in roughly 20 percent of the interviews, likely as a combination of explicit and implicit mentions.

The interviews were also analyzed for relevant correlation through the SPSS program focusing on significant statistical correlations between concepts as measured by a Pearson correlation coefficient.[22] This allowed possible correlation measures of 1 as the total positive linear correlation (each time concept X is mentioned, concept Y is also mentioned), 0 to define no correlation, and −1 as the total negative linear correlation (each time concept X is mentioned, concept Y is never mentioned, and vice versa). To aid the reader, the statistical correlations are visually represented with simplified versions of "solar correlation maps," summarized in figure 3.[23] The closer the "orbit" of a concept to the central issue or concept discussed, the stronger the correlation. To help in this, "planets" (i.e., global city concepts) in the visuals also include Pearson correlation coefficient values. This allows me to highlight key connections between a characteristic discussed in a particular section of the book and specific concepts, generally outlining significant correlations with a Pearson correlation coefficient above 0.5, or a weak correlation of at least 0.3.

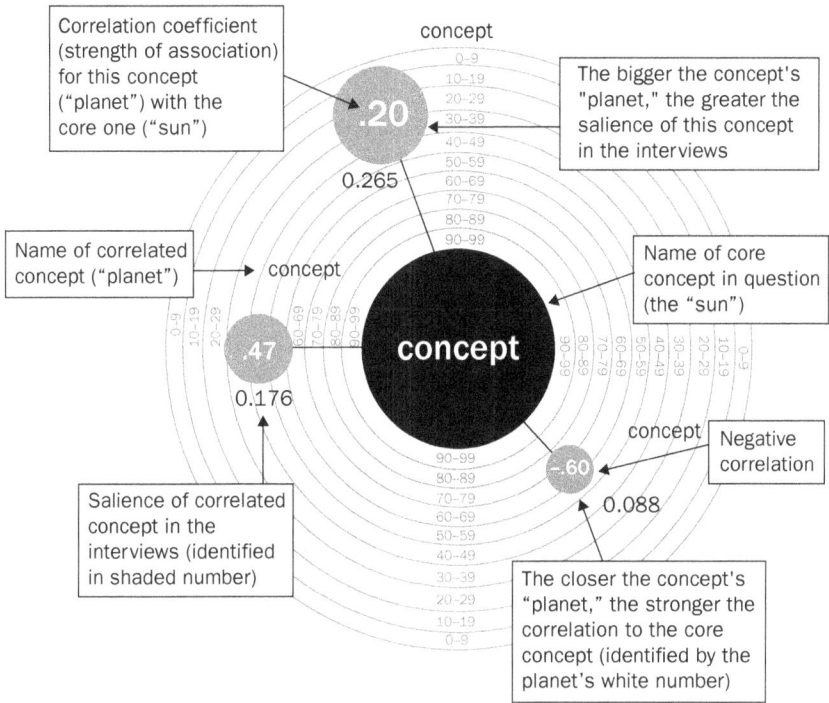

FIGURE 3. Guide to the correlation visuals in the book.

Certainly, answering the question of what a global city is could open Pandora's box and introduce endless narrative and methodological complications. There are many facets of what the global city is, implies, and ought to be. The core concepts behind the idea of the global city range from the idea of hierarchical unevenness among humanity's centers of commerce, to the notion that globalization creates dual cities polarized and splintered between the haves and the have-nots, to implications of these processes on the material, political, and economic reality that urban dwellers have to face on a daily basis. If we want to go beyond the surface of global city-speak often built on anecdotes and stories, a deeper engagement into its global urban imagination that underpins it is needed. This, as I have begun arguing in this chapter, is a composite of multiple concepts and ideas of what makes a place global. From this perspective, making sense of the emergent properties of these concepts, often emerging from broader theoretical traditions, becomes a key empirical puzzle and one I aim to attend to in this book.

As I set out in search of how, when, and by whom ideas existing in the global city scholarship emerge in the everyday discussion about the globalization of Sydney, Singapore, and Dubai, I relied on two methods. On the one hand, ethnographic observation "on the ground" of these metropolises can offer accounts of how these ideas relate to the material transformation of these places. I mainly do so by reporting discussions with my interlocutors about how these cities are globalizing as the entry point into what I hope is a more materially and contextually rich viewpoint than the correlation analysis. This importance in the production of distinction-in-similarity and group making is partly the reason to couple a more qualitative ethnographic analysis of Dubai, Sydney, and Singapore with a method such as correlation analysis that aims to unpack groups and connections that emerge by the encounter of ideas, individual social positions, and the political economy of the global city. Ethnography here is therefore used primarily to convey the grounded-ness of the many ideas underpinning the global city in the lived experience of urban dwellers, but also their materiality—an element that might otherwise be lost in the correlated findings of the other methods used in the book. On the other hand, as noted above, this went hand in hand with a coding of the interviews with my 170 experts. A record of mentions, along with the backgrounds of the interviewees, allowed me some degree of statistical and correlation analysis to identify common connections between notions and backgrounds, while comparing the three cities systematically, but also different types of people across the three cases. The result of this unlikely marriage of qualitative and quantitative work is a narrative that, I hope, allows a grasp of the tangible (material) implications of building and imagining global cities, as well as the often-intangible politics of the global urban imagination.

THE DEBATES

Woolloomooloo: Sydney, 7:00 p.m.

Tucking into an "Italian roasted" bone marrow that would have made my Piedmont-born-and-bread grandmother proud, and chatting about the latest cultural trends of the Harbor City, I am reminded by my hosts Tanya and Yaba, both young and upcoming Australian architects, that the global city is mostly a ground-up exercise, although almost never a fair one. We are at the Larder, the latest of many pop-up diners in Sydney, this time in one of the unused rooms of the fine dining Otto Ristorante at Woolloomooloo, just east of the Sydney Opera House. Pop-up restaurants have become one of Sydney's most popular cultural trends in the past year: both large and small restaurateurs have made profitable use of nonpermanent retrofitted spaces converted to, for example, a three-week Mexican restaurant, a fixed-price Italian trattoria, and a fusion diner serving sushi and Malay specialties. Importantly, these establishments allow dwellers and entrepreneurs to redefine, albeit briefly, spaces and contexts for social interaction in global cities like London or Sydney. These temporary redefinitions of urban spaces have evolved from "guerrilla dining" events popular in South America and, since the early 2000s, in the United Kingdom (UK), which have for the most part been held in unexpected locations with no permits or licenses. Known as "supper clubs," these pop-up establishments were perhaps swimming in murky waters in terms of legality and commercial, health, and zoning permissions. Not surprisingly, the original South American practice of the pop-up restaurant was dubbed "closed doors restaurant" and alluded to the informal nature of these interim redefinitions of private housing, backdoor court-yards, or, in the case of the Larder, unused commercial spaces. Makeshift diners, from their early days, have made use of a variety of nonconventional urban spaces to provide interim experiences that rely not only on the culinary extravaganza of most supper clubs but also on a passing mark on the built-environment fabric of their cities. Londoners were of course instantly seduced by the transient appeal of these initiatives, which quickly gained the attention of major media outlets like the *Guardian*, where they inherited the "supper club" appellative. Like the British supper clubs, Sydney's pop-ups rely mostly on word of mouth and social media networks to harness varied crowds. These crowds comprise mostly dwellers attracted by the culinary and cosmopolitan experience, but also by the exclusivity of the ambiance. Growing in popularity and nonpermanent urban imprint, the pop-up initiative has spread to large commercial names such as Penfolds and even popular media including Channel Ten and its *MasterChef* TV series.[1]

Mixing cultural, gastronomic, and architectural trends, Yaba is trying to convince me that pop-ups might be one of the "best present expressions of the transient, cosmopolitan, and business-driven" nature of the contemporary global city. "But," he continues, they are also a way to "subvert" the "boring" or "unfair way of building" that drives most urban development today. "Subtle changes" rather than street protests. Having seen the location and clientele of the Larder (which are starkly different from those of Ravi and al Ustad in chapter 4), I am obliged to take this with at least a grain of skepticism. Behind the launch of Larder one could spot Fink, a hospitality business well known in the high-end Australian restaurateur scene. Tanya prevents my question, pointing out how we could debate for quite some time the benefit of this mode of global urbanism and the inequalities inherent in a way of globalizing that drives neighborhood change through the influx of more affluent residents and businesses—the definition of "gentrification" par excellence. Perhaps the point of an idea like that of the global city, they suggest, is precisely to "debate" and "develop" what the global means in practice for a city. It requires some departure from conventional models but enough adherence to the current market to be palatable and recognizable, not simply unique. They seem to be riffing out of a Bourdieusian article on symbolic power. Of course, this ethos echoes notions of innovation and opportunity that, as we will see below, have held substantial currency in global city thinking. Yet perhaps most centrally, they engage with Sassen's now-well-rehearsed question, "Whose [global] city is it?"[2] This query surfaces a first contradiction and debate underpinning two more notions at the heart of what a global city is: polarization and cosmopolitanism.

Dual and Cosmopolitan

The debate on guerrilla dining and gentrification at the Larder is an apt point of departure to continue our excursus over the story of what makes a city global. In particular, I focus here on the inherent debates behind the story of the global city in academia but also more practically out of the ivory tower. Questions of inequality are, needless to say, a core pivot of this discussion.

Sassen's *The Global City* is as much a call for attention to globalized cities as it is an account of the socioeconomic consequences on ordinary people. This perhaps less popularly debated consideration from Sassen's 1980s' and 1990s' work brought about the question of the so-called dual city: with global city formation comes urban social polarization.[3] This thesis was developed from some earlier work on the social effects of the economic restructuring of American metropolises by scholars such as Bennet Harrison and Barry Bluestone, who sought to disprove Daniel Bell's 1970s' assumption that deindustrialization would bring about a growth of the middle class.[4] Several authors throughout the 1980s, not least Sassen and Friedmann, argued that the shifts in the occupational structures and industrial bases of the global city's economy were instead resulting in an hourglass effect. This rich-poor division of the city is embodied by the expansion of low- and high-income social groups (or classes) and the consequent shrinking of the middle class.[5] As Sassen later argued, this take on the global city sought to illustrate how the transformative effects of globalization on the world economy, and thus on the economic base of the most globally prone cities, were in turn "creating an increasing polarization of employment opportunities."[6] The employees in Sassen's discussion were perhaps more the people who served us at the Larder and less the entrepreneurs who started it. Cast in this light, the dual-city problem fast became a central issue in much of the contemporary global city scholarship, to the extent that it is now well established as a common crisis tied to the emergence of global(izing) cities the world over.

This is a scholarly moment that sees not only a steep growth in concerns about polarization in cities but also the theorization of those who control the globalization that is shaping these places. Central in the investigations prompted by GaWC approaches in more recent generations of global city scholars, but also by the world of Sassen since the 1990s, has been a more analytically based take on the importance of transnational elites in global city making. Those elites that shape much of globalization and give much of their global bearing to postindustrial metropolises: that loose set of people whom Leslie Sklair termed the "transnational capitalist class," or TCC.[7] This highly mobile stratum of the contemporary society is composed of four major in-groups: a "corporate faction" of executives, CEOs, and their local affiliates, a "state faction" of bureaucrats and politicians, a "technical faction" of globalizing professionals and creative middle classes, and a "consumer-ist faction" of merchants and media, who often compose a "visitor class" in the global city.[8] Members of the TCC can be considered "transnational" in the sense that, explains Sklair, they hold increasingly globally linked interests and project themselves as cosmopolitan as well as outward-oriented individuals, while also maintaining localizing agendas and "local" sociocultural attachments.

The dual-city thesis rapidly achieved well-deserved attention, especially owing to the publication of John Mollenkopf and Manuel Castells's edited volume *Dual City: Restructuring New York* and Sassen's first edition of *The Global City*.[9] In the former, the Big Apple was presented as "two cities, not separated and distinct but rather deeply intertwined products of the same underlying processes."[10] A plethora of empirical studies followed suit to test the polarization hypothesis and unpack the urban dynamics of social stratification in the major postindustrial Western cities.[11] The assumption, of course, has not been free from critics who saw in the "dual city" what Peter Marcuse would later call a "muddy metaphor" for a much more complicated process reflecting spatial reorganization of these cities.[12]

This set of social polarization concerns, however, happened hand in hand with the growing clout of the age-old idea that a global city is inherently a melting pot of a vast multiplicity of cultures. It is, as in both academic and general public parlance, a cosmopolitan hub. Blessed with the attractiveness of its globalizing infrastructures, marketplace of goods, and services and ideas, as well as with a cosmopolitan feeling that distinguishes it from many other conurbations, the globalizing city becomes not solely a strategic magnet for commerce but also a central place in the processes of mobility (social and geographical) that characterize our epoch and a theater for cultural hybridization across societies, nationalities, and religious allegiances. Vast cultural-ethnic diversity, if not "superdiversity," becomes in this view an essential ingredient of the globalization of a city, and a shared characteristic for both the elites as well as the middle and lower classes that tend to service them.[13] Diversely cosmopolitan is often the whole populace of the city, not just the jet setters that might have in some ways hijacked the term "cosmopolitan" by their less chronicled and magazine cover worthy cleaners, servers, nurses and waste managers.[14] A cosmopolitan advantage, many pundits of global urbanism now note, is said to distinguish the global city from many other settlements. Dwellers as well as planners seem to understand the social contrasts and limits of the global city. Yet, when confronted with global city-speak, issues of marginalization are often sidelined by talk of opportunity, international advantage, and competitive thinking.[15] The problem here is that much of this talk equates the "cosmopolitan mix" underneath the globalization of the city to a type of "offer" or "attractive" element, rather than a precondition and consequence.[16] Just as Sassen hypothesized that there might be no global city without also a parallel dual (or splintering) city, the same might be true to some degree of the cosmopolitan mix of global city societies. Yet the story might be, as another subsequent early 2000s debate on the global city highlighted, far more complex.

Splintering and Entrepreneurial

Since the turn of the last century, several urban scholars have been looking at inequality through the lens not solely of its social polarization but also of its physical manifestation through processes of gentrification, spatial displacement, and housing redistribution.[17] As the metropolis opens up to globalization and acquires a more central positioning in the global economy, its physical spaces are reorganized from both within and without—a process is not free from socioeconomic contradictions.

These spatial effects of globalization and urbanization have been the object of scrutiny of an influential study by Stephen Graham and Simon Marvin in the early 2000s, which uses the image of the splintering city to describe this dissociating trend.[18] Focusing specifically on infrastructural developments, the authors underline how the built environment is being "unbundled in ways that help sustain the fragmentation of the social and material fabric of cities."[19] As Graham and Marvin pointed out, major cities (especially in the West) are undergoing an increasingly pervasive socio-spatial reconfiguration: while up until the 1960s metropolises were built around a "modern infrastructural ideal" that focused on the provision of standardized services and thus the interdependence of urban spaces, cities have since then witnessed a progressive splintering of infrastructure resulting from the gradual abandonment of such an approach. As they described it, this system collapsed from a series of interdependent trends rooted in the spreading of economic liberalization, consumerism, and the globalization of urban activities, as well as the availability of more advanced technologies for interurban connectivity and the redefinition of the economic bases of the metropolis in a postindustrial sense, which have all fostered the emergence of a "new infrastructural landscape" for many cities.[20] The contemporary urban condition of global cities is thus one characterized by the emergence of widespread "bypass strategies" targeted toward linking "valued and powerful" users and places so as to elude less relevant urban areas and grid the key functional elements of the city in "premium networked spaces."[21] This fragmentation and re-bundling of urban spaces, in turn, produces "global enclaves" in a vicious cycle of urban splintering recasting and re-dimensioning the way cities are built.[22]

Rescaling and restructuring, however, is not just a material affair. The globalization of cities also implies a deeply political transformation brought about by those very forces mentioned in the scholarship above. In the early 2000s, American urbanist (with, importantly, some political science lineage) Neil Brenner called for greater attention to the political dynamics underpinning the rise of the global city. As he noted, the profit-seeking approaches to urban governance that proliferated during the post-1970s period need to be interpreted as significant expressions and catalysts of "glocalization strategies" oriented toward a "fundamental rescaling" of the spaces, and politics, of the national state.

In this approach, Brenner's work echoes a well-established lineage of urban governance works that is perhaps all too often seen as sitting outside the canons of global city research, and that I, on the contrary, place squarely at the heart of my analysis here. Practically, global city thinking has been affecting the style of city leadership that has emerged in many globalizing cities and the orientation of local governments the world over. This has been well understood in academia ever since the early 1990s. Key in this has been the work of David Harvey, who described how "managerial" approaches to urban governance so typical of the 1960s were, at the end of the 1980s, giving way to "entrepreneurial forms of action" born out of the spirit of the late capitalism of the twentieth century.[23] This approach had been reorienting urban politics toward postindustrial "urban entrepreneurialism" forms of governance and prompting many cities to take the initiative in the economic realm. As geographers like Tim Hall, Phil Hubbard, and Bob Jessop sought to explain in the 1990s, entrepreneurial city approaches are characterized by the move of urban government beyond localized welfare, projecting influence abroad to secure prosperity by engaging wider markets and constituencies, often with a focus on "urban boosterism" and "public-private partnership" as core practices of the post-industrial metropolis.[24] This was no occasional 1990s fad: entrepreneurialism has become a commonplace driver of major urban development investments worldwide and has resisted thorough critique by a wide populace of academics. In fact, in the past few years, debates on the entrepreneurial bases of much urban governance resurfaced in several key journals in urban studies. Scholars, particularly in geography, have been concerned with a reprising of the term "urban entrepreneurialism" and refocusing its discussion more explicitly toward its innovation bases (which, as I discuss in the next chapter, is also one of the central terms of my study), calling for an appreciation of its role in the "statecraft" of local government and of the varieties of entrepreneurialism that are at play in cities—not just a single type across all continents.[25] As we will see throughout the book, a perhaps less critical version of this line of thinking has in fact taken root in practice and in non-scholarly discourses around global cities and their development. While urban researchers pointing at the dangers of urban entrepreneurialism further evolved in conversation with ordinary city critiques, the sense of an emerging global outlook by city leaders has become a staple in managerial and consulting inputs into the leadership of many cities beyond the original ones that scholars looked at in the 1990s and early 2000s, making this a relatively well-established concept in emerging cities like Dubai and Singapore and perhaps with slightly less traction in the still relatively locally focused Sydney.

Discussions on the entrepreneurial elements of the global city, however, also take us directly into dialogue with a set of three further ideas that have in the past decade taken deep root in the minds of many practitioners as well as major urban development stakeholders in the private and multilateral sectors. These ideas, the ingredients of what makes for a global city, emerged more explicitly in practice rather than in what we might call the global city research proper, and have inhabited the borderlands between academia and the built-environment profession. I speak here of the elements of innovation and leadership and the concept of global opportunity. Their emergence is by all means not uncontroversial. In fact, their fast-rising popularity throughout the first decade of the 2000s was one of the major drivers of the kinds of debates, and in some cases rejections, of the global city as a concept altogether. But before we get to this controversy, let me take a brief step through three of these: the idea of urban innovation, the sense of capturing global opportunities to internationalize one's city, and the role of leadership in building places.

Innovation, Opportunity, and Leadership

Is there such a thing as nonacademic, everyday global city-speak? As already pointed out, much of the academic jargon we have encountered thus far has also found its way into the practice. At the same time, there are at least three other notions that, if perhaps most widely brought about by practitioners and fields other than canonical urban disciplines, have wide currency in global city-speak: innovation, leadership, and the sense of global opportunity. They perhaps all deserve volume-length treatises of their own, so my goal here, as with the sixteen notions we encountered earlier, is to simply offer a brief excursus into how they have been shaping global city thinking more specifically.

Innovation, to begin with, is an idea that has a long history and is by all means not just an academic matter; it has already driven the emergence of a field of practice, education, and studies on its own. In its modern conception (as it was originally used in a pejorative sense), what is perhaps the most commonly touted definition of innovation comes from the Organisation for Economic Co-operation and Development (OECD): a process of adoption, assimilation, and exploitation of a "value-added novelty," which typically applies to economic, policy, and social spheres.[26] From that point of view, it is easy to see how major economic and built-environment elites have taken to this concept as a driver of global urbanism. In a 2012 review of the literature on innovation and cities, Richard Shearmur noted how the fact that cities are now seen by many (most perhaps?) practitioners as the "font of economic innovation" is very much a truism in the global North and South alike.[27] Innovation has fast become a key measure of economic success internationally, with measures produced by the global market elites, like the Bloomberg Innovation Index as an annual ranking of the innovativeness of countries or the World Economic Forum's Global Competitiveness Report. Innovation has long been intertwined with issues such as the number of international patent applications, expenditures in research and development, and high-tech industries but has more recently veered to take into account the relationship among innovation, growth, and sustainability. Studies of innovation and cities followed suit, flourishing through the early 2000s in Europe and the United States.

Central in championing this approach was the operation of major economically oriented multilateral entities like the OECD as well as think tanks like the Brookings Institution, which, in the 1990s and early 2000s, became engaged in driving not only "thought leadership" but also capacity building, measurement, and investment in urban innovation. This is at the heart of the OECD's promotion of "competitive cities" thinking as a "new entrepreneurial paradigm" in supporting the spatial development of cities around the planet and driving both innovation-oriented and opportunity-infused urbanism at large. These have been tightly intertwined with the notion of entrepreneurial cities. Fundamentally, the growing popular advocacy for entrepreneurialism, coupled with the production of those "new state spaces" described by Brenner, pushed many cities and certainly much practical (if not academic, at least outside critical urban studies) thinking from government to governance as a view of politics founded on hybrid, public-private, and complex organizational arrangements beyond local government. This is a period of rapid expansion of global city thinking that, perhaps in contrast with (or perhaps perfectly contrasted by) the loud critiques emerging in academia that I detail below, saw the growth of global urban thinking in practice.

Certainly, the popularity of the creative class approach, promoted perhaps most famously by Richard Florida at the turn of the millennium, boosted talk of innovation in global city-speak. Florida's famed 2002 book *The Rise of the Creative Class*, and its related speaking, high-feed consultancy, and popular audience tour, fostered a growing sentiment that successful (global) cities thrive because of their success in the "creative economy" constituted by knowledge-based industries like business, law, tech, and finance and staffed by talented and educated professionals.[28] Here the idea of innovation bridges into elements of cosmopolitanism and transnational elites and stresses the power and value of talent in the construction of a global city—pushing through many of the champions of this creative class a global competition for talent that blossomed among cities in the early 2000s.[29]

In a way, not only was this approach deeply rooted in the elites shaping global cities (and created much scholarly debate against it), but it also very tangibly contributed to divergence and polarization. In fact, fifteen years later, in another attempt at a best-selling intervention, Florida's *The New Urban Crisis* admitted that this blend of innovation thinking also promoted greater inequality among and within global cities. Agglomeration of high-value knowledge-based economies, he noted, eventually benefited "superstar cities" and pushed for a "winner-take-all urbanism" that increased competition thinking in those striving to build global cities.[30] This underscores the sense that a city can, and perhaps should, be built for innovation as an essential element in accumulating "symbolic capital" and standing out while fitting in with the cusp of global talent—something that appears deeply intertwined with urban development. As a director from global real estate group Jones Lang Lasalle put it at a World Economic Forum, "Real estate really is the heartbeat of a vibrant innovation-oriented city."[31] Symbolic power, Bourdieu tells us, is centered on the possession of some degree of symbolic capital. At its simplest, symbolic capital is status or social recognition (or, some would argue, prestige) that empowers those who have it by societal recognition (as capital) and, in turn, allows them to exert influence (symbolic power). Bourdieu sees symbolic capital as "a credit" that is "granted to those who have obtained sufficient recognition to be in a position to impose recognition."[32] In this sense, the capital that sits behind the capacity to exert symbolic power is very much a form of socially approved authority. In turn, this credit allows people to impose meanings and views of the world in a legitimate form. The world is rife with examples of this, from media personalities, campaigners, and politicians to religious leaders and sports stars who are afforded varying degrees of this influence by their social status. Yet the same can apply to material things or indeed immaterial ideas. Similarly, references to innovation in various sectors of urban policy and among city leaders boomed along with the popularity of the "smart city" concept of the early 2000s, where talk of technologically enhanced urbanism became nearly omnipresent across multiple global stages and discussions. Overall, innovation is now a commonplace element of (global) city thinking that is well understood by practitioners and has solid critiques explored throughout academia.

To some degree the idea of innovation has also fostered a more practitioner-based understanding that a key ingredient of global cities is their capacity to capture global attentions, markets, and flows. Relatedly, then, the mid-2010s have also witnessed the progressive rise of another perhaps less academically grounded but globally recognizable concept for many urban development practitioners: opportunity, if not opportunism. As Greg Clark puts it in his *Global Cities: A Short History*, the idea of "capturing a global opportunity" is by all means not new. Italian city-states, for instance, knew full well the logic of leveraging one's international standing and taking advantage of a "geopolitical" positioning—something increasingly well understood by leaders in cities the world over.[33] Yet it is perhaps the boom of advisory firms and surge of business interest in global cities in the 2000s that put this concept at the forefront of global city-speak outside academia. In 2004, for instance, the Boston Consulting Group began speaking of cities wielding the "sources of global competitiveness" by "capturing a global advantage." Cities are seen in this case to be confronted with the fact that "globalization is no longer merely an option but an imperative" and that understanding one's own opportunities to thrive in this world is essential to city leaders and strategists in and outside the public sector.[34] This was echoed by, for instance, the Global Chicago Advisory Committee, composed of powerful corporate interests in the Windy City. Building on Chicago mayor Richard Daley's internationalization strategy, the committee pushed for think tank research (led by Brookings) and capacity building to encourage greater "global fluency" in established and emerging global cities. A key actor in this process has been the Chicago Council on Global Affairs, a nonpartisan think tank based in downtown Chicago that advocated in 2010 for this logic with the aptly titled report *Capturing Chicago's Global Opportunity*. Similar to many other such programs, lobby documents, and discussions, this has become a much-repeated mantra, especially in the fast-rising economic hubs of East Asia (Kuala Lumpur and Seoul, for instance) and, of course, in the oil-rich Gulf. As Clark and others have noted, this was not just a passing fad. The late 2000s and early 2010s saw an explosion of similar business leadership efforts in both the Global North and South from such organizations as Barcelona Global, Pro Bogota, London First, or, as we will see in one of my case studies, the Committee for Sydney. Not surprisingly, one of my case studies, Dubai, made opportunity a major theme of its Expo 2020 global event, including a dedicated "opportunity pavilion" on-site and opportunity-related events to spotlight how the interaction of innovation, creativity, and entrepreneurship can "capture" the global (imagination, attention, and market) "in a place."

Perhaps less academically popular, the logic of opportunity is now well understood by the very elites that global city scholars have long discussed. Yet this also brings us to a third practitioner-driven concept that makes for an important ingredient in global cities: leadership. Once again, as some have argued in urban studies, this is a discussion that remained fundamentally out of the halls of urban research academia. This does not mean that academia is void of research in leadership: plenty of business schools, management studies departments, and organization curricula have made "leadership studies" a central element of their work and a prolific, if not also lucrative, domain of work in universities around the world. The 2010s saw, on the other hand, an explosion of practitioner interest in city leadership and an upsurge in leadership courses in business and management schools around the world. What constitutes effective city leadership has been addressed in a vast literature from scholars in these disciplines, as well as increasingly in the past decade by a proliferation of reports, thought pieces, and events by private companies and multilateral organizations including McKinsey, PriceWaterhouseCoopers, and the World Bank, to name but a few well-known ones.[35] What leadership is, and what constitutes effective leadership in cities, remains mainly the domain of these organizations and of some sparse business schools. As urban geographers and regional studies specialists have begun noting in recent years, the vast majority of urban studies has to date turned a relative blind eye to discussions of leadership.[36] A common contemporary argument is that more general leadership theory focuses on the management of self-contained hierarchical organizations, where power and influence are distributed vertically, while city leadership involves complex networks of overlapping institutions. Cities imply "place-based" leadership processes, "those exercising decision-making power have a concern for the communities living in a particular 'place.'"[37]

Among the limited empirical work conducted to date, the majority are case studies of leadership processes or biographies of particular leaders. Popular audience academic books like Benjamin Barber's *If Mayors Ruled the World* helped push this theme to the fore in practitioner discussions of the global city, painting brief sketches of presumably "successful" mayors from the likes of New York, Seoul, and Bogota, and pushing the sense that leadership is predominantly pinpointed on an individual (generally a mayor), but offering little in terms of more systematic investigation and comparison that might be of help in our cases. In a few rare cases, this approach has encountered the world of management and business. Tangible examples are for instance the Bloomberg Harvard City Leadership training initiative and now the recent $150 gift in 2021 for a Bloomberg Centre for Cities is a collaboration between Harvard Kennedy School of Government, Harvard Business School, and Bloomberg Philanthropies, whose mission is to "inspire and strengthen city leaders" as well as "equip them with the tools to lead high-performing, innovative cities." The overlap with the themes of innovation and opportunity sketched above is blatant. At the outset of the 2020s, leadership, innovation, and the concept of capturing a global opportunity seemed well entrenched in the practice and parlance of the many global urbanists out there. This of course has not been free from a healthy dose of critical scholarly skepticism, perhaps best represented by the so-called "ordinary cities" critique of the early 2000s. In fact, some of the innovative and opportunist themes discussed thus far are perhaps some of the major drivers of the relative backlash against the idea of the global city and in favor of reading urbanism in a more ordinary, postcolonial, and less Western sense.

The Ordinary Cities Critique

A powerful contrast to much 1990s-inspired global city research, and the growing global city-speak of the 2000s, emerged from the postcolonial arena of the social sciences. This movement took issue with the burgeoning practitioner appropriation of the term and its socioeconomic results. According to what is now a large number of urban scholars across geography, anthropology, sociology, and planning, the popularity of global city discussions produced an unbalanced account that has privileged Western cities or Western-like developments in the Global South. This has in part been silencing a vast populace of postcolonial, second-tier, and even suburban realities that forms much of today's urbanization. These approaches have challenged the prevalence of Anglo-American voices in the literature and, more broadly, the "privileging of experiences of large financial centers and associated professional networks."[38] Fundamental in pushing for this critical rereading of the global city has been the work of several scholars that, in the mid-2000s, largely identified with the call for studying "ordinary cities" by Jennifer Robinson and Ananya Roy—geography and planning scholars not surprisingly hailing originally from Southern experiences such as those of South Africa and India. Against the dominant discourse embedded in the global city literature, Robinson and Roy advocated for greater attention to the marginalization that this globalist viewpoint promotes against those cities and localized lives that have remained "off the map" of the global city hierarchies and away from the visibility of the cores of the global economy.[39] These scholarly critiques set to redress an inherent bias in the global city discourse that, according to these authors, is affecting the literature and preventing a full appreciation of global inequalities. It is, as many following Robinson and Roy have noted, a matter of recognizing that some global city scholarship could potentially play a role in continuing this bias and the unbalances of a neoliberal global marketplace. This, as many working in the South and in major emerging centers like Singapore have noted, has engrained a "metrocentricity" in the analysis of global cities and replicates such biases not only through research but also through education. As British geographer Tim Bunnell, writing from the National University of Singapore, illustrated with local and southern colleagues Daniel Goh and Anant Maringanti, much of the effort of the ordinary critique is entrenched in a rejection of a single (dominant) and hierarchical view of the global in the global city.[40]

Here, the language of periphery, which was already present in the 1980s' depiction of the hierarchical unevenness of cities, takes up new meaning to illustrate first, in the late 1990s, a variety of postcolonial experiences in contrast with the work of global city scholars, and second, in the early 2000s, an increasing variety of experiences within global cities themselves. Speaking against perceived limitations of the global city genre, many urban scholars have, however, not simply rejected the idea that these places are changing in relation to globalizing forces and a wider geography of more-than-local flows. For instance, building on the work of Indian feminist critic Gayatri Spivak, urban planners and anthropologists have called for greater attention to the "worlding" of cities to identify the diversity of projects and the practices of making places "worldly"—as localities in dialogue with the world (and vice versa). Here the postcolonial proposal is that we need not uncritically accept the global (or "world historical") logic of how cities are made in relation to globalization, and that we need to recuperate the voice of the "subaltern" and the marginalized when speaking of the processes of internationalization of places. Perhaps not surprisingly, this critique blossomed in a wide variety of re-readings of the global city. Intertwined with other recent theoretical movements in urban studies, such as those adept to studying the geographies of "policy mobility" of ideas across cities, a growth in subaltern as well as more explicitly feminist critiques of the city, or Neil Brenner's latest project describing the challenges of "planetary urbanization," the ordinary thesis approach contributed to a shift in the types of global city studies available. These came, in the late 2000s and early 2010s, from a much greater variety of non-Western perspectives, a wider genre of qualitative analyses (e.g., more ethnographic accounts), and more generally a more nuanced language when speaking of the globalization of cities. They include, for instance, Ola Söderström's study of the related trajectories of Hanoi and Ouagadougou in *Cities in Relations*, Natalie Oswin's *Global City Futures* on Singapore, and Yasser Elsheshtawy's *Dubai: Behind and Urban Spectacle*, to name but a few.

This move, however, did not mean that the tradition of "world" city research, such as that of GaWC, disappeared altogether. Quite the contrary. These ordinary interventions brought to the fore the growth and further solidification of a new generation of world city scholars keen on defending the value and continued relevance of global city thinking. So, while a variety of projects, like those noted above, took a more ordinary view of the global city approach, without altogether rejecting it, the past few years also saw a revival of the early 2000s debate. For example, speaking for the value of global city thinking, Michiel van Meeteren, Ben Derudder, and David Bassens argued that many critiques of this scholarship might have been "hampered by their tendency to be polemical rather than engaging" and might have turned into "gradually routinized straw man rhetoric that emerged as an unfortunate rallying point for postcolonial urban scholars."[41] This straw-man discussion, involving several responses by Robinson and Bunnell, brought about a more explicit conversation about the need to bridge theoretical and academic divisions for a more pluralist approach to studying cities. Bunnell, for instance, pointed at the need not to have to subscribe to be in or out of the "invisible college" of global city research (a term I admit having promoted myself in that form in a 2011 article building on Friedmann). Starkly oppositional academic camps are rarely productive versus the importance for "porosity" and academic cross-fertilization. GaWC scholars like van Meeteren, Derudder, and Bassens also argued that greater openness to engaging across ideological divides and pushing for more collaborative experimentation has to be the way of global city thinking in academia in the twenty-first century. As the mid-2010s progressed, the scholarship on globalization and cities saw the emergence not only of a generation of global city researchers calling for more responsible and nuanced approaches to studying the global city, but also of a more explicitly global urbanism by academics. This was perhaps best crystallized by the confluence of two factors: first, internationally, the more explicit growth of an international "urban agenda" putting cities at the heart of multilateral programs and processes. As Susan Parnell noted, we are at a particular juncture in world affairs where recognition of the global importance of cities calls on experts of urban affairs to take a more proactive stance internationally—as inscribed in the United Nations Sustainable Development Goals and New Urban Agenda.[42] Second, as Karen Seto, Xuemei Bai, and Timon McPhearson, among others, pointed out in some of academia's major outlets, like *Nature* and *Science* (and I include myself here), scholars have pushed for a global urban science and a more proactive role of urban scholars outside the proverbial ivory towers of their campuses.[43] So as we saw in the previous chapter, we enter the 2020s in a productive place for academics to bridge beyond the study of the global city and an engagement with its political economy, and we can look back at a century's worth of concepts and ideas that make this term more than a repeated trope.

What Is in an Idea?

What emerges from this excursus in the global city genre, and its critiques, is a complex nuance of ingredients forming what we would otherwise be simply inclined to call a global city as a catch-all term. The phrase stands in for a complex body of meaning. It is the result of an at least century-old tradition of thinking that acknowledged the centrality and hierarchical unevenness of cities in the geography of the world economy, and society more broadly. It highlights the importance of gateway but also agglomeration functions that some cities perform in a more than local sense, and the socioeconomic but also very tangibly material implications of this global positioning. It also underscores the analytical possibilities to understand these phenomena, as well as the inherent dangers and northern biases of globalist thinking, gesturing toward the need to think of what remains off the map and not simply buying into a catchphrase—a mission I have taken up here with the explicit purpose to unpack the genre of global city-speaking, not just its academic writing, and its implications for the ways we see emerging cities.

Several of these arguments overlap and are intertwined. In my investigation, I do not delineate a clear line between global and world city, or whether global or ordinary interpretations are preferrable. Neither will I attempt to draw a tally of the most common tradition of thinking since, as I outlined above, this line of investigation of a globalizing urban condition builds on a mix of these debates. Hence, we embark here on a journey to understand how these ideas "hit the ground," as Sassen put it time and time again, and whether they do so differently in the apparently different cases of Singapore, Sydney, and Dubai.

My goal is to see beyond uncaring repetitions or straw-man rejections of the term and push us (scholars and practitioners) toward a more tangible discussion. Certainly, as we saw happening at the NSW Art Gallery at the beginning of chapter 2, "global city" is a persuasive idea. Yet as I sought to illustrate here, we could take statements about the globalization of cities more seriously rather than dismissing them. This is a view on rhetoric that scholars in the humanities have held for quite some time: rather than dismissing rhetoric as simply synonymous with something shallow and deceptive, we can unpack it by looking into, rather than beyond, its meaning. Unfortunately, the term "rhetoric," much like the term "Machiavellian"—often simply taken as a synonym of "cunning" rather than, as originally professed by the Florentine author, an approach that is strategically oriented toward one's own state interest—has been ditched by many outside classical studies. Similarly, the "global city" and its practical instantiation in policymaking and planning the world over has often been dissed by academics subscribing to more critical readings of urban studies. Yet "global city" has in this sense become a "rhetorical device": a technique to persuade listeners to consider an issue, or indeed a place, from a particular perspective.[44] What that perspective is, how it takes shape, and what are the elements of its worldview (or "worlding") are the subject of much of this book and, I argue, can be read by considering the more nuanced elements of global city-speak detailed in this chapter. Yes, Bunnell may be right that all too often the scholarly debates have been quibbling about "fine grain" definitions and "nomenclature"—and I certainly subscribe to that view.[45] Yet, as McNeill pointed out, global city-speak (and I would add its underlying urban imagination) carries power: a very *symbolic* one, I argue throughout the book.

From this point of view, we could argue that the twenty concepts in the book represent, in Bourdieu's lexicon of symbolic power, a series of "symbolic forms" structuring the urban imagination. They are instruments for constructing reality and representing it both in spoken words and intrinsic imaginaries. Symbols are perhaps the most fundamental instruments of social communication and integration. Language, math, the economy (with money, for instance), politics, and much more all rest on shared systems of symbols, which make possible the consensus that allows people to make sense of social relations and, at the same time, maintain and construct divisions. The color red (versus green) makes a fundamental difference in the system of mobility across our streets, just as the word "push" (versus "pull") provides a fundamental instruction as to how to operate a fundamental division, like a door, between distinct spaces. The language of today's global urbanism is an influential mode of global urban "thinking" that is far from extinct or indeed resolved in one of the many debates this scholarship has witnessed in its century-odd history. I chose to focus on the nuances within the rhetoric of the global city to understand the elements that make this device, and its genre of speaking and thinking in general. The global urban imagination, especially in a time of populist inward backlashes against globalization, might be here to stay in many cities and city leaders. I encourage us, then, to ask ourselves, to paraphrase the vignette that kicked off the previous chapter, what "we talk about when we talk about global cities."

THE RISE

Al Seef creekside: Dubai, 4:00 p.m.

Strolling along the water on the right-hand side of Dubai Creek, a few minutes on foot from the original fishing and pearl diving settlement of the Emirate, I catch a glimpse of wooden water taxis (*abra*) crossing from the opposite shore as evening falls on the city. My Emirati friend Saeed is taking me through a series of low-rise streets lined with Arabic *bayts* (houses) built in seemingly traditional materials and shadowed by several of the iconic *malqaf* (or *barjeel*) traditional wind-catcher towers designed to ventilate the buildings. I am meeting Saeed to chat about his experience with the development of the 2015 Dubai Strategic Plan (DSP) and its replacement with the 2021 successor a few years later. The DSP's tagline, "Dubai ... where the future begins," seems at odds with our promenade. The plan was issued with the ambitious 2015 goals of 11 percent growth in the GDP to reach US$108 billion (nearly achieved and just short of $105 billion in 2015) and a target of $44,000 per capita (missed and ending at $25,000 in 2015). I am asking about the future and the process of planning for a global city future, but Saeed is keen on reminding me that "the future begins in the past" and he makes a point of this with our visit to this area just next to the Al Fahidi historical residential neighborhood of the 1890s.

We are walking into the brand-new development of Al Seef, alongside the creek, making our way through what at first sight appears to be the original Bastakiya in the old Bur Dubai. First built by Persian merchants hailing from the Bastak county in modern-day Iran, relatively run down for most of the past

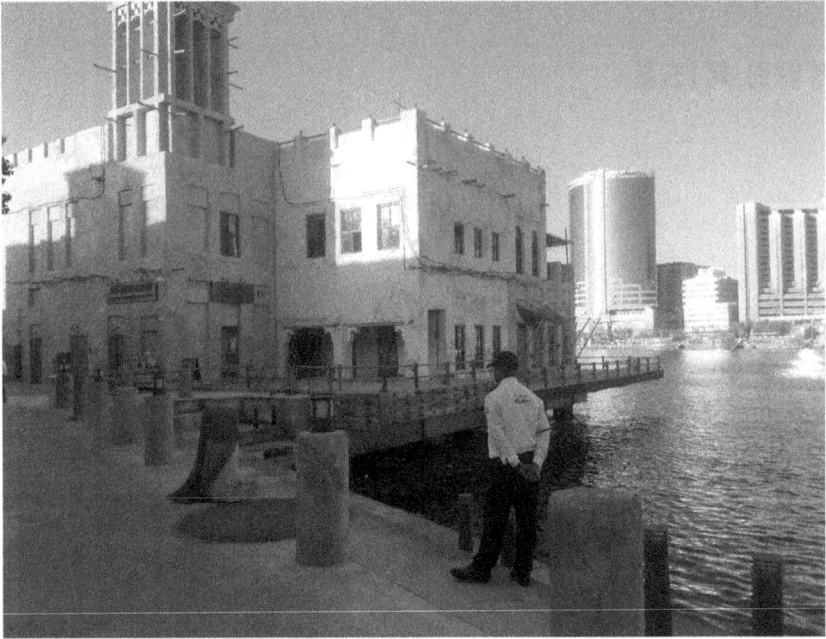

FIGURE 4. Al Seef creekside.

century, and an object of a 1990s redevelopment by the Historic Building Section of the Dubai Municipality, the creekside area changed dramatically in the past year. It feels, at least at first sight walking along the lime and fossilized mixture walls and wooden beams protruding from the buildings, like a jump back in time to Old Dubai. It is, in reality, a quite meticulously reconstructed replica of that time, down to the faux wooden beams and the *malqaf* towers. There are even fishing nets hanging on the railing by the docks.

The Al Seef development is a project of Meraas Holding, a developer launched in 2007 (when Dubai Strategic Plan 2015 was rolled out) that is also behind other popular Dubai mixed-use destinations like the open-air mall of City Walk in Satwa and the walkability oriented La Mer beach. The area is a site for a new imagery of Dubai moving from the hypermodern glitz of the skyscrapers downtown to a distinctive Middle Eastern feel in the heart of the old part of town. One of the hotel chains housed in Al Seef, Jumeirah, promises guests "a step back into enchanting Arabia" but where "comfort and tradition come together" in a "glimpse into the past in the heart of Dubai." Saeed's tone indicates that he is perhaps not fully persuaded, but he mostly agrees. Some of what Meraas is doing is helping with offering a more varied experience of what the Emirate is without necessarily soaring hundreds of meters into the sky.

Jumeirah is a Dubaian international luxury hotel chain active since 1997 and now under the overall control of Dubai Holding, whose majority shares are owned by the ruler of Dubai Sheikh Mohammed. It has been a staple of luxury accommodation in the Gulf, in addition to large international companies like Sheraton and Hilton. Along with Al Seef, Jumeirah has also unveiled Za'abeel House a few meters down the creek. In its almost container hotel-like shape, it is designed for those looking for a more "modern" access to this part of town, although it still offers a low-rise and relatively understated alternative to some of the eccentric skyscraper hotels on Sheikh Zayed Road or Dubai Marina. Al Seef is one of the newest developments in the city, but Dubai is, at the time of writing, again set to break the record for tallest structure on the planet. "Old habits die hard," sighs Saeed, as he takes me around the block and we continue our discussion on the planning of Dubai's global aspirations.

The feeling that surrounds our conversation is that global ideas about the city are constantly, and often hurriedly, translated into a very localized materiality. The urban imagination of Dubai as a global gateway and destination ends up in very tangible manifestations of glass, concrete, and people performing activities key to sustaining the edifice of the global city, often unequally. Tim Bunnell, in his work on Asian urban aspirations, has stressed how material consumption is not only an important component of many people's aspirations and urban imaginations, but also one that may be entangled with wider claims to social inclusion and political rights.[1] One could get this same feeling strolling around Singapore and Sydney too. Saeed and I debate at length whether, despite the obvious commercial purpose and faux historical appeal of near-theme-park quality—down to brand new wooden renditions of 1950s electrical switches installed across the development by Siemens and fake 1960s public phones hanging on corners—this might be a positive development in the city.

We continue our walk away from the creek, and a few minutes later we are in a distinctly more modern built environment and have reached our selected dinner spot. Al Ustad is a classic Iranian-descent kebab diner that sits anonymously on a busy road in Al Fahidi. Like the perhaps even more rustic Ravi in al Satwa, Ustad is sparse on décor and is miles away from the westernized experiences of the grand hotels downtown or along the beaches. Its clientele is predominantly local. The limited menu offers down-to-earth good barbecue and low prices. After several portions of yogurt mutton and a jovial explanation by owner Majeed as to why the restaurant has made it onto the pages of the *National* and into the best travel guides, Saeed is still busy trying to convince me that the idea of Dubai's "future begins" tagline needs to be read in relation to the story behind the present-day stereotype of the city. What echoes here, perhaps still poorly understood in global city-speak, is the necessity to understand the globalization of these places in their historical grounding and trajectory.

When it comes to global cities, the processes and governance dynamics that lead to their ascent and sustain their globalizing centrality remain largely overlooked. It is necessary to consider not only the worldwide flows that influence these metropolises but also, as Kris Olds and Henry Yeung put it in the case of Singapore, the "differential pathways associated with global city formation processes" and therefore the sheer variety of evolutions that lead to the emergence of a city as "global."[2] Put it simply, there is no one trajectory to global city status. Despite Saeed's admirable efforts as one of but sixteen people explicitly bringing this theme up in the 170 interviews for the book, history is not a popular, although not a forgotten, topic of my conversations in Singapore, Sydney, and Dubai. It is not absent, recording a relatively average role throughout in comparison with other key concepts behind the idea of a "global city" (scoring a total salience of 0.159, on par with the total average of 0.156), but it is less common than the impact of elites and gateway functions in shaping global city-speak.

What I attempt to do here, by picking up Saeed's (and Olds and Yeung's) message in the next few pages, is to put the rise of our three global cities into context and unpack the pathways to global city formation that underpin them. I do this not only to offer a brief primer to those unfamiliar with the three settings of this book but also to piece together a set of further elements central to the rhetoric and thinking about global cities today. In describing how Singapore, Sydney, and Dubai emerged on the world stage, I illustrate the idea of the emergence of global cities from, and relationship with other places still, "off the map," as Jenny Robinson put it. I also note the incidence of the sense of capturing a particular (global) opportunity needed, especially in business thinking, to make it as a global city in a particular historical time.

The Rise of Singapore

As the official Visit Singapore website puts it, "The story of Singapore is rich with twists, turns and triumphs." Accounting, and developing a narrative, for the history of the island has been a fundamental component of nation building in Singapore. The modern and much-recounted story of the city-state typically starts on 9 August 1965, with its independence from Malaysia and with the founding-father figure of Lee Kuan Yew, a lawyer turned politician in the mid-1950s, a founder of the now-ruling People's Action Party (PAP), and first prime minister when Singapore gained autonomy in 1959. Lee was instrumental in navigating the complex separation from British colonial rule, first as part of the short-lived federation of

Malaysia in 1963, and then from Malaysia after the tumultuous race riots period of 1964. Often recounted by Singaporean officials as a characteristic of Lee's vision, the new Republic of Singapore had a tightly intertwined relationship with global city planning from its early days. As Singaporean commentators regularly note, this traditional strategic mind-set was ingrained in the city's first generation of leaders owing to the limited resources available during the last period within the Malaysian state and continues to this day as a central concern of policymakers. The original 1819 trading post founded by Stamford Raffles on the island, and subsequent British colonial development, was in practice the only key asset for the small state that split off from Malaysia (shortly after its founding in 1963) for unreconcilable ideological differences and racial rifts that led to an expulsion of the city from the Malaysian federal government in 1965—a rare case in which the current advantageous (as we will see in chapter 5) governmental positioning was in fact granted to, rather than called for, the city-state. Singapore's swift emergence as an "Asian Tiger" with high growth rates between the 1970s and 1990s surprised many and followed a path similar to the success stories of Hong Kong, Taiwan, and South Korea, averaging a sustained 6 percent growth per annum in that period. Within this rise, the Singaporean government took a strong role in a tightly controlled planning system almost entirely directed toward ensuring economic prosperity and social stability.

In this sense, Singapore represents perhaps one of the original contemporary global cities that perceived itself as such, as Singaporean sociologist Chua Beng Huat noted, well before the term reached any popularity in the social sciences. In fact, as the country started on a path toward more explicit internationally driven industrialization to attract foreign capital, it also took a decidedly outward-oriented approach to its development as, for instance, one of the founders of the Association of Southeast Asian Nations (ASEAN) in 1967. In the 1970s and early 1980s, much of the city's governing structure and rapid economic development took hold on the island. This saw the establishment of the Economic Development Board (EDB) and the development of industrial estates located within the Jurong area through the then named Jurong Town Corporation, established in the east of the island in 1968 by EDB to manage the structural needs of rapid industrialization. Throughout the 1970s, Jurong, and the island in general, saw not just a growth in industrial sites but a diversification of the revenue sources of the Singaporean economy, with, for instance, the establishment of oil refineries on three of the offshore islands south of Jurong (which to this day account for nearly a fourth of Singapore's exports) in some of the city's initial land reclamation efforts—now a staple of Singaporean development. Yet it is perhaps in the 1980s that we see Singapore emerge as the type of global city we know today. With a slowdown in international investment in the city's industrial capacity, and the already blatant natural and manpower limits, Lee Kuan Yew's government began to reach out to the world more explicitly and entrepreneurially. The year 1981, for instance, saw the launch of Singapore Changi Airport and Singapore Airlines and an expansion of the Port of Singapore as a major regional hub, and along with that a specific national program (the Operational Headquarters Programme) designed specifically to attract Southeast Asian head offices of major international companies; these projects were part of a strategy that mirrors ahead of time the formulation of command and control functions popularized by Sassen and the GaWC analyses of global cities at the end of the 1980s, while mirroring quite clearly the gateway functions so typical of the definition of "world city." Some tourism and more markedly short-term business visitors began rounding out the international profile of the city, which in the late 1980s and throughout the 1990s looked explicitly to its regional neighbors to offer a competitive advantage while continuing with strategic development of core island assets like the Mass Rapid Transit system launched in 1987 but part of the same 1971 strategic plan that led to Changi Airport.

The mid-1970s also saw the establishment of the Urban Redevelopment Authority (URA), chiefly tasked with managing land use planning and responding to the need for more strategic development of the island beyond the pressing overcrowding of the center. Via the URA and the 1966 Land Acquisition Act, which gave ownership of the vast majority of the island to the state along with a carefully managed sale of sites program of private sector engagement, Singapore has managed a tight control on its built-environment expansion. Singapore embodies the idea of a "property state" in that it has used real estate and urban development powers to foster and direct the growth of the city on an international stage. It also represents an unambiguous case in which the rhetoric of globalization has become policymaking, as testified explicitly in the city's 2010 economic strategy seeking to cast itself as "the Global City in Asia," which is very much in line with, as well as in competition with, Hong Kong's branding as "Asia's World City."

Environmental and sustainability concerns, as well as cultural development ones, gained a more explicit role in Singapore's development in the early 2000s, when the city sought to cement not only its now pivotal regional role but also a more explicitly prime positioning on the global scene. Here, concerns about the "beautification" of Singapore, the development of a new class of sustainability-oriented assets, and greater appeal to the international leisure industry became increasingly central in the government's mind-set. Seeking and receiving international recognition has been key to this. For instance, the World Economic Forum's 2015 Global Technology Report named Singapore as the most "Tech-Ready Nation," and the city-state regularly features among the most internationally recognizable innovation hubs on the planet with the highest de-

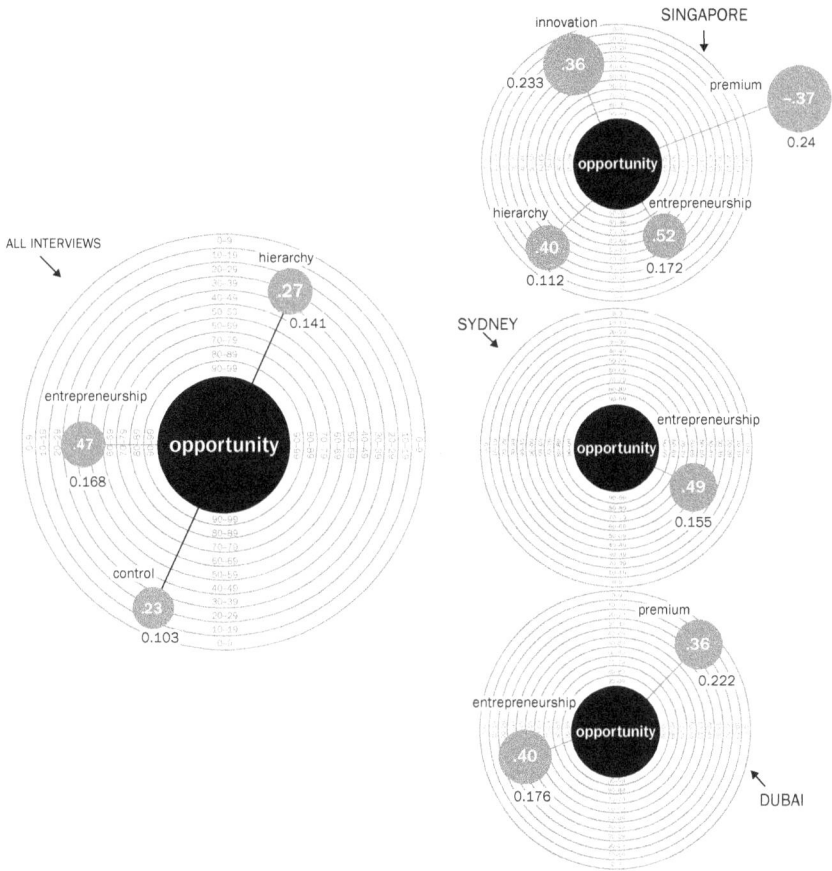

FIGURE 5. Mapping "opportunity" in global city-speak.

grees of digital penetration and technological experimentation. Tech and innovation (a key theme we will look at later), however, have gone hand in hand with the production of a Singaporean experience embedded not just in advancement and sustainability but in a certain type of culture too. As Singaporean geographer Lily Kong noted, the city's cultural policy of the early 1960s and 1970s focused on the harnessing of arts and culture for nation-building purposes, but in the 1980s and especially in more recent decades it recognized that the arts and culture had a clear tourist dollar potential and that they could function as a subindustry in themselves, accounting for a lively arts and culture scene as a key ingredient of global city making. This has been, in the view of many commenting on the development of Singapore, linked to the issue of capturing a global opportunity. Yet interestingly, in my conversations for this book, the appreciation of the opportunity element of the global city idea is far more present in Dubai (a higher-than-average salience of 0.167) than in Singapore or Sydney (very low salience of 0.078 and 0.095, respectively). Not surprisingly, discussions of leveraging opportunity in Singapore are linked with ideas of an international hierarchy of cities and of the role that innovation plays in global city making. Overall, the story of the rise of Singapore as a globally recognizable hub tells us much already about the specific framing of a place as globally oriented and speaks directly to international flows. Yet it also once again testifies as to the need to read developments, and plan forward, with a historical sense that in some cases can become part of the city's global identity.

The Rise of Sydney

Even though Sassen described it as "Australia's only global city" as early as 1994, Sydney has traditionally occupied a rather marginal position in the world city literature.[3] Honored only by sporadic mentions alongside far more famous urban centers, and relegated to the margins by a lack of internationally available publications, it was considered a "secondary city" for much of the twentieth century. Peter Hall initially sidelined it as "sub-global" in the 1960s, and three decades later GaWC was still cataloging it as an "outer" second-level world city in its first urban ranking.[4] These considerations, however, might give a false impression that Sydney has a recent history. Rather, the development of the Harbor City dates back to an eighteenth century (by all means problematic) colonial history first as a penal outpost and increasingly as the major settlement of the federated colonies of the Commonwealth of Australia at the turn of the twentieth century. It is perhaps after the 1920s and more markedly in the following postwar period that the city began moving beyond a manufacturing base, relying on large infrastructural works. And since the 1970s, it has diversified more explicitly as an outward-oriented hub for a variety of world city functions. Sydney has since moved to center stage in both popular and academic discourses. The urban development of the capital of the state of New South Wales has been pinpointed on the problematization of its economic base in relation to the "global" from the mid-1970s, when, after twenty years of mass-production "long boom" started in the 1950s, the city underwent a substantial restructuring. Owing to the changing integration into the world economy of that period, the sprawling metropolis underwent a progressive shift away from heavy manufacturing toward information and service industries that, between the mid-1980s and mid-1990s, formed the bedrock of Sydney's globalizing economic base.[5] This was facilitated by Australia's deregulation of its financial system in 1983 and by a growth of interest and investment from the Asian Tigers, including Singapore, Taiwan, and Hong Kong, in the early 1990s. Since then, the city has, according to many, rapidly surpassed its national peers to become Australia's core settlement. "Tell Melbourne it's over, we won," boasted the *Sydney Morning Herald* on New Year's Eve in 2003, a defeat that was conceded by the same Victorian premier Jeff Kennett, and more generally a rivalry that endures to this day.[6] While it might be a somewhat complex endeavor to assess whether the Harbor City can be declared a globalization "winner" vis-à-vis its long-standing national rival, it is indisputable that Sydney has become the country's key mobility hub and primary link with the world economy. It has gained, beginning in the mid-1990s, a growing national and international importance by housing in its Central Business District (CBD) a financial hub that includes the Reserve Bank, the Australian Stock Exchange, and over 48 percent of the top five hundred Australian companies.

Even in the wake of the 2008 global financial crisis, Sydney has proved capable of a positive performance thanks to the overarching stability of its key financial institutions, and it represents one of the best cases of the "West to East" shift in the world of international financial centers.[7] This went hand in hand with a growing integration into, and quite clearly dependency on, the world economy and related unavoidable recognition in a plethora of rankings and general reporting on cities. In particular, Sydney's experience in the 1990s and its affirmation in the early 2000s have witnessed a growth in its global profile as a key destination. Its tourism industry expanded progressively to become one of the key economic development priorities for the state and central local governments—with the City of Sydney (occupying the innermost part of Sydney's twelve thousand square kilometers) as the prime beneficiary of this approach among the thirty-five local authorities in Sydney. Yet this gateway function was well ingrained in the history of Sydney not just from its colonial days but even more markedly from a boom in Mediterranean and subsequently East Asian migrants after World War II. In this sense, tourism is not the only prime influx of people and investment, with the education sector also fueling the growth of the city as the major Australian hub for this ahead of Melbourne, and growing cultural industries that are now well established on the world's stage.

However, Sydney's global fortunes (and the associated problems) cannot be explained by global processes alone. The city's ascent in the world urban hierarchy is not merely a consequence of worldwide realignment. Rather, Sydney's increasingly central positioning on global financial, information, and mobility "highways" is the result of a complex mix of flows and networks that have not just been shifting eastward but are also consciously sown by various actors involved in the city's governance. Sydney's ascent is not exogenous; rather, it is the result of a conscious political process aimed at repositioning the metropolis in the contemporary world system, similar to some degree to Singapore's story. What is perhaps starkly different, as we will see in chapter 5, is the governance setup of a city that is split among thirty-one local authorities (with the City of Sydney as the second-oldest one in the whole country), a much broader state government, and limited federal influence from the federal government in Canberra.

Ever since the 1990s, authorities in Sydney have followed an increasingly entrepreneurial style of governance, shifting from the management-style approaches of the 1970s and 1980s to a more opportunistic, business-oriented, and outgoing edge.[8] Sydney has also been the object of aggressive liberalization, with a conscious agenda by the parties involved to promote mostly through neoliberal policies, as Australian urban scholars like Pat Troy point out, a focus on global competitiveness.[9] In the mid-1990s this took a progressively explicit global city framing at both the state and local (City of Sydney) levels, as noted in the 1996 *Sydney as a Global City* discussion paper developed by Australian planning scholar Glen Searle for the New South Wales government. As another Sydney-based academic, John Connell, summarized in the 2000 book *Sydney: The Emergence of a World City*, talk about urban development in Sydney was at this point highly intertwined with a global discourse even though the local academic community, highly active in casting a critical eye on these trajectories, was already pointing at the often unproblematic use of an increasingly common language of globalization.[10] Here, an interesting difference between Sydney and Singapore is that the nature of critique by Sydney-based academics already diverged quite substantially from that in the city-state. If in the 1990s and early 2000s (with some level of generalization) urban scholars in Singaporean institutions focused mostly on understanding why and how the city was globalizing and pointing at specific areas lacking attention for the central government, in Sydney academia progressively developed a more explicit culture of critique. Also different is that in Sydney, perhaps due to the lack of metropolitan governance, it has been the private sector that has advocated even more loudly for a global orientation of the city. This has been echoed, for instance, in the increasingly central role of entities like the Committee for Sydney, a major business leadership organization gathering key commercial interests in the city, throughout the first part of the 2000s, and a key factor in metropolitan governance. Yet, as noted above, the sense of capturing a global opportunity is very limited in conversations about the globalization of Sydney—essentially the second-least-discussed issue after metrocentricity—and a fundamentally economics-driven point of view, as this concept was raised in more than half of the interviews with Sydneysiders with a business and economics background versus limited mentions across all the other profiles. Nonetheless, the recent history of Sydney speaks quite clearly, just like Singapore, of a con-

FIGURE 6. Sydney's "green, global, and connected" marketing outside Town Hall.

scious framing of the city as a global place—something that has to do with a sense of grounding, or "placing," globalization in and through Sydney.

A Grounded Rise

In Sydney, this process of emergence from the margins of the world cities hierarchy has taken what might at first be interpreted as an almost opposite form of urbanization to Dubai. Besides promoting the preservation heritage landmarks, local authorities and planners have progressively sought to diversify the landscape of the "towns" and ethnic neighborhoods that constitute the non-Anglo-Saxon texture of the Australian society, like Little Italy in Leichhardt just west of the City of Sydney or "Vietnamatta" in the Cambramatta suburb further inland toward Liverpool. Certainly, local authorities have more than a vested interest in promoting these spatial features, which are not only a source of local distinctiveness but often also attractive hubs for tourists and residents in search of particular culinary, cultural, or even more generically "ethnic" experiences.[11] Chinatown is a particularly fitting case in this sense. The City of Sydney has long taken special care of its core ethnic neighborhood, with interventions dating back to 1972 and the redevelopment of Dixon Street, central axis of the area, to better suit the needs of its growing Northeast Asian community. Now widely regarded as the Chinese heart of the city, the area has in the past few years seen the city council going to great lengths to integrate specific "ethnic" plans into its strategic initiatives, like the *Sustainable Sydney 2030* strategic plan, which set out the City's vision in 2008. This strategic approach partly mirrors the region-wide *City of Cities* approach sketched by the New South Wales government within which the City has to operate, but it is not solely a spatial differentiation process: planning localized distinctiveness within the City of Sydney is also a process that aims to depict the Harbor City as a cosmopolitan hub capable of offering and conjugating a multiplicity of different "ethnic" lifestyles. As the study leading to the Chinatown redevelopment noted: "The overriding purpose for improvements to the Chinatown area is to upgrade and enhance its special character which is unique to other parts of the City: to respect, protect and build on the area's historic links with Chinese culture and the Chinese community, together with the growing influence of other Asian cultures and communities, while recognizing the area's importance to contributing to the vitality and diversity of Sydney as a global City."[12] The planners' substantial attention to projects like Chinatown demonstrates there is also a need for smaller urbanism that creates the essential conditions for such cosmopolitan identity for the global city beyond the postcard memories of the transient tourist and into the mundane experience of the global city dweller living the everyday life of these metropolises. Despite the upward scalar abstractions inspired by intercity competition and big-picture thinking, planners often demonstrate a willingness, where not a concern, to produce global cities from below.

As Donald McNeill emphasized in relation to the City of Sydney council, there is a growing awareness among local government officials that the "globalized" spaces of central business districts and key commercial neighborhoods might run the risk of becoming bland and devoid of meaning while, on the other hand, culture and livability features are a central component of a global city's competitiveness.[13] As McNeill notes, the *Sustainable Sydney 2030* vision was extensively influenced by Danish urban designer Jan Gehl, who before that was associated with "the large-scale pedestrianism of Copenhagen" and "whose advocacy of urban design and place-making as a means of improving the social life of central cities" had been noticed and applied in Melbourne already, with the task of producing a "lively, engaging city center" for Sydney.[14] This pervasiveness of imported design rationales in Australian planning is not limited to major developments only. For instance, as part of the effort to "elevate" design in Sydney, the State Environmental Planning Policy on "Design Quality of Residential Flat Development" (known as SEPP 65) was introduced in 2002 to implement "principles for good design" to residential flat buildings in all of New South Wales. One crucial consideration that is in many cases overshadowed by the global city discourse, however, is that design in this case is not just an instrument for iconicity. Rather, the authorities in Sydney, and in a similar way in Dubai, have been focusing on the role of high-standard built forms because of their capacity to lift the quality, and even more importantly the perception, of these cities' living environments on par with perceived global competitors. The aspiration here is not just one of quality but also an underlying imagination that sees these cities as competing onto global economic circuits. Yet this does not mean that globalization happens purely from above. Rather, as we will see more in detail in chapters seven and eight, it is embedded in localized processes of governance too. For instance, these directives aimed at improving the designed status of the city are tightly influenced, at the local authority level, by the presence of bodies like the North Sydney Council's Urban Design Advisory Panel or the City of Sydney Council's Sydney Design Advisory Panel, which is tasked with "assist[ing] the City in its promotion and delivery of world class urban design, architecture and sustainable and inclusive design in Sydney's buildings and public spaces."[15]

As with the idea of premium connections, the sense that globalization is put in place and grounded via global cities is not a relic of 1990s global city thinking. Rather, the eighteen-to-twenty-five age bracket of our experts commonly referred to this feature of global cities—perhaps even more than their older counterparts. Possibly because of the complicated jargon here, but also because it appears in global city texts in many different ways, the idea of the "materially grounded" nature of the global city was never mentioned explicitly but was one of the most common implicit (i.e., discussed with synonyms) concepts in nearly a third of the interviews for this book. The private sector and local government, far more than national government experts, are mostly where this attention is placed, oftentimes and quite logically next to discussions of premium connections and gateway functions inherent in global city building. Here, those experts who identify as architects or with architecture backgrounds are by far the most common users of this idea, especially alongside the sense of how the global city articulates globalization through a "place." As I will illustrate more in depth in chapter six, the "placing" of globalizations through the specifics of a located city is a central tenet of global city thinking. Yet it is perhaps more tightly intertwined, as figure 5 below illustrates, with the global city discourse in and about Singapore than that in Sydney, where placing such as the one described above is perhaps limitedly only linked to the worlding of the city as a global hub.

The Rise of Dubai

Staring down at traffic-clogged Sheikh Zayed Road from Dubai's numerous sky-scrapers, a foreign observer might have a hard time visualizing that the city was a cramped village of fishermen until the mid-nineteenth century. Yet, the Emir-ate has come a long way since its 1833 establishment by Sheikh Maktoum bin Bati. Despite suffering an acute epidemic of smallpox in its original settlement (the Bur Dubai), and then a devastating fire in its marketplace (Deira), the city has undergone a rapid evolution from its preindustrial conurbation to a postin-dustrial center in a little more than fifty years. Dubai has grown faster, and has grown more recently, than both Singapore and Sydney, and perhaps we can think of Dubai as part of a third wave of "new" global cities that have gone from off the map to on the global map. Its pearl-based commerce of the nineteenth century was fast replaced by trade with South Asia in the early 1900s and boosted by the discovery and burgeoning of the oil industry in 1966—something that has fueled, according to some, a "super-fast" urbanism that embodies its great-est comparative advantage with the other cities in question here.[16] In 1971, the sheikhdom formed a union by joining forces with Abu Dhabi and presenting an intricate Islam-inspired constitution to the five other former states of the Trucian Oman, which, having lost their British tutelage, gathered in the present-day United Arab Emirates. The UAE's resources economy also supports, at least in Dubai and Abu Dhabi (and perhaps more markedly in the former), progres-sive growth in other sectors, especially in real estate and logistics but also to a mounting degree in tourism and some "creative" and innovation work. Begin-ning in the mid-1970s, Dubai engaged in planned expansion of its banking sec-tor and its Jebel Ali port and also developed a lucrative trade relationship with Iran during the First Gulf War with Iraq in 1980–88. As in Singapore, taxation and land management formed the core of the incentives to attract international capital and included a strong policy of low taxes and free zones such as Jebel Ali Free Zone, minimal business barriers, and the branding of the city as a stable enclave within the political turmoil of the Middle East—a geopolitical theme we will return to later in this chapter. A diversification of Dubai's economic activities, mainly to reduce its dependence on declining oil reserves (which today account for only 5.1 percent of the GDP) and seek the status of "developed econ-omy" by 2010, was central to the concerns of the ruling family and the govern-ment in the 1990s and even more explicitly in the early 2000s. In this sense, commentators noted how the Emirate has "happily embraced globalization" and grounded its entrepreneurialism in an open-door economic liberalism that has often been in tacit contrast with many regional neighbors.[17] Large tourist-oriented developments also began to appear and were scattered across the sprawling urban landscape in this period, illustrating the changing priorities of the city's governance and its attempt to attract not solely capitalist elites but also high-income customers by establishing itself as an exclusive leisure destination. Dubai soon grew to become one of the world's top immigration hubs as its rulers explicitly sought to make of this approach a fundamental tenet upon which to brand the fast sprawling Middle Eastern metropolis. At present, the national Emirati group is said to constitute well under 15 percent (or even 11 percent by some estimates) of the whole resident population, with those of Asian backgrounds (Indian, Pakistani, and Bangladeshi) accounting for nearly 85 percent of the expats.[18]

The governing elite is headed by one of the descendants of the ruling family, Sheikh Mohammed bin Rashid al Maktoum, Dubai's ruler and the UAE prime minister, who has held solid control over the expansion and diversification of the Emirate's activities. Yet plans for expanding and diversifying proved rockier than predicted when the global financial crisis hit later that year, spiking on worldwide markets in September 2008. Many wealthy foreigners were reported to have fled Dubai as market prices precipitated to a historical low. Despite the diversification strategy, the effects of widening recessions and stock market crashes have significantly impacted Dubai. Although the ruler promptly dismissed the possibility of jettisoning the 2015 plan, strategic revisions were rapidly under way, as the sinking demand for real estate and low oil prices have (for the first time) forced a reality check on the ambitions of the Emirate and a necessary rapprochement with its oil-rich neighbor Abu Dhabi. The many iconic developments that first appeared as work-in-progress in the Emirate, from the tallest building in the world to an Atlas-shaped archipelago, raised more than a few eyebrows in the Western media. To a degree, Dubai has improved its comparative advantage on some of the classic command cores of the world's economy by emerging as a "winner" in the crisis, much like Singapore, Sydney, and Beijing, against negative performances by more traditional hubs such as Tokyo, Frankfurt, and Brussels.[19] But it is important to understand that beyond the limelight (and global media attention) of the high-rises in Downtown Dubai, the city has also spent considerable capacity to become a global mobility hub, mirroring to some degree many of Singapore's logistic achievements in maritime and air traffic.

Recognition of the importance of this gateway function in between continents, not just as a destination, is embodied in the development of the new Al Maktoum International Airport, designed to host up to sixteen cargo terminals with a prospective capacity of twelve million tons and serving up to 160 million people a year (Atlanta, currently the largest airport, can handle about 90 million). It promises to provide the Emirate with a global hub twice the size of

London Heathrow. The project will not replace the current International Airport, but will soon be connected to it through a revamped 40 kilometer highway and a prospective high-speed railway. This logistics-oriented approach has found approval as some key Dubaian businesses such as Emirates Airlines have continued an almost steady rise to worldwide centrality. The city's flagship company, for instance, is now the world's fourth largest in terms of international passengers carried (just behind the main American airlines) and the second largest in terms of freight ton kilometers flown, behind FedEx. Along with the rival Qatar Airlines, the success of Emirates has recently taken the helm of gateway functions in the Gulf: as neighboring Abu Dhabi–supported Etihad Airways underwent heavy losses and strategic setbacks in the early 2010s and had to scale back to a much more limited international role, Emirates' business further fueled the hub strategy of Dubai as a key stopping point for people and goods between Asia and the West.[20] This gateway mentality is, in Dubai, often matched by some historical referencing. Not surprisingly, local officials now methodically point to how Dubai started its worldwide ascent not with the famed ports (Rashid, Hamriya, and Jebel Ali, respectively in 1967, 1975, and 1979) but rather with the opening of its International Airport in 1959. The development of thirty free trade zones adjacent to these regional and global logistic hubs also played a fundamental role in capitalizing on global opportunities in international markets to become rooted flows going through the Emirate.

Externally oriented logistics have gone hand in hand with further development of services within the city itself. For instance, the launch of the brand-new Dubai Metro in 2009, set to become the longest automated metro network in the world with more than 70 kilometers of track, was a step toward addressing Dubai's chronic traffic problems. The early 2010s post-GFC visitor who expected to find deserted malls or empty highways might be met with some disappointment. The Emirate authorities, whether in the shape of the royal family, its subsidiaries, or the municipal government, have maintained a rather firm hold on the planning of the city even after the troubles of 2008. While the city might be the last of our trio to achieve global city recognition, it is also now a well-established presence in the global imaginary. This is what many urban developers, local governments, and even national governments around the world have been referring to as the "Dubai model"—an aspirational trope that has fascinated many aspiring global cities the world over. Dubai has conjugated centralized control with an openness to flows and influences from across the more globalized echelons of the world city hierarchy. As noted above, it has built clear assets to capture global flows, as with its ports and airports, along with a suite of facilities that cater to the economic elite and big business, as with its five-star hotels and free trade zones, side by side with heavily government-driven national champions like Dubai Ports and Emirates. Yet it has done so by importing, more and more explicitly since the 2000s, the model of Singapore (and Hong Kong) based on clustering economic activity and offering beneficial conditions in terms of both tax incentives and a more lenient laissez-fare and internationally oriented culture than most of its (often troubled) neighborhood.

Key to this, and to the emergence in other cities' imaginaries of a Dubai model, has been its characteristic physical growth in the early 2000s, which more than anything else in the public imaginary has represented the ambition of the Emirate to be seen as daring and unique in its reach for global visibility.[21] Yet it is also important, as narrated regularly by several scholars and perhaps best embodied in Yasser Elsheshtawy's classic *Dubai: Behind an Urban Spectacle*, to recognize how throughout the 1990s and even more extensively in the past two decades the city has also seen a sprawling reality of urban dwellers, dwellings, and local economy well beyond the glitz of the five-star hotels—an issue I pick up more explicitly in chapters 9 and 10 of this book.[22] Overall, however, we can argue that what the three short stories recounted here have in common is not only their intertwined fortunes with the global economy but also a historical background: the current currency they can afford globally is a result of globalization pathways that date back to the 1970s, not a novelty of the 2000s as many assume, but a result of these cities' capacity to capture the opportunity to place themselves on a global system of flows, mobility, and capital. They have gone, to paraphrase Robinson, from off the map to on the map of the global economy by mediating the perception that they are a secondary or "developing" kind of city and emerging as a much more commonly accepted set of referent points in the global urban imagination.

THE TRAJECTORIES

Dubai Museum of the Future: Madinat Jumeirah, 11:00 a.m. "You have to see things in perspective." My interlocutor, Majed, is of Egyptian origin but has long served as a senior adviser to the ruling family. In the unforgiving lunchtime heat, we briskly make our way between the main pavilion of the Madinat Jumeirah Conference Centre, site of the World Government Summit (which Dubai has hosted regularly since 2013), and a purpose-erected square white hub across the faux creek that surrounds the Madinat. The hub hosts the now-regular Museum of the Future exhibition, which I was lucky to get a sneak peek of, courtesy of a friend. Majed is keen to illustrate how Dubai is charting a path that other global cities should follow. His hopeful narrative is one of continuous backward-forward jumps between tradition and the future, which he illustrates by taking me through the Dune-shaped 2015 Expo UAE pavilion set in Milan. The pavilion was designed by London-based Foster and Partners Architects to create a link between the traditional desert-rooted history of the UAE and the hypermodern innovation in energy efficiency and augmented reality. Majed speaks of the traditions and "trajectories" that link the history of the global city to its "[path]way" to global success.

The Museum of the Future pavilion organized by the Dubai Future Foundation at the annual summit has been a regular attraction of the event since the 2016 exhibition.[1] The Foundation, at the pinnacle of the Emirate's Dubai Future Agenda, represents a certainly not insignificant AED 1 billion (approximately US$272 million) Future Endowment Fund. In the eyes of the ruler, the foundation is to replicate the role of the ninth-century Grand Library of Baghdad, also known as the "House of Wisdom," not so much as a place of preservation and translation but chiefly as "a global model for sciences and a platform for innovators from all over the world" as Dubai continues in its "usual" business of "shaping the future."[2] Rest assured, this is no summit exhibition gimmick, Majed stresses, waving his index finger. The museum is getting its own US$136 million futuristic building located just under the iconic Emirates Towers along Sheikh Zayed Road, designed (and partly 3D printed) in a hollow oval shape and standing out clearly as a statement at the beginning of the main artery across the city. Yet the (building's) "content matters" even more than the "usual" visuals that make it into CNN reports and architectural magazines, says Majed. They should be inspiring because, in his view, Dubai is trying to "stand out" from the crowd in a way that is tangible, grounded, and progressively recognized.

Kicked off in 2015 with the goal of building the world's first "Office of the Future," a fully functional 3D-printed building, the museum and foundation hold particular importance in Dubai's bid to further diversify its basis from logistics and leisure (and real estate speculation) and to embrace innovation as a core credo of how to build a global city and putatively foster a "creative class appeal" unique to the Middle East.[3] This is not just a matter of playing a role in the "future *of* Dubai," Majed stresses, underplaying Dubai's effort in the Florida-esque "war for talent," but rather building Dubai as a key player in "business of *the* future"—a "global city of innovation," that is. Yet even this quintessentially future-oriented point of view, as the start of this vignette notes, is very much embedded in an imaginary that sees Dubai both in a historical trajectory (of growth) and in relation to a variety of other cities (competitors and peers). The relationship with these peers, and whether they can grasp, as he says, Dubai's uniquely oriented and fast-growing "capital" in the business of futures, is vital to the "survival" of the city.

Ola Söderström has echoed this approach by demonstrating how even "off the map" cities in the Global South are enmeshed in transnational relationships that determine their growth. Illustrating this in Hanoi, Vietnam, and in Ouagadougou, Burkina Faso, Söderström called for closer attention to the "politics of translocal connections" as clear determinants of the intensity and orientation of the "trajectories" of urban development.[4] Standing out still happens in relation to a group, and in relation*ship* with the members of that group—be they regional or global centers of influence. Once again, this reminds us that symbolic power does not take place in a vacuum but rather is very much the "stuff" (as Bourdieu put it) of social relations. It also underscores, perhaps not so clearly in the words and imagination of Majed and those closer to the sheikh, that these trajectories hit the ground in Dubai and intersect with those of many different interests in and for the city—creating a complex reality of networked urban governance. As British

FIGURE 7. Inside the Museum of the Future.

geographer Doreen Massey put it apropos of London, "Multiple trajectories come into collision" in a global city, a place whose own trajectory's "gaze sweeps the planet."[5] Majed shares some whispered insecurity here: it very much depends too on a complicated dance of "sort of politics" behind "the scenes" and across a variety of more or less informal councils (as we will see below, named *majlis* in the Arabic tradition). Understanding how these politics play out is very much an exercise in contemporaneously appreciating future orientations and the historical processes that led us here, in relation to places other than Dubai, or indeed Sydney and Singapore.

Urban Governance Trajectories

The creation of governing relationships between those who control the city and those who live under such rule is no short-term feat. Even behind the myth of super-fast urbanism, Dubai, just like Sydney and Singapore, can showcase both historical and international trajectories. Hence, as several authors, including Chris Davidson and Kristian Ulrichsen, have pointed out, understanding Dubai's governance requires more nuance than many popular commentators give away.[6]

It encompasses (soft) authoritarian rule, strong developmental visions, a lean and efficient state apparatus, active market interference, reliance on the market mechanism, and a pragmatic (not ideological) approach to development. This means developing a more nuanced view of the Emirate while not condoning the city's centralization of authority.

Dubai's neoliberal "informalization" has deep roots in the Emirate's history that go all the way back to Sheikh Maktoum bin Hushur's effort in 1901 to establish Dubai as a free trade area to attract migrants from the port of Lingah on the Persian coast. A "protection agreement"[7] was arranged between the sheikh and the merchants, who saw the free tax status of Dubai (1984) as key to their economic aspirations. This was a strategic move that has had significant implications for the development that followed in the twentieth and twenty-first centuries, setting up the system of "financial patrimonial-clientelist favors" in exchange for the merchant/business class's complete political compliance.[8]

This is not to say that Dubai's history is not void of political resistance. Inspired by shifts of power in the region (Kuwait in particular), Dubai's merchants sought in 1938 to impose reforms on Sheikh bin Hushur. This move sought to bring practices of merchant-ruler relations from the formal backstage and informal front-stage politics to a formalized front-stage politics, and in doing so left ripple effects on the shape of "experimental" urban politics in Dubai. The merchants did not depose the ruler, but instead installed a fifteen-member majlis (a sort of common interest assembly, something I detail more in depth below) with the ruler as president. Central in this move was that much of the reformist campaign did not take place in just a subpolitics setting but also included members of the rulers' extended family. Critically, this move enhanced the importance of informal practices, leading to the creation of a permanent but relatively hidden structure of the Emirate's urban governance. During the period that the merchants' majlis was in operation (which was less than a year), it created a number of important institutions, including the municipal council, planned for a social security system for the elderly, elected new customs officials, and established an education department. In 1939, the ruler took advantage of backing by the British to dissolve the majlis and regain control. Yet some of those structures formalized in the merchant experiment retained importance throughout the decades and resurfaced after the independence of the Emirate as central to the formal governing of the city by the sheikh.

Critical in this power transition was the institutionalization of formal politics in the "backstage" of urban governance. This predominantly takes the shape of consultation and access via a system of *majâlis* (plural of *majlis*) that is today a common political tradition of the Gulf States. To be certain, this is backstage because majâlis in Dubai do not have any formal consultative or legislative powers. Yet they are an expanding boundary between a formally sanctioned space of engagement (where discussions of policy change are possible among Emirati) and the formal process of government that can be seen from the outside and on the surface; however, they are still not directly accessible by wide international audiences, like those at the formally sanctioned "informal" policy talk at conferences like the Dubai World Government Forum. If in the previous ruler's tenure (Sheik Rashid, 1958–1990) the majlis consisted of a set group of leaders that functioned in place of a formal government organization, at the turn of the century and throughout Dubai's global city expansion in the early 2000s, this took on a broader meaning, ranging from informal sessions at which (some) expats are welcome to exclusive meetings among senior government officials and/or business leaders. As I have argued elsewhere, this appreciation of Dubai's urban politics calls for a deeper sense of how governance is structured in the Emirate, paying attention to the system of majalis interest groups that, starting with the immediate proximity of the sheikh and spanning the city's ruling class, characterize the shape of much of the politics in Dubai. Hence, it might paradoxically be that in Dubai, even more than other Western cases, the politics of informal urbanism are an extensive and varied element of how the city's governance has been and is developing.

To be certain, Davidson already noted in the early 2000s how the Emirate's internal social relations are partly depoliticized via what he called "sovereignty bargains" between the ruling family (and its extended Emirati circle) and foreigners who move to and trade with Dubai. The line between informal and formal is blurry, represented mostly by the physical presence of authority (the ruling family's majâlis) or its closest advisers. These are people like Mohammed Abdallah al-Qarqawi, who heads Dubai Holding, Sultan Ahmed Bin Sulayem, who heads Dubai World, and Mohammad bin Ali al-Abbar, who heads the Department of Economic Development and Emaar—the Emirate's largest government-controlled property development firm. Quite rightly, then, Dubai's present governance is highly dependent on social relations embedded in informal settings. Ahmed Kanna has taken this view to depict the Emirate as the quintessential "corporate city" with the sheikh as its CEO, and to narrate how the development of the city takes place via a complex structure of engagement with its foreign citizens and depoliticized nationals.[9] Dubai authorities themselves often refer to it as such in informal spaces like summits and unofficial engagements with international dignitaries.

Looking at this history, Martin Hvidt argues that this governance setup significantly limits the ruler's ability to deviate from the present path-dependent and strong pro-business development course. Such a policy change would endanger the development project he is heading.[10] For Hvidt, the sheikh is under constant threat that some of the business elites might leave the country in order to seek better opportunities elsewhere, and thus he is forced to accommodate the wishes of the new internationalized business class in policy formulation and execution. Thus, the majâlis continue to provide an important informal consultative channel between the ruler and the citizens in Dubai. As Emirati political scientist Abdulkhaleq Abdullah suggested, one should think of it as a two-tier system: a first tier of the traditional government departments (e.g., Dubai Municipality) and a second tier erected during the rule of Sheikh Mohammed around his Executive Office, which manages all new developments from megaprojects to free zones and ports. The creation of the office went hand in hand with the consolidation of an even broader system of formal backstage governance that linked the merchant and business classes: previously heading these activities were more than sixty separate entities, which merged in 2005 and 2006 into Dubai Holding and Dubai World, two giant holding companies. This has condensed some informal politics, conducted in front of the international public, and formalized backstage politics, mainly in majâlis format, away from the public eye and among Emirati, around core issues of the city's urban development.

Central in connecting the wider realm of the majâlis of the merchant/business community and the closest majlis of the Executive Office has been the "closed doors" rhetoric promoted by the sheikh. As Hvidt puts it, "The *majâlis* and the open-doors policy provides a range of informal channels through which the business community can, and does, interact with the leadership on all levels."[11] The multiple roles of leadership and the high degree of state control of economic actors provide close ties between the public and the private sector.[12] The government has fostered an organized set of partly private actors who can provide useful intelligence and the possibility of decentralized implementation of essential state policies. Hence, the ruling elite in Dubai has thus far managed to formally sanction and bolster the importance of informality (both within the privacy of the closer majâlis and on public stages) to diminish the risks of rule alteration from backstage or circumvention and subpolitics that is today almost altogether absent in the city's politics. There remains little, therefore, in informal subpolitics that can circumvent this authority structure in Dubai, whether we look at the built environment or more broadly. As Kanna noted, this structuring of formal-informal political relations has "demobilize[d] citizens" by conflating consumerism with progress and modernity and creating a "flexible" citizenry that regularly balances Islamic traditions with modernity where explicit front-stage "politics somehow disappear."[13] As we will see in more depth on the question of "cityzenship" in chapter 10, this is perhaps one of the most fundamental problems in the construction of Dubai as a global city today. It has become a key determinant in maintaining all but Emirati in a "transient" state,

Elsheshtawy has argued in his starkly critical *Temporary Cities*, and perhaps represents the main difference between the governance of Dubai and that of Sydney and Singapore. Unable to be opened up to even a minimal degree of internationalization, while still engaging only a small percentage of Emirati in public life and offering little space to the new generation of more global citizens who have grown up in an internationally connected Dubai (not the pre-2000s version), it represents a fundamental Achilles heel of the fast-rising metropolis. Yet even in this context there emerges, as in Sydney, some important evidence as to the relative privilege afforded to business in the shaping of the city and in the architecture of urban governance that determines how Dubai, like the Australian metropolis, goes "global"—a theme confirmed in Singapore too.

Path Dependencies

Trajectories imply a degree of "lock-in" in the inertia of urban governance that characterizes cities like Sydney, Singapore, and Dubai. Again, this does not mean that politics remain still and devoid of change. The first efforts to regulate the evolution of the Emirate date back to 1960, when Sheikh Rashid bin Saeed al Maktoum entrusted the British architect John Harris with the task of systematizing the development of Dubai's infrastructure. Harris's master plan focused on essential urban features that the city lacked almost entirely, including a system of paved roads, basic utilities such as water provision to more than eighty thousand households, and city lighting. The plan was rather modest in its scope, especially because of the limited financial situation of the Emirate at the time, but it made some important steps in terms of calling for zoning for residential, industrial, and commerce areas, as well as promoting the idea of a new town center beyond historic Deira.[14] It was the discovery of oil at the end of the decade, as well as the growing role of the Emirate as a commerce hub, that led to a renewed version of Dubai's master plan—once again authored by Harris in 1971. While recommending continuity in the same zoning (now "section") approach, the new vision called for an expansion of the Dubai Creek area and a better connection between the two sides of the city, Bur Dubai and Deira, to be developed through two bridges and a tunnel capable of accommodating the increased number of cars—a problem endemic to the city to this day. Likewise, the plan made provisions for better connections with the newly built Port Rashid, which was to open in 1972.[15] The 1970s, then, saw a "period of planned suburban growth" characterized by a progressive emergence of the Sheikh Zayed axis between the Creek and Jebel Ali as the "new Dubai" commercial and financial heart of the city.[16] The problem of managing Dubai's expansion, however, persisted and the government produced a variety of "structural" updates to its basic master plan to try to keep pace with a fast and unregulated urbanization. Aimed at re-charting the expanding conurbation, these visions culminated in the early 1990s with the *Dubai Urban Area Strategic Plan, 1993–2012*, which sought to establish clearer zoning guidelines for the city, but whose actual impact remains dubious.[17] At the turn of the millennium it became clear to planners and officials in the Dubai municipality, and not least to the reigning family, that the city required a more specific strategic direction in terms of managing the almost uncontrolled growth of both major corporate developments and smaller dwellings. Besides, starting with the *Five Year Plan for Dubai Urban Area*, designed to cover the first decade of the 2000s, the Dubai municipality showed some key concerns in terms of population dynamics, and in particular as to the faith of the central areas of the CBD; with most high-income residents relocating to wealthier suburban areas, several parts of Jumeira (al Satwa mostly) were witnessing a sprawl in DIY retrofits of low-income households.[18] This led to a profusion of strategic visions concerned with a large array of urban issues from heritage conservation to traffic management and infrastructural improvement, such as the *Structural Plan for Dubai Urban Area* or the *Strategic Urban Growth Plan, 2000–2050*, which were limited not only in terms of specific planning but also in actual implementation capacity. In this sense, while one could argue that, contrary to the widely held view, Dubai is the quintessential unplanned metropolis, there have been a number of efforts toward providing some strategic direction to the city's urban development. The most visible of these attempts was perhaps manifested in the *Dubai Strategic Plan 2015*, which was issued on the eve of the global financial crisis (2007). The document, branded under the tagline "Dubai . . . where the Future Begins," took stake of the 13 percent economic growth rate of the past years and formulated an ambitious plan to make Dubai a more integrated, environmentally sustainable, and even more modern metropolis. The impacts of the global economic downturn, however, would soon challenge these expectations in the wake of unprecedented economic turmoil and a collapsing real estate sector. The plan has since become an object of substantial revisions in a process in which the government has demonstrated substantial awareness of the impact of the crisis, with an all-out scrutiny of all components of the strategy.[19]

Up until this point, with perhaps the original Harris plan being the only exception, the influence of the ruling family and the Dubai government in planning the specific direction of the Emirate had remained relatively limited. Interestingly, the Dubai Municipality, which has jurisdiction over municipal services and maintenance and was established as early as 1954 by the then crown prince of the Al Maktoum family, has remained a largely technical body with very little impact on policymaking. This is evidenced by the directorship of the body, held by a civil engineer, Hussain Nasser Lootah, who replaced another long-serving engineer and public administrator, Qassim Sultan al-Banna, who had been in charge since 1985.[20] The overall role of the municipality, then, has to date been largely detached from the overarching policymaking structure and mostly confined to the implementation of strategic decisions from the Dubai government and the ruling family—or, at best, expert consulting on metropolitan planning issues, as with the process that led to the *Dubai Strategic Plan 2015*, first issued in February 2007 and then partly revised in light of the financial crisis. Compared with the planning experiences of London and Sydney, which we will encounter in the following chapters, the strategies set out between the 1970s and 2008 were limited in reach and broad in strategic direction. Most of these documents sought to identify general areas of necessary and desired development, and some of them indicated specific zoning requirements. But the overall approach to urban development in Dubai has long remained a relatively relaxed laissez-faire one whose only real constraints were those imposed by the international markets. The city witnessed aggressive economic neoliberalization in respect to the rest of the Middle East, with a growing inference of "external" (read: international) actors and capital, which in turn shaped the development of the city throughout the late 1990s and early 2000s.

Colonial Legacies

Inevitably, when recounting the trajectory to global city status of many cities beyond Europe, colonial heritage and postcolonial ties are of central importance to detail today's realities. It might be useful, then, to begin by considering the relationality of some early plans that set the course for these three cities' emergence to worldwide renown. In London, this strategic thinking originally took the shape of the 1944 *Greater London Plan*. Prepared by professional planner Patrick Abercrombie and based on his earlier draft "County of London Plan," the *Greater London Plan* was devised to seek a holistic solution to the expanding conurbation of the British capital and eventually became the blueprint for London's postwar reconstruction. The plan is widely regarded for its lasting impact on the city owing to its big-picture vision for London's growth in the 1950s. This is perhaps best represented by Abercrombie's proposal for the establishment of a "green belt" around London. This area would be kept free of development and would surround the broader conurbation, separating the outer country reserved for agriculture from the "green belt ring" to be used for Londoners' recreational activities and the central city for the built environment. Abercrombie's plan was to remain a fundamental imprint on the emergence of London as a dominant world city.[21] The plan and more generally the early efforts toward a coordinated development of London have had some direct connections to analogous attempts in Sydney and Dubai. In the 1940s the Australian metropolis had just topped one million inhabitants and inaugurated the iconic Sydney Harbor Bridge, but it was also suffering quite substantially from the aftermath of the Great Depression and the Second World War. The area where the city was located, known as Cumberland County, was one of the few that after the war was governed, albeit briefly, by a region-wide council (known as the Cumberland County Council and in place from 1945 to 1964). Under the *Local Government (Town and Country Planning) Amendment Act 1945,* the council established provisions for a comprehensive local planning scheme for the city. The *County of Cumberland Planning Scheme*, which was to go into the annals of Australian history as Sydney's first plan and one of the first key metropolitan area development plans in all of the country, was released in 1948. Unsurprisingly, owing to both the colonial legacy and the popularity of the *Greater London Plan* among British-trained planners, the plan drew much inspiration from Abercrombie: it introduced land use zoning and suburban employment zones, as well as the idea of a green belt for greater Sydney. Yet the plan, as well as the council, was met with growing and strenuous opposition from property owners, industrial sector developers, and other layers of government. In response to these mounting pressures, the Cumberland County Council was dissolved on 19 December 1963 and replaced by the State Planning Authority. The limbo in metropolitan planning lasted until 1968, when a new vision for the Sydney region was released: the *Sydney Region Outline Plan*. This plan abandoned the green belt–satellite city concept in favor of linear development. Unlike the *County of Cumberland Planning Scheme* before it, this plan was never made law, and while this, in theory, enabled greater flexibility and change, it allowed much less control over planning in the metropolitan Sydney region. This change was from a legally enforced metropolitan plan to one based on objectives and principles, without the comprehensive detail that had been a vital underpinning of the *County of Cumberland Planning Scheme*. For a long time, then, Sydney was without a citywide strategic direction—a void filled only much later by the initiative of the government of New South Wales described above.

Dubai, on the other hand, presents us with some similarities with Sydney, albeit on a much smaller scale. The Harris 1960 and 1971 master plans were in fact devised for growth in the Emirate but had to deal with a much more limited urbanized area, as well as with fewer planned original settlements. Harris's experience in the Gulf began with smaller-scale developments—in particular, the construction of Doha's state hospital in Qatar in 1952, whose contract he won through a competition at the Royal Institute of British Architects. Yet, when Sheikh Rashid bin Saeed al Maktoum called him to Dubai for the master plan, Harris was very much working in the shadow of Abercrombie with his focus on zoning and strategic networking of key metropolitan hubs, but he had little engagement with notions of parklands and green belts owing to the obvious adverse environmental conditions of the city. Likewise, considerations of open spaces and public use of the built environment, besides some key technical developments such as the lighting system over the main roads of Dubai, were equally sidelined because of the concurrent financial limitations and specific cultural and religious needs of his employers, who very much favored some evident lines of continuity in the city's development with some traditional Islamic canons. To find a comprehensive and growth-oriented approach like Abercrombie's or Cumberland's in Dubai, perhaps we need to consider Harris's work in relation to the later *Dubai Urban Area Strategic Plan, 1993–2012*, which sought to establish clearer zoning guidelines for the city and aimed at reconceptualizing the planner's vision in relation to the needs of an emerging commercial hub for the Gulf, although with dubious impact on its effectiveness. However, as with Sydney and London, the Harris plan laid the bare bones of the metropolitan evolution of the Emirate: if London was to be defined by the green belt and parkway systems, and Sydney was shaped by the focus on the bay and the centrality of the harbor with functional satellites in the west and southwest, Dubai's linear development from Deira through Bur Dubai and forth to Jebel Ali also owes much to its original master planner. Likewise, the early policy transfer resulting from the popularity of Abercrombie's experiment as well as the colonial linkages made it possible that in all of these cities the emphasis on networking among core metropolitan hubs for commerce and public life was embedded at an early "globalizing" stage. Yet to find even more direct parallels on the strategic *global* city emphasis of these three metropolises we need to look ahead, to the 2000s.

For instance, it is almost impossible to understand the governance of the Emirate by paying exclusive attention to its formal governmental bodies. Rather, a key institution that shapes politics and policymaking in the Emirate, as well as almost all layers of Emirati society, is the system of majâlis. A majlis ("sitting place," for which majâlis is the plural) is generally understood as a social gathering among people with a common interest. Historically, majâlis have been a cornerstone element for Arabic rulers to relate to and consult with their citizens, although the practice is more generically understood in societal contexts other than those involving rulers as a form of informally regularized exchange for deliberating, debating, and exchanging information. This means that while in the presence of a caliph high or other dignitary, the majlis takes the shape of an appointed and consultative body or council, and the practice trickles down to other layers where governing overlaps with civil society, allowing for those in charge to discuss pressing issues with those who are subject to rule.[22]

Rarely are majâlis invested with formal powers over the rulers' decisions, although they oftentimes can substantially influence opinions and raise issues of key concern. Yet as Christopher Davidson pointed out, even this institution has evolved into a more modern function than its traditional and medieval concepts, focusing on a variety of complex issues and contributing to the governance of the Emirate.[23] The majlis is essential in the sheik's rule today as it allows him and his lieutenants to maintain semiformal relations with the business and civil society elements key to Dubai's prosperity. This takes the shape of a hierarchy of majâlis where not only nationals but also invited guests are allowed into the inner proceedings of the ruling family and its closest collaborators, and conversely where new collaborations and central political connections are forged over tea, sweets, and discussions on current affairs.[24] Hence, as Martin Hvidt noted in a study of governance in Dubai, this "provides a range of informal channels through which the business community can, and does, interact with the leadership at all levels," which in turn allows the rulers to organize a set of "partly private actors who can provide useful intelligence and the possibility of decentralized implementation of essential state policies."[25]

From "Off" to "On" the Map

So, could we argue that, at least among those who have a grasp of historical trajectory, the "ordinary" critique of the global city idea is in fact equally graspable? Jennifer Robinson's critique that the global city discourse, and imaginary of what makes a global city, leaves much "off the map," especially when it comes to Global South cities.[26] Some of the evidence above may lead us to conclude that the same logic extends quite fittingly to all of those places that for at least part of their history have been out of the dominant global imaginary. Perhaps a logical corollary would be to ask whether, in fact, Sydney, Singapore, and Dubai have now "emerged" and represent some of that very imaginary that dominates how the general public, urban practitioners, and indeed academics think of cities globally. But how well understood is this sense of emergence and exclusion in these places, and how well recognized is the long-lived legacy that sits behind it?

The importance of a city's historical trajectory stands out particularly in my interlocutors in the twenty-six to thirty-nine age bracket, where it features in numerous explicit positive and negative mentions, something that is also common in the forty-to-fifty-nine age bracket. Divergence of opinions, and "negative" scores flagging interviewees who do not feel the historical trajectory has substantial impact on the city's current globalization, tended, at least in my conversation, to emerge from a discussion as to whether the contemporary period and conditions (or "wave") of globalization are fundamentally novel or a continuation of a longer-lived process—mostly in the private sector. Nonetheless, in these discussions a sense of history (denied or relied on) remains explicit and inherent in the ways experts see the evolutions of Dubai, Sydney, and Singapore. This also perhaps makes the larger group of global city practitioners and academics aged twenty-six to fifty-nine the most historically aware. In this group, and in a few cases outside this group (twenty-five and younger or sixty and older), it is principally governmental employees at national or other layers of government beyond the municipal that record the highest mentions and most common discussions of history. This perhaps appears in many of these conversations as historically embedded in national politics: it might be the case that, especially when national and city politics do not overlap (as in Singapore), the global city is forgetting its urban history. This echoes Robinson's and others' concern that the global city developmentalist discourse through which most cities in poor countries are assessed, especially by Western lenses, is fundamentally lacking in qualities of city-ness characteristic of these places. Yet, as I highlight in chapter 9, this does not mean they lack in materiality.

Interestingly, especially given the strong "founding" narrative of Singapore and the resurgence of historical "roots" in Dubai's developments, it is in fact in Sydney that discussions of historical trajectories of the global city register the highest salience, with over one-third of the experts including historical considerations in their interviews. This is often in relation to issues of development from the original colonial settlement and attachment to its British colonial heritage, which along with mentions of the historical evolution of local politics and the historical relationship with the national neighbor / rival Melbourne account for the most common narrative here.

This evidences that there are, in fact, some historically built-in "comparative gestures"—as Robinson would call them and as I detail in more depth in chapter 12.[27] London is a recurrent presence in the minds and strategies of planners and politicians in Singapore, Sydney, and Dubai. So how do these strategic practices relate to the British capital? One obvious starting point is the direct colonial connection at hand here. London's global history is intertwined both with the extensive legacy of the British Empire and with the development of the present world system.[28] Thus, London has long been recognized as a central pivot for world affairs, and, unsurprisingly, the endorsement as a "global" city dates back to long before this term was given currency in the 1960s. Confirmed as the quintessential archetype of the global city, along with New York, London has since occupied a steady presence in the headlines of the scholarly literature and at the top of nearly all urban rankings. A key feature of these historical evolutions is that both cities can demonstrate a similar early British colonial heritage. Dubai became a protectorate of the United Kingdom in 1892 against the Ottoman threats from the North and particularly because of its privileged positioning for trading with the Gulf and South Asia. Sydney, on the other hand, was founded as a colony of the empire in 1788 and quickly became the chief British and Irish immigrant gateway for the gold rushes of the 1850s. These cities' imperial heritage allowed for early referencing back to the "core" in Singapore, Dubai, and Sydney. Embedded within the wider frame of the British empire, but also subjected to London as the model of geopolitical centrality, the three cities have since their early days had to confront a networked system of politics, commerce, and culture, which might have provided some very early bases for the internationalized thinking now at the heart of Singapore's, Sydney's, and Dubai's global city strategies.

The sense of what lies off the map and what is left out when speaking of the global centers of the world's economy is, as we saw in chapter 2, now deeply rooted in the urban imaginary and parlance of social scientists working outside these cities. The key point here is one of limited urban horizons, where assumed global places take precedence over more ordinary and mostly sidelined realities, and where little is said of the politics (and of the academics) that cause these places to exist on the map while excluding others. An interesting process that we see happening in Singapore, Sydney, and Dubai, then, is that of progressively placing these cities on such a map, with increasing recognition by the powers that move the global economy, and recognizing the politics that this process entails—a key theme of the next few chapters. This sense of being off the map is not lost across my interviews: although less salient than a recognition of the importance of history and generally below average in respect to other terms, the idea is still relatively common across the three cities and relatively more so in Sydney and Singapore than in Dubai.

Clearly this idea is far more rooted in academia than in other sectors (to the tune of four times as much)—with nine of its thirteen explicit mentions discussed by academics. Planners and social scientists, within or outside universities, and generally the broader generation of those between ages twenty-six and fifty-nine are in this case those who most commonly embrace the sense that certain cities have been or are off the map, relegated outside the assumed global geographies articulated by major global cities. Those with an architecture background, save for only one expert in Sydney, seem not to be familiar with or are not inclined to discuss global cities in these terms at all. The idea has very limited currency among local government officials and was even refuted by a number of my interlocutors who have a business and economics background. Key here is also the way we speak of what is "off the map": the vast majority of nonacademic interlocutors speak of their own city on and off various established global geographies, rather than acknowledging the presence of other cities that might be sidelined by a focus on the

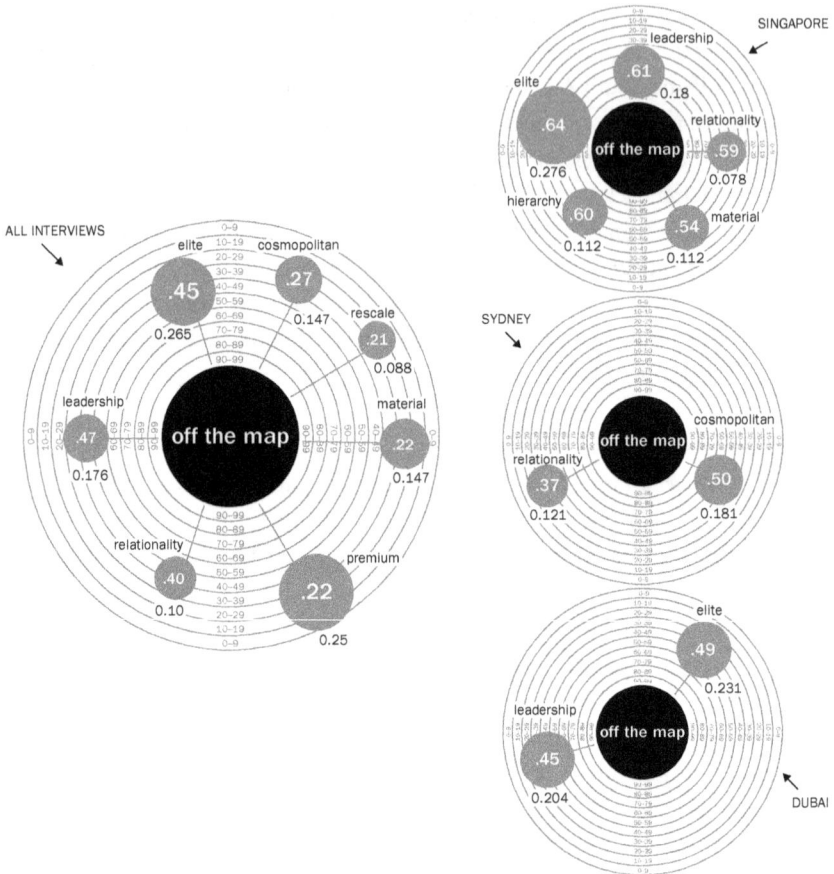

FIGURE 8. Mapping "off the map" in global city-speak.

global centers of power. Not surprisingly, then, the sense of what is off the map today (and was in the years that led to the rise of these cities) is in Singapore, Sydney, and Dubai often emerging when recounting the place of their cities in world affairs, not so much when speaking of other contexts.

Considerations of what is off the map from the global city discourse have, perhaps unsurprisingly owing to the similar scholarly lineage in postcolonial thinking, strong correlations with the idea that global city thinking is inherently metrocentric (biased toward the core of the city, and core cities in the world system). This is particularly the case in Singapore, possibly because of the better-developed and more extensively used global city discourse in the city-state, but also because of the important concentration of postcolonial scholars in the city, predominantly at the National University of Singapore, as well as those who have graduated from departments and courses that have embedded this sensibility in their curricula. The correlation between speaking of "off the map" and speaking of "metrocentricity" in Singapore is, in fact, the strongest (a 0.74 coefficient) of all the linked concepts in all interviews for this book. Dubai, perhaps at the opposite end of the spectrum, offers a limited choice in terms of this academic community, with most critical urban scholars writing on it being based outside the Emirate, as well as a comparatively smaller number of professionals who have undergone this type of education. Interestingly, of the three cities, Sydney is the only one that has a clear correlation between conversations as to what is off the map, or indeed of how the cities have emerged from off the map, and the sense of hierarchy between global cities. Quite simply, the correlation between discussing history on or off the map and hierarchy is, aside from Sydney (a 0.6 coefficient), lacking in the vast majority of my interlocutors' views—a key element of developing a perhaps more nuanced and certainly more explicit political realization of the differential power that cities yield on a world stage, and of the impact this has on purportedly "less global" cities. This is even more important because it might appear, then, that by missing a more explicit sense of history and trajectory, elites in at least Dubai and Sydney might be "missing a trick." But symbolic power depends on the degree to which "the vision proposed is founded in reality."[29] The process of historicizing and contextualizing a city in relation to a long-lived global lineage, as we have seen in Singapore, is particularly important for elites and authorities to manage the reality they govern from. The challenge, however, is not to simply reengineer this sense into the cultural scene but to make it part of people's habits and everyday experiences—the *doxa* Bourdieu speaks of as a core field of symbolic interaction. Nonetheless, this implies drawing boundaries that further shape the imaginary of what these global cities are.

In cases where my interlocutors discuss what is off the map, we often relate this conversation not just to cities away from the place we are focusing on, but also to what is not accounted for in the built form of their cities: metrocentricity is not just about other urban centers (as we will see in chapters 9 and 10) but also about what is out of the "metro" in Sydney, Dubai, and Singapore—echoing, for instance, Australian conversations about the suburban realities of Western Sydney and rural-urban splits in the character of "global" city living around the New South Wales capital. This connection is particularly strong in Sydney (0.5 correlation), where in many cases interviews that discussed the dominant "cosmopolitan" character of the global city also brought up discussions of what is left off the map. Thinking of the implications of what is left off the map is also, especially in Singapore and Dubai, correlated to conversations about the role of elites in shaping the development of these cities, showing strong correlations with speaking of leadership in Singapore, where the national story recounted above clearly echoes the place of the nation's founder Lee Kuan Yew in lifting the city from off the map of relative colonial anonymity to global hub. This is echoed in Dubai, perhaps a little less strongly but with some sound correlation, with the Al Maktoum family, but is absent in Sydney, despite its having an increasingly proactive mayor like Clover Moore for the past fifteen years.

What we learn from these conversations is that history matters fundamentally to delineate the path dependencies that global cities embark on but also what symbolic system they become entrenched in. As French sociologist Emile Durkheim underlined well before Bourdieu, the existence of symbolic systems depends on a "logical conformism" between individuals who agree on their meaning and share some basic understanding of the essential language they are expressed in.[30] This is indeed evident if we think of the tacit agreement on the basic grammar structures that give meaning to sequences of words in every language, but several straightforward analogues can easily be found in cities. Colonial heritage plays an important role in all three cities, but their explicit efforts at painting a "global" city image have also brought their development into continuous dialogue with the symbolism of what accounts for a global city and the determinants of that viewpoint. The trajectory from off the map to on the map, however, remains poorly discussed and often devoid of political considerations, especially in relation to the understanding that the international geography of global cities is an uneven one and hierarchical differentiations are a central feature of this world system.

THE DISTINCTION

Chilli crab: Singapore, 11:30 p.m.

My old schoolmate Yi Ling and I are treating an academic visitor from the United States to a late-night meal of Singapore's famed chilli crab just off *lorong* 25 (Indonesian for 25th "hallway") in Geylang. The area, perhaps one of the least touristy parts of the center of the island, is peppered with local eateries and the odd prostitute soliciting attention from passers-by in the smaller *lorongs*. Anthony, our guest, is in for a treat. Said to be created for her mobile pushcart stall by Cher Yaw Tian and her husband Lim Choon Ngee by stir-frying mud crabs in chilli and tomato sauce, the dish is now well recognized by international elites like CNN Travel and local authorities like the Tourism Board as a national treasure. Our restaurant, a local institution known as "No Signboard" restaurant, was started by Ong Kim Hoi as an unnamed (hence its name) seafood hawker stall at the Mattar Road Centre in the 1970s and now has franchises in three of the island's major malls.

I am more of a black pepper crab and *mantou* (northern Chinese steamed buns) person myself, but we indulge our visitor in a quintessential local experience that, he feels, is "Singapore on a plate." Rich in its possibly slightly fabricated backstory, object of a bitter early-2000s dispute with the government of Malaysia, recognizably Southeast Asian but still familiar in its components, and popularized by the likes of Conde Nast Travel and Lonely Planet guides, the dish gets him talking about the unique global advantages of Singapore. In this instance, for example, he explains to us how Singapore is actually the greenest global city on the planet. He is referring to the Massachusetts Institute of Technology's release of

FIGURE 9.   Singapore: global and cosmopolitan (plaque at Henderson Waves).

Treepedia, a project by Senseable Cities Lab that analyzes Google Street View imagery of cities to calculate the percentage of each scene containing plants, trees, or other green spaces into a Green View Index, a measure of twenty-seven cities in which Singapore is first, followed by, you guessed it, Sydney and nearly double the result of London. Yi Ling and I saw this presentation a year earlier at MIT's Singapore campus, but I indulge our interlocutor to understand the logic of what makes the city unique. Anthony's logic is deeply impacted by the dynamic of symbolic power. Singapore is distinctive because of its externally validated, in fact ranked (see chapter 11 for more on this), uniqueness, but it also stands out in familiar terms. Whether it is the chilli crab or the green canopy around town, we speak of relatively distinctive offerings but in relatively graspable and commonplace features of major cities around the planet. Key international flows and actors play a core role in this, but explicit local strategies have sought to tap into the symbolic systems these flows and actors operate in, and capitalize on, their appeal.

This logic is not a complex scholarly theorem: its roots are tightly intertwined with the logic by which Singaporean authorities have built the city's distinctiveness over the past four decades. In Singapore we encounter tangible evidence that the idea of the global city is by all means not simply the heritage of academic thinking, or that it emanates just with the core metropolises of the Global North. Quite the contrary. An explicit usage of this terminology has been historically embedded in the growth of Singapore. Since its early days government leaders have been constituting a continuing rhetoric, and time and time again restated the global city as an objective and a model to be followed in the developmental trajectory of the city-state. Perhaps one of the best examples of this, Yi Ling reminds me (as she is a better urban historian than I am), is the case of the now-famed 1972 "Singapore: Global City" speech at the Singapore Press Club by Sinnathamby Rajaratnam, then foreign minister and one of the architects of the Singaporean independence in the mid-1960s. In a relatively tongue-in-cheek rebuttal to detractors of the city-state's success, Rajaratnam sought to solve the "mystery" of why post-independence Singapore was not collapsing. Was Singapore's success, "which some people find worrying and others somewhat irritating," just "an illusion created by a cunning arrangement of mirrors"? Here the minister observed that the solution to this "puzzle" was that, at the time, Singapore was "transforming itself into a new kind of city—the Global City."[1] Speaking at the same time as early global city writers like David Heenan and Stephen Hymer (both early users of the term in the 1970s), Rajaratnam was not borrowing from the heyday of these global city theorists but perhaps more explicitly from British historian Arnold Toynbee and his idea of cities "embracing the world" throughout history, with some less explicit echoes of Peter Hall's notion of the "world city" in this and other speeches.[2] For Rajaratnam, the path ahead is clear: it is a "global character which distinguishes this type of city," and it is its connectedness to the fortunes of other planetary hubs that makes its unique. "Global Cities, unlike earlier cities, are linked intimately with one another," he says to spur Singapore to embrace its embeddedness in the global (economic) system. Distinction is vital to the global city, but it needs to happen in a reality where cities are interlinked, and where global flows and fortunes are determined by relatively common terms of a global game.

Symbolic power does not come without contrast and globalization appears to many as the only viable developmental pathway in an interconnected age. The importance of this is reiterated over and over by Singaporean authorities. For instance, in 2011 the deputy prime minister Wong Kan Seng noted how for Singapore "becoming a global city is not merely an aspiration" but "a prerequisite for our survival," as "closing our doors would only turn us into an island of no consequence, unable to provide for our people. We will become irrelevant to the world." Not surprisingly, Wong's intervention referred explicitly to Rajaratnam's 1972 "global city" speech. Centrally, though, the deputy prime minister highlighted an important balancing act. Singapore's leadership sees itself as custodian of the city and seeks to maintain a global outlook. In his words, global cities are also "centers of change [. . .] open to constant flows of people, capital, technology and ideas: to thrive, global cities remake themselves from time to time, implementing bold initiatives that the rest of the world study, and perhaps eventually adopt."[3]

While we could think of this as originating in the study of "world city functions" typical of the late 1960s with Peter Hall or the late 1980s and early 1990s with Friedmann, Wolff, and the GaWC program, younger generations have strong echoes of the idea that the global city articulates globalization through a "place." The data show that the eighteen-to-twenty-five age bracket of our experts commonly refers to this feature of global cities, perhaps even more than their older counterparts. Equally, the sense that cities become anchors of globalization by offering a key place on spaces of global flows is common among those who mentioned at least one Global South city in their discussions, signaling once again an expansion of global city thinking, but also of the geography of networks and connections linking global cities to global markets.

The idea of placing globalization, generally well understood across conversations with my interlocutors (at an above-average overall salience of 0.171, the sixth most commonly referred to concept), offers a series of interesting correlations in our three cities. Just as in Dubai, a city that we could argue was physically built with globalization in mind, interviews in Singapore display some strong correlations between the idea of putting globalization in place and the sense of the materiality of the global city. Global-speak in both city-states often links the need for international connectivity with a sense of required material transformations on the ground, be they a recognition of the importance of logistic hubs, mobility amenities like airports, or, mostly in Singapore but increasingly in Dubai too, the production of globally oriented districts and neighborhoods. Curiously, perhaps at odds with the growing popularity of "innovation districts" as a conduit of grounding globalization into innovation-focused areas of the city, evidence to the contrary has emerged in my study.[4] Interviews on Singapore also display some negative correlation with the idea that innovation is central to the global city: my interlocutors seem unlikely to discuss this innovation-driven determinant of the global city when speaking of the way the city-state anchors global flows in place (I pick up this curious negative correlation around the way global city strategies are being developed in chapter 8). Not surprisingly, our Southeast Asian case has an equally strong correlation between the placing of globalization and the production of premium connections that create privileged access to certain spaces of the city. In Singapore, then, this sense of placing globalization is correlated not only to the idea of elites but also to the way Singapore and Singaporeans narrate their story of globalizing. This link between placing

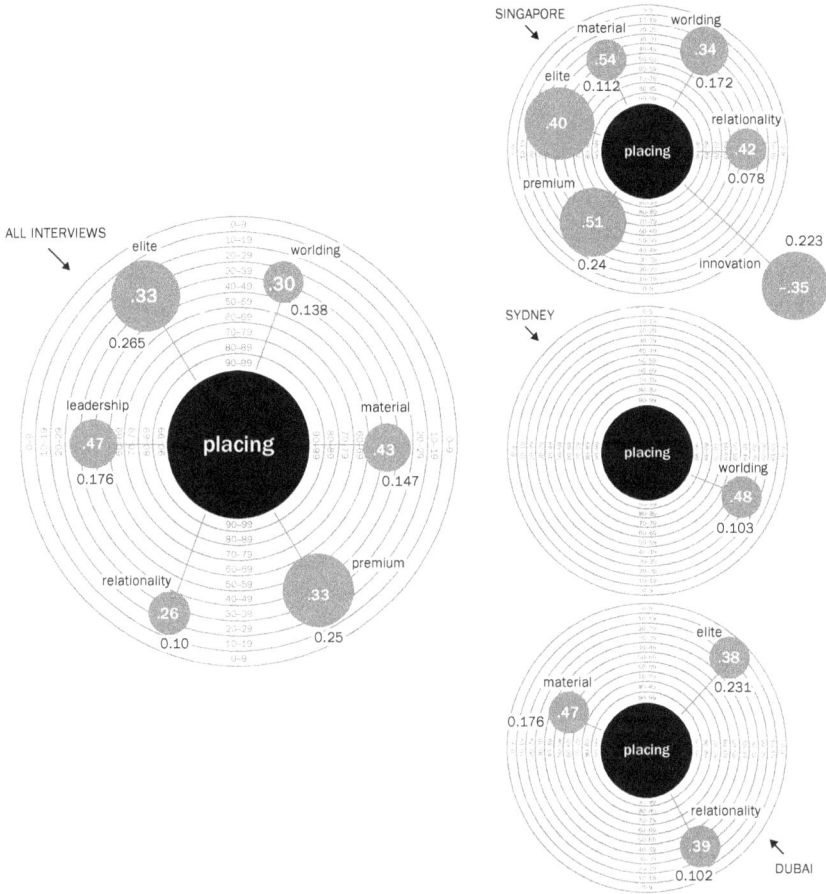

FIGURE 10.   Mapping "placing" in global city-speak.

and worlding is, interestingly, the only notable correlation in Sydney, where my conversations elicited little relation to the elements of elites, materiality, or premium connections. Yet the story of making Sydney into a global destination again presents us with familiar dynamics of symbolic power.

Destination Sydney

Since the urban boom of the mid-1970s, and even more markedly from the mid-1990s with the growing importance of its CBD as a financial hub housing the Reserve Bank and the Australian Stock Exchange, Sydney has been developed around a twofold global city strategy.[5] As Peter Murphy and Sophie Watson underlined, Sydney has centered its globalization on the themes of tourism and business, linked by the strategic branding of a Sydneysider lifestyle rooted in the cosmopolitan, modern, and relatively inexpensive features of the Harbor City.[6] In this view, Sydney's characteristics are supposed to appeal to both the transient visitor in search of the Australian experience and the corporate (middle to high) class looking for a livable but styled settlement. Tourist branding required the development and marketing of icons such as the Opera House and Bondi Beach, the improvement of mobility infrastructures to house greater numbers of transient users, and an emphasis on special events like Mardi Gras, New Year's celebrations on the Harbor, and megaevents like the Olympics.[7] In addition, Sydney has proved capable of sustaining the parallel growth of a business-pitched reorganization that has been pinpointed on similar, if not often analogous, developments: efficient mobility hubs to house global flows of not just people but also capital, information, and goods; prestigious corporate spaces such as Aurora Place and 126 Phillip Street; and cultural institutions that are compatible with and often contingent on many of the same complexes that form the visitor-oriented urban substrate. Positioning a metropolis as a postindustrial service city allows for manufacturing cores to be moved away—or indeed eliminated—from tourist and business paths, thus providing more flexibility in the rebranding and redeveloping of city spaces. Further, these configurations can coexist in the same Sydneysider lifestyle worlding, selling the Sydney experience and commodifying the urban into a product to be consumed in either the short term or the long term. Likewise, they have both equally found fertile ground in the liberalization, pluralist, and demand-oriented approach that, as we will see below, the city has followed over the past decade. Like Hong Kong and Shanghai and several other growing Asian world cities, the Harbor City has been built to compete on a global scale with other strategic sites of globalization, with local governments taking the lead role in both the political and physical construction of Sydney as a global city.[8]

As this lifestyle brand has, arguably, borne fruit, the Harbor City slowly integrated a third theme to its global city model: sustainability. Although some movements toward more integration between planning and environmentalism have been present since the 1970s and in alternate phases in the mid-1980s, the increasing centrality of green narratives and developments in Sydney has been emphasized only since the 1990s.[9] This was inaugurated by the Australian Labor Government's "Building Better Cities" plan in 1991, which prompted some ad hoc arrangements to address growing sustainability questions such as the inner docks renovation in Ultimo.[10] To be sure, this move toward a more ecological approach to city redevelopment is not unique to Sydney or Australia. Embodied by the 1992 Rio Summit (the Earth Summit) and its major outcomes—the so-called Agenda 21 and the UN Framework Convention on Climate Change—the global environmentalist movement and the progressive global governance efforts to implement sustainable-oriented policies echoed around the whole globe. Indeed, cities themselves took up advocacy and governance roles promoting cross-national initiatives through international initiatives such as the United Cities and Local Governments organization, the Cities Alliance, and, later on, the Climate Leadership Group. So, to understand Sydney's green reinterpretation of the global city idea, we need to explore how the Harbor City has integrated this "environmentalist" ethos into its twofold lifestyle approach, and what governance dynamic underlie it.

Green is nowadays a key element in the construction of Sydney's global image. It is, even before becoming part of actual urban planning, a lifestyle re-branding and a re-problematization of the city's identity in the imaginaries of global audiences. What this means in practice is that the city has to act accordingly both through the definition of a new urban narrative and through the re-configuration of its features to suit the changing discourse. If this means a paradigm shift for some metropolises, especially in the East (Hong Kong, Shanghai, Seoul, to name a few), *greening* Sydney is instead relatively easy: the city's identity is already substantiated by an environmentally prone image of the Harbor City that is solidly rooted in its lifestyle branding, be it visitor or business oriented. Ever since the 1988 twin development of Darling Harbor and the First Fleet anchorage, which now hosts Circular Quay and the Opera House, Sydney's dramatic growth in tourism and corporate activities has been tightly tied to the "café harbor society" stereotype of a green and livable city open to all kinds of guests, from the backpacker to the financial elite. This, however, should not downplay that there are some separate areas of urban and architectural development that do not overlap between these two categories. Business-oriented planning, for instance, requires interior space configurations and preferential pathways that have (and in most cases are meant to have) little connection to public areas. Nonetheless, Sydney remains one of the most striking cases of intertwining between the two. This intersection has fueled a demand for more green spaces like Hyde Park and natural attractions, and greater connectivity with the various areas of Sydney Harbor National Park, such as Watsons Bay in the far east end of the city. Arguably, the green theme has progressively acted as a linkage between the vacationer facade of the city and its corporate core, enhancing the attractiveness of the "leisure dimension" that "differentiates Sydney from other [world] cities in the Asia Pacific region."[11] Thus, reinforcing the role of culture as the glue between the operationalization of political power and the attraction of capital has been further enhanced by a greening of the Sydney-sider lifestyle that certainly appeals to both audiences. In turn, the escalating prominence of green solutions to city planning and architecture has slowly modified the patterns of consumption of the city's major urban spaces, redeveloping large central areas such as the CBD, Bondi, or Manly to fit the new dominant green ethos.

In this view, local government authorities in Sydney have taken up a vast array of initiatives aimed at improving its livability and aligning with global standards such as Agenda 21. For example, the CitySwitch initiative, a national program to reduce greenhouse gas emissions by improving the energy efficiency of office spaces, has been endorsed and promoted by Parramatta, North Sydney Council, and City of Sydney Council with the patronage of NSW Department of Environment, Climate Change and Water and in coordination with other state capitals such as Brisbane and Canberra. Climate advocacy and awareness events like Living Green or the Earth Hour are widespread throughout the year, with more-targeted campaigns promoting green practices such as cycling or car sharing usually led by the inner local government authorities. Public-private partnerships on sustainability themes between Local Government Authorities (LGAs) and companies are also a rising phenomenon.

The most influential imprint in this direction by the New South Wales government is the metropolitan planning strategy known as *City of Cities*, released in December 2005 by the minister for planning Frank Sartor and currently under review. With a substantial focus on sustainability and globalization, this state-led scheme has envisaged differential development based on a classification of Sydney's LGAs in a set of "strategic centers" with different functions. Namely, the LGAs have been ranked as "global Sydney, regional cities, major centers and specialized centers." Importantly, this view has outlined which parts of the overall conurbation "have national and international significance" (North Sydney and the City of Sydney) and which are instead major logistic hubs (such as the airport, Olympic Park-Rhodes, or Randwick Education and Health precinct), distinguishing these from "regional" service centers (such as Liverpool and Parramatta) and other sublocal communities (such as Campbelltown).[12] Likewise, the strategy has also indicated which areas have the potential, but are not presently developed, to acquire "major center" status (such as Cambramatta and Leppington).

While the plan theoretically opens up for broad participation, a few local actors have led the globalization of the metropolis and its recent environmentalist turn. The City of Sydney Council, in particular, emerged as the most active green agent of the past few years. This growing concern with environmental responses to climate change and urban livability is probably best epitomized by the aforementioned *Sustainable Sydney 2030*—a vision for a green, global, and connected metropolitan center originated in a series of public consultations and cooperation with various key international planners (such as Lendlease property management corporation) as well as architects Jan Gehl and Ken Maher and culminated in a policy document issued in 2008. This project aims to revolutionize and revitalize the metropolis's core with environmentally oriented developments and an emphasis on sublocal community improvement, setting the City of Sydney's "City of Villages" internal diversification policy on a course similar to the NSW's *City of Cities* initiative, but on a different scale. As the document points out, Sydney's inner city is thus supposed to become "internationally recognized for its environmental performance" (thus, green), "Australia's most significant global city" (thus, global), and networked within and outside its boundaries (thus, connected).[13] Perhaps we can notice here the most distinct representation of the correlation between the idea of worlding and the sense of putting globalization in place: a central place (almost unquestioned, with metrocentric critiques rarely emerging in Sydney conversations) that grounds the distinctive globally green character of Sydney in the distinctiveness of central Sydney councils and the City of Sydney LGA in particular.

While I do not wish to undermine the sustainability qualities of this strategy, there are some daunting signs in this approach. In this sense, the *Sydney 2030* strategy is not just pure corporate greenwashing on the metropolis's core—for instance, City Hall has inaugurated the 2.6 kilometer Bridge to Bridge route to expand the cyclable area of the CBD by creating a bike path between Sydney Harbor Bridge and Anzac Bridge, and this has been developed within the broader public consultation frame of the strategy. Yet, the growing marketization of these environmental developments and the vastly uncontested nature of such process have raised skepticism in civil society and academia alike. Green solutions are, in fact, increasingly presented not solely as necessities of an expanding metropolis faced with internal environmental problems and transnational climate change dangers, but also (if not predominantly, in a somewhat commodified form) as accessory features of Sydney's lifestyle branding to promote the Harbor City in the global marketplace. Little political contestation beyond some electoral squabbles has to date taken place on this crosscutting re-worlding of the city. This is tantamount to a move that, as Sharon Zukin pointed out, leads to a selective urban "upscaling" aimed at providing physical support and programmatic narratives to the "universal rhetoric of growth" fueling global cities at large.[14]

Within this strategy, sustainable developments have progressively become less and less a matter of global ethics (almost never present in policy and planning documents) and transnational collaborative endeavors (rarely mentioned); rather, they have morphed into a matter of urban performance in the global marketplace and a factor of consumer satisfaction for the city's users. This adversarial and market-driven worlding (almost at odds with the way Ananya Roy and Aihwa Ong use the term), in turn, prompts some critical reexamining of whose "spaces of dependence" are at stake in these strategies and rhetoric. Who is being targeted in this spatial reconfiguration and who has a substantial role in the governance of this greening are key matters that cannot be sidelined. This, of course, hints at another place of this study, on the shores of the Arab Gulf, whose global ambition might be even clearer than Sydney's.

Ambitious Dubai

Mohammed Alabbar, chairman of Dubai's real estate titan Emaar, had a recurring expression to describe the rationale behind his developments: "We aim," he says with compelling assertiveness, "to create a global landmark."[15] In the first decade of the 2000s, just like Sultan Ahmed bin Sulayem of Nakheel Properties and Mohammed al Gergawi of Dubai Holding, he had to carry out the epic implementation of Sheikh al Maktoum's vision. The Emirate's planners were tasked with building, where not creating anew on a sandy tabula rasa, an instantly recognizable image that testifies to Dubai's ascendance while also feeding the ruler's compulsion to set standards on a worldwide scale. Alabbar's statement was not abandoned to rhetoric. As the city quickly grew in both regional importance and urban extension, Dubai embarked on a "frantic quest for hyperbole" that has since symbolized its attempt to ascend to the Olympus of global cities.[16] Function had for long not been the primary concern in a land of endless anonymous horizons and (once) seemingly bottomless financial availability. Until the crisis struck, form was the key focus of architecture in Dubai, whose fundamental criterion is setting the standard of hypermodernity as the city that mastered a hostile nature around itself and led the evolution of urbanism in the twenty-first century.[17]

Lacking a strongly preconceived historical image, the Emirate allowed for an easier construction of a global city facade. However, while this "historical vacuum" can offer much space for place promotion, it can also hinder the formation of a convincing brand of what Dubai is—an identity that to date remains relatively weak. In order to solve this distinctiveness puzzle, the governing elite has emphasized the creation of landmarks and world-class structures capable of "controlling" and dominating architectonically the development of a unique urban identity.[18] By doing so, the Emirate has embarked on an almost unprecedented (with the exception of Las Vegas) attempt to create a set of predetermined "experiences to be consumed" by foreigners who constitute the natural target of a city where a relative minority is indigenous.[19] Dubai's ruling class has learned that, in the present "society of spectacle," global audiences in the West as well as in the richer strata of the Global South can be captivated through a proficient usage of symbolism, hypermodern imagery, and promises of growth.[20] In this context, monumental developments and high-tech public spaces are supposed to rise as cornerstones of the city by creating an instantly recognizable skyline, with a boosterism-ridden architecture concerned with making "nowhere suddenly in somewhere."[21] Dubai has perhaps long been seduced by the so-called Bilbao effect and the potential of "wow architecture" of defining a city's image in the eyes of foreign audiences.[22] Not least, it has spearheaded the promotion of a "Bilbao effect strategy" across most of the region, to Doha, Riyadh, Abu Dhabi, and beyond, through what has become known as the Dubai model: not just a planning approach but a broader entrepreneurial growth strategy (something I expand on in chapter 8).[23]

Nonetheless, the Emirati fixation with the iconic is not simply a whim of its multibillionaire leaders, as many Western commentators have argued. Iconicity is, in Dubai, a crucial pillar of the worlding of the city by the dominant elite and of the entrepreneurial narrative that has been put in place to assert the Emirate's vibrant presence in world affairs. It is a testimony to the city's dynamism and proof of its commitment to (hyper)modernity. Iconicity is also often intertwined with a search for innovation and competitiveness that has to be reflected in unparalleled constructions. In the early 2000s Dubai sought to become, in the words of Alabbar, "New York in the making."[24] Rather than a caprice, the impressing eccentricities of the hopeful global city are a vivid sign of its urban entrepreneurialism. In order to develop a global influence, however, Dubai's architectural icons need to adhere to those widespread stereotypes that represent modernization and power. As the theory of symbolic power tells us, symbolic objects are significant only if recognized as such: they depend on logical conformism between individuals who agree on the meaning of a symbol. To create an icon that has significance (and consequently influence) over a widespread audience, one has to relate to the symbolic systems shared or understood by as many as possible in such an audience—the "dominant" culture. Dubai needs to locate itself prominently within the global imagination of the audiences it tries to reach. This is not just about putting itself on the map as an exotic location, but rather speaking the language of a globalization it tries to master. The logic of "putting globalization in place," then, is essentially pinpointed on doing so in an intelligible way: it has to, first, conform to the broader language of what counts as global internationally in the eyes of those whom Dubaian authorities seek to persuade (tourists and business elites *in primis*); and, second, it has to do so in a sufficiently different way to garner some degree of power beyond pure conformism.

Skyscrapers are obviously the most common example of this, but there are other features that reify progress today: mobility hubs such as ultramodern airports or international trade centers occupy much of the global imaginary of what twenty-first-century globalization is. They are the "signs of modernity" and some of today's most "obvious candidates for housing globalized flows, whether metaphorical or material."[25] Similarly, first-class hotels and shopping malls denote the vitality of the business and tourist industries, and environmentally viable mass developments are the latest in world-class engineering and urbanism. In this context, the ability of the Emirate lies in its mirroring and enhancing of dominant symbols of modernity. Being "modern" is, in current world city-speak, maintaining a globalized entrepreneurial edge that is reflected in prominent urban restructuring—mostly geared toward efficiency and sustainability—as well as in the vitality of one city's transformative and advanced producer services economy. This does not imply that Dubai needs to change its understanding of what a modern metropolis is, but rather that it has to conform to, and excel in, such globalizing approaches. The "icons" that are sprawling around Dubai are not ends in themselves: symbolic power is a transfigured form of other types of power, be they economic, religious, or political. Icons are Dubai's means for global reach. Sheikh al Maktoum underlined this himself in a 2009 interview: "We are not growing in order to be a model for its highest building in the world, best airports, and most luxurious hotels, and the largest seaport and man-made islands: the Dubai model is beyond that."[26] Symbolic developments are the means to narrate and unfold the city's move to establish a place for channeling the major flows of globalization, and to do so in the language of the dominant form of global urbanism. The Dubai model is about reaching primacy in the latter.

A startling example of this search for a recognizable positioning in the imaginary of the global audiences was the construction of the spectacular Burj Khalifa: the tallest building in the world. The Burj, inaugurated on 4 January 2010, was officially renamed Burj Khalifa in honor of the president of the UAE and ruler of Abu Dhabi, Sheikh Khalifa bin Zayed al Nahyan, in an unexpected act of submission by Sheikh Mohammed to Dubai's wealthy neighbor. Yet, "Burj Dubai" remains the most common branding of the building in the media, popular imagination, and even official presentations such as that of the inauguration, which showcases the story of the skyscraper to endless queues of visitors seeking a ticket for the panoramic terrace on the 124th floor. It soared into the Emirate's cityscape in a little more than four years, at the impressive pace of one floor every three days. With a record height of 828 meters, the spire was already a dominant presence in the urban fabric before completion. This highrise—whose elevation was kept secret until its grand opening in 2010 by the firm that designed it, the American Skidmore, Owings and Merrill—is reminiscent of the Mile-High Illinois envisaged by Frank Lloyd Wright in 1956 for Chicago but never realized.[27] It embodies the classic human fascination with towers, symbols of power and dominance that have occupied the urban imaginary for centuries. As the construction evolved, this skyscraper attracted interest from all over the world, with investors of all nationalities rushing to secure a spot in the new Emirati icon during a two-night frenzy in 2007 when office and habitable spaces reached exorbitant prices between US$3,000 and US$4,000 per square foot.[28] Even the Burj, however, was eventually affected by the real estate crisis, with prices dropping substantially, but it remains a successful driver of attention, media coverage, and investor interest to this day.

The high-rise symbolizes Dubai's quest for uniqueness and primacy in the global city hierarchy. In this race, it also shows concerted effort of all the key players of the Emirate: the sheik, local government, major stakeholders, and transnational capitalist elites. Emaar, the developer of the Burj, has targeted the marketing of the skyscraper, which offers a multifunctional hub pinpointed on its Armani Hotel & Residence housing 160 suites and 144 cutting-edge apartments, toward the latter of the key players. Moreover, the building is the pinnacle of a much wider Emaar development known as Downtown Burj Dubai, which is spread over five-hundred-odd acres of Dubai's CBD, alongside Sheikh Zayed Road, with an estimated US$40 billion capital investment.[29] Of course, the development does not stop at the Burj Dubai in terms of world-class standards: immediately below the tower is the world's largest shopping center, the already operating Dubai Mall, circled by a boulevard that in Emaar's initial vision was capable of rivaling the Champs-Élysées in width, length, and prestige. Adorned with an aquarium that is listed in the *Guinness World Records* and an ice hockey rink that is three times thicker than those in the National Hockey League, the mall boosts the Emirati fascination with water spectacles. As the progressively dazzled shoppers make their way through the mall toward the Burj Dubai, the top-ranking boutiques leave center stage to another urban champion occupying much of the adjacent thirty-acre lake—the Dubai Fountain. Designed by Los Angeles–based WET Design to replicate and, needless to say, amplify its previous design of Las Vegas's Bellagio Fountain, this gigantic water spectacle sprays an average of twenty-two thousand gallons of water to a height of 150 meters at any given moment, with multiple cycles of color-shape combinations.

This iconic downtown enterprise is reminiscent of a similar project: the Kuala Lumpur City Centre (KLCC) and its Petronas Twin Towers building development. Set to become the tallest edifice in the world at the end of the 1990s, the KLCC has a narrative similar to that of the Burj. As explained by Tim Bunnell, "The building is seen to both image Malaysia as a 'world class' national player (and Kuala

Lumpur as a 'world city') as well as to promote new 'ways of seeing' among citizens."[30] In this sense, both cases demonstrate how the iconic high-rises are more than simply consequences of urban speculation, which is often indicated as the original reason for skyscraper development. Petronas Towers, just like the Burj Dubai, "cannot be understood merely as a function of land values" and has to be appreciated beyond its aesthetic value in its social role.[31] Key developments like the Burj fast become the tip of the sword for the city's quest for global status. The symbolic function of the iconic skyscraper in the contemporary metropolis is to define the presence of the city on a world stage, while also constituting the identity of the locals through a preponderant symbol. As Ada Louise Huxtable prosaically put it, "The tall building probes our collective psyche as it probes the sky."[32] The icon becomes a powerful defining element for the local identity, and thus a representative image of what the urban communities in Dubai, Kuala Lumpur, Sydney, London, and the like are. In this sense, it is not surprising that leaders have sought these developments as "pinnacles" of their visions. Indeed, as KLCC represented Prime Minister Mahathir Mohammad's aspirations for Malaysia, the Burj embodies Sheikh Mohammed's idea for Dubai. However, if Bunnell could justly argue that Petronas Towers was also a "space of contest" where there was, in its initial "socialization" phase vis-à-vis its urban community, a "sense of popular problematization," the same might not be true for our Emirati behemoth.[33] The Burj is used by the rulers to ascertain a local identity in relation to a migrant population, but this does not necessarily translate in either the assimilation of the expats or the construction of a more multiethnic Arab societal basis. The "citizenship" of Dubai seems to remain confined to either its original Emirati lineage (a mere 10 percent) or the transient elite who, perhaps not so paradoxically in a city built for its business-based visitors, often owns far more "right" to the city than longer-term temporary migrants residing as the city's middle and lower classes. As noted by sociologist Leslie Sklair, "The dominant forms of architectural iconicity for the global era are increasingly driven by those who own and control the corporate sector."[34] The Burj is no exception. Cutting-edge apartments, offices, and hotels within it were mainly designed and marketed toward them and are mainly built to house globalizing flows. Even if the degree of exclusion appears to be minimal (indeed, almost anyone can enter the Dubai Mall), the form and function of the development have a preconceived notion of the "in-built user" that is hardly tailored toward low-income inhabitants.[35]

As the case of Downtown Burj Dubai illustrates, the Emirate's development sought to impress and set the meter of comparison for what a modern global city is on a global scale, topping on measurements and audacity, while convening a dynamic-innovative image of the metropolis. In this, the Burj is not dissimilar from its "predecessors" Burj al Arab and Emirates Towers, which played a similar role in shaping the city's identity in the early 2000s. Likewise, it is self-referential: Dubai is an almost mandatory prefix for most of the developments, and even if the official denomination was changed at the last minute in a rather unpredictable sign of submission to the Union and its oil-rich neighbor Abu Dhabi, the name "Burj Dubai" remains the most widespread way to refer to the behemoth, used not only by the popular media but also in several official documents and in the building's inauguration exposition itself. More importantly, the construction and rhetoric of the skyscraper are reflexive of a straightforward strategy that was until a few years ago core to the Emirate. As Sheikh al Maktoum saw it, Dubai was to be "number one in the world, *in everything*."[36] Contrary to, for example, Foster's "gherkin" Swiss Re tower in London, the Burj Dubai seeks to make this statement loudly and visually: it does not rely on a "civilized dialogue between the tower and its nearest neighbors" but rather stands out and informs the *entire* skyline in order to shape the image of Dubai as a whole.[37] This logic seems to have returned (if it ever left) to London with a new rival to the Burj: the London Shard. The iconic becomes, in this paradigmatic policy, a trampoline for the wider world. It epitomizes the means by which Dubai seeks to convince others of its progress and its participation in the "international" while also trying to capture the global audience through the soft power of its symbolic capital and the global visibility of the urban spaces that it rests on.

Different among Equals

What do we learn by recounting how Singapore, Sydney, and Dubai have sought to cast themselves as different, but on often relatively common terms? What does paying attention to the dynamics of symbolic power tell us about the ideas and logics of global city thinking in these cases? As noted at the end of the previous chapter, a key and perhaps underappreciated idea behind some global city research is that of understanding the hierarchical unevenness of the world city system. Certain places and certain elites play a more dominant role in current international affairs than others. Cities and elites "central" to the contemporary economy skew current affairs toward them and perhaps relatively away from more peripheral, "Southern" contexts and people. As I noted when discussing the issue of understanding the importance of recounting what is "off the map" in global city thinking, Singapore is the only city of the three where most of my interlocutors' discussions displayed some degree of correlation between this idea and hierarchical thinking—essentially grasping the power politics that both global city-speak and tangible connections imply. This is not yet the case in Dubai and Sydney.

Appreciating the (not so) hidden hierarchy of global city thinking is a fundamental tenet of the postcolonial critique of writings like those of Sassen and Hall. Yet there may be some hope for the newer generations. It is among the youngest (aged eighteen to twenty-five) age group of experts interviewed for this book that we find the most explicit appreciation for the hierarchical unevenness of global cities. Perhaps somewhat surprisingly, civil society experts seem to engage in this type of thinking the least. This might be because the majority of the conversations with civil society veered toward being highly localized and centered on specific local matters rather than, say, intercity competition or global networks, and this is also in stark contrast to the private sector, whose experts regularly mentioned hierarchical differences between cities in their interviews. In this sector, as with terms like "transnational elite" and "gateway functions," there is little to no disagreement on the influence of hierarchies of cities (e.g., in the financial or logistic sectors) on the way a city globalizes and the impact this uneven global geography of human settlements has had on Sydney, Singapore, and Dubai. Among the three cities it is definitely the latter that sees the highest salience of this idea in global city thinking. The Emirate scores almost twice as high as Sydney and Singapore, which are generally well aligned, when it comes to acknowledging the hierarchical disposition of cities internationally and when it comes to integrating this in the way experts in Dubai see the city's evolving. Perhaps quite logically, and independently of whichever city they hail from, it is interviewees with a business and economics background that seem to have the greatest sense of hierarchical unevenness, and far more so (thirteen out of twenty-one interviewees) than even architects (three out of seventeen) or planners (four out of twenty-four), who should purportedly be more familiar with the global city literature. The central concept to be grasped here, then, is that of unevenness: as already well articulated by Bourdieu in his original discussion of symbolic power as imbued with violence and subjugation, there are inherent power relations embedded in the pursuit of distinction. Who controls, or seeks to control, this practice is the subject of the next chapter.

THE LEADERSHIP

Baniyas Square Station: Dubai, 2:00 p.m.

It is a Monday afternoon in October when my Emirati friend Maitha and I, while waiting for her driver to pick us up outside Baniyas Square Metro Station (just a few minutes east of Deira's Gold Souk), stumble upon an unusual sight. The crowds of commuters, who are dressed in all sorts of working-class attire and encompass a vastly mixed Middle Eastern–South Asian variety of "locals," are suddenly parted by a fast-moving group of Emiratis in white *thawb* (the classic ankle-length white robe), followed by a few police officers. The group emerges from the Metro station amid a wave of murmurs from the crowd. Several individuals hold up their mobile phones to capture the occurrence. "Oh! Even *he* takes the metro," remarks Maitha. A few seconds later I spot the "he" in question: Sheikh Mohammed, flanked by several aides, is indeed not an everyday sight for the average Dubai Metro commuter. Yet scenes like this are relatively familiar to those of us who have attended forums like the World Government Summit, where it is common to come across local dignitaries. Dubai's ruler is disappearing into the background when Maitha starts singing his praises, knowing I have been reading his book *My Vision* for my research. Not so subtly subtitled *Challenges in the Race for Excellence*, the short tome of the sheik's musings is indeed a gold mine of quotes for my research on the entrepreneurialism at the foundation of the global city idea. "I know what you are thinking," she says, "but you'd be hard-pressed to tell the story of Dubai without the sheik: it's like Lee Kuan Yew in Singapore, no?" It is hard to dispute that. Indeed, certain individuals are key to the story I am trying to tell about my three cities. Leadership emerges time and again as a core ingredient of the recipe for international success in the urban age. Yet we are also often confronted with its limitations—a consideration that takes me back to a previous conversation with Maitha.

The setting was breakfast on the morning after the fireworks and light spectacles of the opening ceremony for the Burj Khalifa, televised worldwide in January 2010. The day before, Sheik Mohammed had surprised the media and many nations with a remarkable initiative: "This great project deserves to carry the name of a great man: today I inaugurate the Burj Khalifa."[1] After six years of the skyscraper appearing as "Burj Dubai" in newspaper headlines and TV reports, the sudden change in dedication of the newly minted tallest building in the world impressed many who would not have expected Dubai and its ruler to bow to another Emirate. The change of name occupied pretty much the entirety of our chat over a luscious serving of *luqaimat*—a local dish of deep-fried batter with sesame seeds drizzled with date syrup. "People just don't get it's not just about money," Maitha tells me. It is also about a "brotherly" connection, in a move from "going solo" to realizing the need to rely on Abu Dhabi. The official naming of the building after Abu Dhabi's Sheikh Khalifa bin Zayed Al Nahayan was coupled with a profoundly nationalist display characterized by UAE flags and official statements, not least underscored by a skydiver landing at Sheik Mohammed's feet carrying a UAE-flagged parachute. The international community, Maitha told me, might "not be easily fooled" by this, but her bets (likely winning ones) were on much of the non-Arabic world to misinterpret the "brotherly" gesture. The problem, perhaps, is that when translated into English and Aglocentric thinking, the reading of brotherly relationships might lose some key elements of reciprocal giving, seniority, and clan rapport that pervade this in Arabic. As a scholarly piece by researchers at the University of Victoria on the naming of the Burj put it, this gesture embodied how "fraternal commodification agreements can be used to enact new 'global urban imaginaries.'"[2]

The international story was perhaps less subtle. As many put it then, Dubai, crushed by the pressures of the global financial crisis, was forced to lean on its richer neighbor. It is now widely known that the sister Emirate supported Dubai with a hefty US$10 billion bailout while the Al Maktoum's sultanate was on the brink of defaulting on its Dubai World debts in December 2009.[3] In what was then widely heralded as the ultimate gesture of submission to Abu Dhabi, Sheikh Mohammed decided to theatrically rename the Burj Dubai as the Burj Khalifa. This situation led many commentators to question the independence and authority of the ruling family in Dubai. Yet this was but a part of a larger line of questioning that, as some of the few academics researching the Emirate at the time later noted, criticized the actual room for maneuvering left to the Al Mak-

FIGURE 11.   Downtown Burj Dubai during the development phase.

toums in a context so dependent on the ebb and flow of the global marketplace. Maitha, and some scholars more recently, is adamant that there is a substantial element of "brotherly" gestures here but that this is not family "like an American or Brit would think of"—something maybe I can get "as an Italian," she concedes. Coming from someone very close to the ruling family, who at times is softly outspoken for a more gender-balanced "new" Arab world, this certainly piques my interest. Indirectly, this makes the story of leadership a far more complex one than one just about leaders. Taking a peek behind the image of the sheik in Dubai, the national founder in Singapore, or the mayor in Sydney becomes necessary to better understand leadership in the context of the system (of urban governance) that underpins those who lead.

This deeper look into leadership tells us that in spite of financial obligations to its neighbor and of the expanding neoliberal climate in Dubai, authority remains relatively one-tiered—even many years after the 2010 episode. Dubai's governance is still solidly centralized despite the growing influence of business actors and the relative political-economic dependence on Abu Dhabi, and this structure fundamentally impacts the production of the Emirate as a global city. To grasp the clout of leadership on the global city (idea and place), it is important to underline what key drivers allow for the continuation of this management and how

Dubai's (monarchic) government has managed to maintain a strong hold on its development process over the past few decades, but do so by understanding the underlying politics upon which this leadership rests. These, as I illustrate in this chapter, are not just local matters but rather a fundamental element of the domestic-international relationship that places city leaders as key "middle-men" between the street and the globe.[4]

Once again Maitha seems spot-on. Leadership might not be the key ingredient of the global city recipe, if such a thing actually exists, but it certainly is a fundamental one and indeed a factor that the scholarship has often ignored. "Tell me that this is so different from your other places?" she challenges me. "And that you can tell your story without Lee Kuan Yew's nation [in Singapore] or 'Team Clover' [in Sydney]?" It is hard to dispute this. Yet leadership, as I have argued with my colleagues Elizabeth Rapoport and Leonora Grcheva in *Leading Cities*, is often largely ignored in the academic literature on global cities. This is a theme that comes predominantly from the practice and the media/business discourse around the globalization of cities. From this viewpoint, the role of leadership in shaping the globalization of cities is, at least in the three cases in this book, well recognized. Across all my conversations, leadership shows seven direct correlations, with "off the map" the most connected of the twenty core concepts underpinning this book—even ahead of the idea of elites. Leaders are a fundamental piece of the puzzle of the global city and key drivers of the global system of valorization that underpins global urbanism. In short, Maitha is probably quite right in saying that it is hard to tell the stories of Dubai, Singapore, and Sydney without referring to particular individuals and their place in how global cities are built.

In Dubai, the role of leadership is evident (at a high salience of 0.204) and quite clearly correlated with the idea of being (and recognizing what is) "off the map." This is not just about the fast rise of the Emirate from anonymity to recognized global hub. It is also about Dubai's recognition of realities that, owing to its emergence, are becoming more directly linked to global circuits of goods and people, as with major African capitals or central/south Asian cities that are now regularly serviced by Emirates Airlines. The sheikh and the ruling family are regularly pointed at by the vast majority of those who recount the story and challenges of the Emirate; and the need for, the downsides, and the impact of leadership are well understood across all my interlocutors. Perhaps less salient (at 0.181) in Singapore, leadership still echoes soundly across the conversations in and on the city-state, where the closest and strongest correlations are again on questions of what is "off the map" but also with the relationality of the idea of the global city. Leaders in Singapore seem to be inevitably linked (essentially every other conversation) with what connects the city to other cities. Only in

Sydney, however, is the discourse of leadership, with its predominantly nonacademic roots, intertwined with the discourse of "command and control," with its long theoretical lineage in global city research present in urban studies since the early 1980s. Here, perhaps, the impact on local and state government of a previous generation of scholars well familiar with this terminology, as with Australian geographer Glen Searle's work in framing "Global Sydney," has some incidence on the connection between these two elements of global city-speak. Interestingly, and somewhat related to this, it is in two distinct generations that, overall in all three cities, the idea of leadership has its strongest interconnection with other core ideas of global city-speaking: the eighteen-to-twenty-five and forty-to-fifty-nine age brackets of my interviewees display significantly higher degrees of correlation with other terms, perhaps pointing at a return of a greater attention to leaders after a degree of lesser interest and impact in the past few decades. And finally, but again interestingly, no evidence of direct or indirect engagement with the idea of leadership is present among the architects I spoke to: while planners, social scientists, and business/economics-trained interlocutors all display some degree of salience of this term, and STEM-trained people follow a little behind, the way the architectural practice frames the globalization of Sydney, Singapore, and Dubai seems interestingly devoid of references to the leaders of these places. "You can't, however," admits Maitha, "compare Dubai and Singapore with the rest." Is the leadership of these places so different from the rest, and so much that it tells us little about other cities beyond the Gulf and Southeast Asia? A closer look at global city-speak might, in my view, tell us otherwise.

Urban Entrepreneurship in Action

Contrary to the experience of many widely referenced cases of global cities typical of urban studies such as those in North America, the centralization of policy-making in Dubai and Singapore is not the result of progressive aggregation of divided municipalities. If in many of those cases the dynamic that brought many of those cities under the control of a single and overarching institutional framework has been characterized by progressive annexation of discrete governing bodies, in our cases the Emirate and the Asian Tiger have historically been underwritten by, respectively, the monarchical structure of the ruling Al Maktoum family and by the parliamentary role of Lee Kuan Yew's People's Action Party (PAP) since the heydays of the two cities. Likewise, if in many cases one-tier systems have progressively disappeared or have witnessed an inverse fragmentation, Dubai's and Singapore's political systems have witnessed a substantial continuity owing to their relative city-state positioning. Yet this seems more and more often a repeated truism than something commentators (and many urban scholars) grasp. Rarely do we spend time recounting the political-legal structures behind the places we speak of. This is perhaps a slightly dull political science and legal theory exercise (feel free to turn to the next section of this chapter if you think so), but also one that is quite telling for us to speak of global cities in a less simplistic manner and gives more weight to the urban governance structures in place in these fast-rising global hubs. Let me take Dubai as an example.

Dubai is part of, and gives name to, one of the seven Emirates. It is the second largest after Abu Dhabi. The United Arab Emirates are generally described as a constitutional monarchy federated with seven "city-states" anchoring these within the UAE. This means that Dubai's system of government is formally characterized by a ruling monarch that is to act unchallenged as head of state within the parameters of a more or less explicitly defined legal frame. This was drafted in 1971 along with the overarching constitution of the UAE. Legally, Dubai is subject to the federal government but retains the capacity to administer a large number of matters grouped under the rubric of "internal affairs" as well as the legal system of the Emirate, which, in contradiction with all the other Emirates besides Ras Al Khaimah, remains independent from the UAE Federal Judicial Authority. Leadership is enacted here within an ambiguous legal-political positioning.

It is important to note here that key to these "internal" matters is the right to control business licensing and international business governance, which has to date allowed the ruling family to maintain a solid hold on the development of the Emirate. More specifically in legal terms, Dubai's system has been heavily influenced by both its British colonial heritage and Egyptian law connection. This made it heavily dependent on civil law principles and on the broader Islamic Sharia framework that constitutes both a guiding principle for the Emirate's administration and a direct influence on the local Islamic population through a dedicated court. In this legal landscape, the ruler of Dubai maintains almost complete control of the government framework, particularly through a crosscutting capacity to enact and adjudicate laws, as well as to determine the Emirate's political direction on a wide variety of matters. This privilege extends to his family and is passed from one generation to the next. Not surprisingly, many authors have pointed at Dubai as a modern sultanate, although this characterization tends not to be espoused by the nationals themselves, who generally emphasize the modern Arab nature of the Emirate and its quasi-city-state nature.[5] Dubai is legally not free from the federation, but there is very little discussion that the Emirate, along with its richer neighbor Abu Dhabi, is solidly in command of the destiny of the UAE, while also retaining substantial sovereign prerogatives on a number of fronts. Yet, as has often been the case since the early 2000s, Dubai has been somewhat wrongfully paired with other nondemocratic regimes, like China. Seeing the crosscutting control by the ruling family, as well as the nonexistent civil society influence on matters of state, the international press has generally overlooked the complexity of governance in Dubai and its Arab roots—often left to the domain of Middle East specialists and bundled to some degree with other non-Western cases.

Leadership is perhaps best understood, then, not just as the person who embodies it, like the Sheikh, but as a distributed affair that rests on a deep edifice of urban politics. In this sense, leadership appears far from just a privilege of Western societies and needs to be read more widely within the broader context of "urban governance" of these cities. Seen from this angle, Dubai's form of government, indissolubly intertwined with the family's patrimonial network, has been criticized in many cases for representing "little more than an extended system of patronage" where public and private blend together with no clear-cut boundaries.[6] However, according to Ahmed Kanna, the system of governance in Dubai has fast evolved to make this city a "corporation" with the sheikh as CEO in command of a relatively successful experiment in modernizing the Emirate through a mix of Arab culture, neoliberal policy, and tight control of internal affairs.[7] Mohammed himself, for instance, is the founder and current major shareholder (99.67%) of Dubai Holding, the state-led company that manages twenty sectoral developers ranging from real estate to entertainment. This governance system, however, does not end up diluted in loose ties, informal gatherings, or dissociated decisions. Dubai's growth is firmly in the hands of the Al Maktoum, who since the early days of the Emirate have sought to set a path toward internationalization and, in the early 2000s, toward a global city profile.

Certainly, the tactics displayed by the ruling family and its executive do match quite closely the academic reading of the "entrepreneurial city." In this sense, Dubai has quite clearly embodied at least the typical characteristics of entrepreneurial cities the scholarship has recognized since the mid-1990s.[8] It has rigorously pursued innovative strategies, which is reflexive of a purposeful aim: that of achieving a global city status comparable to London and Tokyo. Likewise, it has sustained this venture with an entrepreneurial narrative targeted at global elites in an effort to brand Dubai as the archetype of success. If, as Jessop has pointed out, the presence of innovation with an explicit purpose distinguishes the real entrepreneurs from those "that happen for whatever reason(s) to perform well economically," the Emirate seems like a paragon of the former.[9] Strategic planning is certainly not left to the textbooks but widely applied and easily allowed by the authorities to key corporate actors in order to seduce a global audience. Indeed, Dubai's goal is to carry the day in the "race for excellence," as the sheikh puts it in *My Vision*.[10] A race that few would dispute, even in the sheik's tighter circles, requires Dubai, but also Singapore and Sydney, to become an "entrepreneurial city."

As geographer John Lauermann noted in an essay on municipal statecraft, entrepreneurial tactics such as speculation and risk taking on municipal finances, place branding, or interurban competition are nowadays simply "standard operating procedure" for many local governments and city leaders the world over. Importantly, entrepreneurialism is not to be read as just the domain of profit-seeking neoliberal approaches. As Donald McNeill pointed out on the story of the emergence of Barcelona as a globalizing city under the tenure of Mayor Pasqual Maragall in the 1980s and 1990s, we need to read these entrepreneurial tactics beyond the synonym of "boosterism," and we can equally apply them to both left-leaning governments and relatively conservative leaders like those of Dubai and Singapore. Sydney, also chronicled by McNeill, is a case in point here when it comes to the impact of independent mayor Clover Moore in shaping the internationalization of the Australian city. This way of highlighting entrepreneurialism is, Lauermann and McNeill quite rightly argue, not just about growth but very much an ethos entrenched in most, if not all, global city thinking as a way for municipal leaders to link local matters to wider circuits of capital, people, and ideas. In spite of the economic downturn of the early 2000s, Lauermann notes, the entrepreneurial spirit of the global city has proved remarkably resilient—something that the story of Dubai, but also those of Singapore and Sydney, confirms quite clearly. Not surprisingly, then, entrepreneurialism is, in all three cities, tightly correlated with the idea of global opportunity we discussed in the previous chapter. This is especially true in Singapore, with the other cities trailing closely. The leader recognizes the possibility of playing a role in the (uneven) geography of globalization and facilitates the city's rise to worldwide recognition—several interviewees, whether we were in Australia, the Gulf, or Southeast Asia, argued with me on this point. The issue of innovation has been central in nearly all of these conversations. As *The Leopard*'s famous quote puts it to chronicle the long-lived changes of Sicilian society through time, things might have to change to remain the same. Entrepreneurially engaging in the "business of change"—innovation, that is—might be a telling reason why many global cities have attained worldwide fame.

Building a Space for Innovation

Although the idea of the "creative city" has extensive currency among practitioners, this is another case of a term that in fact has a fourfold incidence among academics, where the salience score is nearly four times higher than in general among experts. This is an ironic parallel to the idea of cities "off the map" developed by scholars who are almost diametrically opposite to Richard Florida and those espousing creative cities credos. Overall, then, innovation records only a medium degree of salience (0.162, like ideas of history or entrepreneurship) in global city-speak when we bundle together scholars and non-academics. It is generally low in Dubai and Sydney and much higher in Singapore (0.233), where perhaps this type of global city thinking has found roots across the spectrum. When it comes to correlations, then, innovation seems to have strong links with acknowledgments of the importance of elites in Sydney, signaling how these features have been intertwined in the partially unequal development of the Harbor City. It also displays some connections with place and opportunity in Singapore, perhaps not surprisingly illustrating how the most innovation-savvy city of our triad has also grasped the importance of building spaces for the "creative class" (something that Sydney and Dubai have captured perhaps only more recently) and seizing its role in capturing global opportunities. Interestingly, innovation is also one of the few cases where we can spot some degree (–0.23) of negative correlation: we can notice that talk of materiality and material assets of the global city, driven mostly by the forty-to-fifty-nine age group, tends to result in ignoring innovation as a key feature, and vice versa.

But this trend might be changing in the younger generations (below the forty-to-fifty-nine age bracket). Central players for global city development, such as Dubai's ruling family, Singapore's PAP, and Sydney's central local authorities (City of Sydney *in primis*) or the executive of the New South Wales state government, have been progressively putting emphasis on "elevating design" to produce world-class built environments that appeal to both the visitor class and the more permanent dwellers. A central reasoning here is that designed spaces go hand in hand with maintaining a strong grip on the highly mobile transnational class that seems to be able to determine the global fortunes of metropolises worldwide. In this sense, while often not particularly savvy in terms of global city scholarship besides the odd reference to scholars such as Sassen, many of my interlocutors are certainly familiar with Richard Florida's best-selling "creative class" lingo. Florida's *Rise of the Creative Class* described of the (presumed) transformative potential of this broad group of "creative professionals" engaged in the knowledge economy and their role as a driving force of urban change, chronicling how creativity holds fundamental power on the global marketplace.[11] For instance, in several interviews in Sydney I was pointed toward the necessity for the Australian metropolis to retain its prime role in international design, art, and cultural circuits as a central asset defining the Harbor City's rise to the top ranks of the world's urban hierarchy. In more than one instance, many of the basic considerations in Florida's work were embedded in the "global city strategy" thinking of Australian, Emirati, and Singaporean experts, almost to the extent of direct citation in some cases, as a middle-aged planning officer from North Sydney more or less inadvertently demonstrated: "We also need to focus on creating a 'people climate' not just a business climate."[12] I must admit I had initially overlooked this direct connection, and in at least four different cases I took these expressions to represent the broader societal emergence of a transnational class discourse and only later discovered the almost *verbatim* reference to Florida while processing some interviews.[13]

British geographer Jamie Peck justly underlined not only how these creative-city strategies are "predicated on, and designed for, this neoliberalized terrain" but also how this increasingly popular urbanist mantra has the capacity to inspire a growth in competition and the precariousness of a city's global fortunes. As Peck rightly puts it, creativity strategies "were in a sense pre-constituted for this fast policy market," as they "empower, though only precariously, unstable networks of elite actors, whose strategies represent aspirant attempts to realize in concrete form the seductive 'traveling truths' of the creativity script."[14]

Certainly, this thinking has received some sound degree of scholarly validation. Harvard economist Edward Glaeser, another common speaker on the circuit of global city pundits, has long argued in this direction, pointing out that the varied social milieu of the globalizing metropolis, and its vast human capital, is a necessary precondition for the global success of cities in a time of spatial dispersion.[15] What makes these places unique is, in fact, not just the aggregate of their corporate headquarters and financial workforce or the ratio of airline traffic and goods shipments they totalize. Global cities are the combination of all these features, which, rearticulated through the unique density and magnetic boundedness of the global city's urban fabric, produce further advantages. Metropolises thus also become knowledge bases of pivotal importance not solely for the circulation of information and ideas but also for their production and hybridization.[16] It is not surprising, for instance, that the vast majority of the world's top research institutions are located in the top tiers of most urban rankings, clustering in and around places such as London, New York, and Tokyo. Moreover, understanding the attractiveness of the reflexivity of these metropolises further substantiates the need to see global cities as social milieu, where face-to-face contact and the lure of a global lifestyle are as important as the location of producer services to put these places on the map. Interestingly, the terminology here does not percolate through in conversation with those with an architectural background, where the term registers no explicit or implicit mentions. On the other hand, this issue is hotly debated among those with planning and social sciences backgrounds and is mentioned most commonly by those working in the private sector. However, we should perhaps be careful in thinking of generational splits: the eighteen-to-twenty-five age bracket of interviewees has largely disregarded this issue, even displaying some degree of negative correlation with the idea of gateway functions when speaking of innovation, and vice versa. Yet, it is undeniable that much strategic thinking in cities, whether conscious of innovation or not, is increasingly shaped by a sense of cities relating to each other and urban models traveling internationally.

A Bridging Role

The evolution of a global city, as British designer Deyan Sudjic noted, "depends on their engagement with the political context of the world."[17] When discussing a city's evolution and current trajectory, global city-speak is by nature prone to take into account the broader "international" context in which these cities are seen to emerge. This is the case when speaking of global city planning. If by definition the profession of the city planner "exists in continuous interaction with the system s/he is planning," when it comes to global cities, such a system necessarily extends to a wider geography constituted by international hierarchies of cities, interconnected global markets, and competitions between different world city functions.[18] Equally, it also necessarily depends on global professional circuits such as those of globally influential architectural firms like Foster and Partners or SOM, and multinational urban developers like Lendlease that determine much of the global engagement of these cities and city makers. A very similar case can be made for city leaders. Yet this also highlights a central dimension of global city leadership that is rarely considered central in the scholarship: leadership in these globally connected places plays a bridging role between the needs and realities of everyday city management and the global circuits of capital, ideas, politics, and culture shaping globalization. Global city leadership, then, perhaps not differently from diplomacy, may be a matter of "two-level games": a careful balancing of domestic and international politics.[19]

Introduced to the study of diplomacy in 1988 by American political theorist Robert Putnam, this view on politics describes international negotiations between states as consisting of simultaneous political "games" on two "levels" happening contingently at both the intranational level (i.e., domestic politics) and the international level (i.e., diplomatic politics). Neither a purely inward (domestic oriented) nor a purely international (outward oriented) analysis, suggested Putnam, can account for the outcomes we witness in diplomacy. The explanation for the dynamics of international politics sits in the interplay between the two—something commentators of the United Kingdom's politics around Brexit are likely familiar with. While perhaps intuitive to some, oversimplification in one or the other direction is often the case when explaining who "governs" the faith of global cities. Certainly, balancing pragmatic local/domestic matters such as managing waste on curbsides or zoning streets for parking spaces and outward/ international matters like enticing multinational companies or taking part in a multicity campaign to fight climate change is what gives city leaders a unique bridging position. This has been widely celebrated by those who believe mayors may be the planet's best answer to the limits of state politics, especially when it comes to making international commitments—on climate change and migration, for instance—and tangibly taking real steps to implement them. This bridging role that city leadership can play, and more broadly the in-between role of urban governance in relation to linking international affairs to everyday lives on city streets, is critical for redefining the rights and duties of urban dwellers the world over. Yet it is important to highlight here how the emphasis on the leader in much global city-speak often represents a convenient reference for that most visible touch point between local matters and global issues.

Yet understanding that city leadership rests on two-level games implies thinking of the localized political pressures that sustain its capacity to "go global." Essential to the governing of global cities and exerting symbolic power on an international scale are three key elements of authority: its resourcing, its legitimacy, and its institutionalization. These are by all means not simply localized features. For instance, the mechanisms of internal legitimacy are intertwined with the external legitimacy afforded to the leadership of a city by peers, the media, the private sector, and other governmental entities from outside the confines of the city in question. Leadership needs to regularly reiterate its relevance and "mission" to its citizenry, and this might often involve, especially in nondictatorial but yet not democratic societies, deploying entrepreneurial tactics inward rather than outward. For example, Singapore's PAP after Lee Kuan Yew's leadership has had to play a delicate balancing game with its electorate to maintain a formalized grip on the city-state's government. While it would be easy to presume that Singapore's rise has gone hand in hand with a tightly centralized grip by its ruling leadership, a little political history might dampen this truism (perhaps just as with Dubai). While expanding its global visibility and control of logistics in Southeast Asia, the city-state government experienced tumult in the early 2010s. PAP's so-called new normal politics followed a very poor performance in the 2011 general elections and represented an effort to partly reinvent itself to regain its hegemonic role in an essentially one-party system. Key determinants of the modest success, which at the end of the 2000s and the start of the 2010s seemed to hint at a shift in majority rule, had been issues surrounding rising housing costs and declining quality in the city's public transportation systems. So, while the city-state was flourishing internationally and reinforcing its status as a global city, very tangible domestic issues that had to do with housing quality, affordability, and capacity to move across the island at a reasonable cost were putting substantial pressure on its leadership. This led to some relatively substantial strategic shifts domestically. It pushed toward the 2013 Single Singapore Citizen policy, designed to give the changing single-dwelling populace of Singapore the opportunity to purchase "built to order" public housing, and was followed shortly thereafter by the 2015 Fresh Start Housing program, which subsidizes apartment living for families with young children. Yet it also allowed the government, and in particular its Ministries of National Development and Housing Development Board, to once again publicize internationally its innovative credentials and, on the back end of domestic pressures, further strengthen the appreciation by many cities and private actors of Singapore's role as a new global city. In both discourses, whether oriented to domestic or international audiences, the housing reforms were communicated in a markedly clear Singaporean way. They entailed telling stories of the nation's success to build housing of quality for many people on the island, while continuing to improve for, and listen to, its citizenry. Of course, the story of the successive elections is much more complicated than just one of housing and transport issues, or indeed global projection, but many local commentators pointed at the importance of this relationship in pushing PAP more squarely into power, winning 69.9 percent of the popular vote, 10 percent more than in 2011 and far ahead of the opposition's Workers' Party, sitting at merely 12.5 percent. As Kenneth Tan notes, the government enacts this effectively through periodic "national-level public envisioning exercises" through which the people may be persuaded (rather than forced) to comply with the dominant ideology, rally around a consensus defined as the national interest, and thus maintain order and stability that, in the first instance, benefits the dominant interests of the elite.[20] These, as in the housing story, have a double audience in local citizenry and global markets, whose relationship the PAP leadership has rather effectively bridged and negotiated over its rule on the city-state. This reminds us that it is important not to simplify and "flatten" the leadership of global cities—even in the most centralized of contexts—but rather think of it as a bridging reality enmeshed in two-level games between local and global. This is, evidently, a function of the delicate "glocal" balancing act we considered in the previous chapter when discussing the trajectory of urban development in global cities. Leadership's in-betweenness opens up many possibilities to "go global" with a direct link to everyday urban matters, but it also raises fundamental questions as to the nature of urban politics in today's tumultuous world politics.

Perhaps in Singapore and Dubai we might be in luck in noticing this balancing role freed from the more complex structures of Western countries. Yet Sydney too offers fertile ground to capture the bridging position of those who lead the city. Certainly, we can recognize that our three cases have had limited formal political pressure from "higher" executive authorities at federal and national levels—something that is obviously altogether absent in Singapore. In Sydney and Dubai, the Australian and Emirati federal governments have had a relatively limited direct role in city politics, leaving urban planning to local and state authorities, and influencing these "transversally" only through their fiscal policies and (especially in the British case) constitutional prerogatives. With limited funded support for local projects, regional and local authorities have had to reinvent their managerial role at the urban scale, taking up more and more entrepreneurial approaches to metropolitan planning in order to muster resources from the city's global economic base. A difference here is perhaps that of Dubai's economic ties with Abu Dhabi which remain to date murky at best. Moreover, the cases analyzed here also point us to the importance of understanding urban governance processes not just through complex nature as intertwined with the private sector, but also as not antithetical to government per se. Centralization in Dubai and Singapore, and some degree of pluralization in greater Sydney, have in fact taken place not only because of, respectively, pure top-down imposition and absolute bottom-up splintering of authority structures. Rather, all three cities remind us that these governance alignments are in place with a substantial degree of complacence by the variety of both governmental and nongovernmental actors involved in the production of global city pathways. On the one hand, in Sydney the state government of New South Wales has taken part in the decentralization of entrepreneurialism and the broadening of the global city initiative by allowing substantial degrees of laissez-faire in policy-making and, even more importantly, private inference in strategizing for global growth. In Dubai, on the other hand, corporate actors, expats, and consultants have generally accepted the necessary sovereign bargain that, while removing most political rights and almost all space for authority contestation, has allowed substantial room for maneuvering in terms of development, investment, and global linkages. Singapore, perhaps, stands in between these two extremes as what appears to me as the most balanced of the three cases, often managing two-level games precisely as such rather than almost always outwardly oriented (as in Dubai) or inward focused (like Sydney).

Although debates around devolution and the shifts of power between central and local governments might seem commonplace in "urban" talk in many Western countries like the UK and the United States, this is far less the case in global city-speak. The idea, perhaps best embodied in the work of Neil Brenner on the rescaling of the state through the city, that the layers of governance superimposed on the global city are being reshuffled remains a relatively uncommon one across all of the expert conversations in the three cities, where it represents (with metrocentricity) perhaps the least used concept when speaking of global cities.

A caveat is in order here: "state rescaling" featured explicitly as a mention in 6 of the 170 conversations for this book, more than the terms "entrepreneurial city" (only twice) and "globalization in place" (three times). Yet all direct mentions, as well as half of the indirect (synonym-based) ones, came from academics. Quite simply, when we talk of global cities in Dubai, Singapore, and Sydney, we rarely speak of the ways their governance structures are being cast and recast by their globalization. This theme is most common in Sydney, with Dubai and Singapore experts seldom venturing into discussions of the redefinitions of the boundaries of politics and government. This is perhaps partly understandable, because Sydney's positioning is far more explicitly nested in other layers of government (federal and state, to begin with) and because the governance of Sydney, as we have seen here, has over the past few years increasingly become a central issue in the Australian city, especially when it comes to metropolitan governance. Yet something bigger is at work here. Almost no expert interlocutor for this study touched on bigger reconfigurations of governance beyond the local-central dynamic or around metropolitan governance matters. In Dubai, for instance, a few (nine) experts brought up issues of political shifts in relation to the connection between the governance of Dubai and the broader influence of the UAE federal authority. This was, however, almost exclusively to debate the shadow of the power of Abu Dhabi and the ruling family over the growth of Dubai, especially around the 2008 crisis and successive bailout by the richer neighbor in the wake of debt challenges by the Dubaian authorities. In several cases, Dubaian experts in metropolitan government positions even denied that this relationship with Abu Dhabi has tangible implications for the transformation of government in Dubai, pointing at the fact that, despite some financial troubles, the structure of governance in the Emirate has undergone little to no substantial reform in the past decades. Similarly, if even more markedly, shifts in governance structures are hardly noticed in Singapore, where no higher (e.g., federal) authority is superimposed on the city-state and where little is conceded as to the impact of globalization on the city's governance. But this may signal an even deeper issue that has been pointed out by several scholars engaging in the global city literature: oftentimes, despite extensive talk of political matters like inequality and socioeconomic rifts, global city-speak struggles to engage directly with its politics and its governance implications. As Roger Keil, and John Friedmann before him, pointed out, there remains a "political deficit" in global city thinking whereby processes of globalization, socioeconomic restructuring, cultural and class confrontations, and material reconfiguration of the city often take a far more central stage than more traditional political science questions around who governs and what "politics of urbanism" are at play here. Incredibly, there remain today few scholarly treatises on either the leaders or their citizens. Centrally, symbolic power as a form of representation of reality implies that power itself does not sit simply with the symbolic capital of individuals (e.g., the status of elected mayor or community organizer) or the tools and media used to deploy it (e.g., strategic plans or speeches), but rather in the relation between these and those who are subject to (and participate in, says Bourdieu) symbolic power. Symbolic power as a "power of words" to give order, Bourdieu explains, "lies in the legitimacy of the words and of the person who utters them, a belief that words themselves cannot produce."[21] The relationship between the leader and those that are governed is central, and highly political, and yet silenced in much discussion of the global city. This tells us that leadership, then, matters fundamentally but not in isolation. Even important figures like Lee Kuan Yew and the sheikhs of Dubai are embedded in a complex structure of global city politics. This in turn puts pressure on the governments and leaders of these cities from both outside the geography of the city itself, owing to the need to engage globally, and within, even when the system appears centralized and unitary. If government matters for the way we tell the story of a city's globalization, then, we should not forget the wider politics in which it is embedded— that which we call "urban governance."

THE GOVERNANCE

Global Cities Forum: Chicago, 1:00 p.m.

"That's the mayor of Sydney, isn't she?" asks Jonathan, a planning colleague from the World Bank with whom I had a previous foray into disaster management in cities. I only manage to mutter a confused "Well, no . . . I mean, to a degree. . . . Which *Sydney* are you talking about?" Perhaps not the most flattering display of my Australian credentials. We are at the Chicago Global Cities Forum, which, much like the World Cities Summit in Singapore, gathers in the North American city a list of international dignitaries of the global urbanist kind: mayors, experts, pundits, architects, and policymakers, among others. The person in question, Lucy Turnbull, has more correctly the title of chief commissioner. She oversees the Greater Sydney Commission (GSC), which was set up in 2015 to provide a regional "strategic" view across greater Sydney. Putatively, the mayor of the *city* of Sydney, intended as "Council of the City of Sydney," is Clover Moore, in charge of the CBD's local authority within greater Sydney since March 2004. Then again, Moore succeeded Turnbull at the helm of the City Council, as the latter was briefly mayor (the first female one, after seventy-eight men, nonetheless) and then commissioner (a temporary office) in 2003 and 2004. I concede that part of the reason for Turnbull's invitation to the forum is that she is the first lady of Australia, as her husband, Prime Minister Malcolm Turnbull, currently heads the Liberal Party, presently holding the majority at the federal level in Canberra. Jonathan, who prefers straightforward and simple answers, looks decidedly puzzled. Yet the confusion does not stop there. Shortly thereafter, at the forum's traditional (and exclusive) "Night Owl" drinks session on the rooftop of the Park Hyatt, Jonathan looks at me even more bewildered. After briefly introducing him to Claudio (Orrego, that is), whom I present as former "Mayor of Santiago, Chile" and a great advocate of urban resilience, I repeat my poor local politics performance. While waiting for two more Nomi Bar signature drinks served in copper gnome-shaped cups, I clarify to my friend that Orrego was actually the *intendente* of the regional government (province) of Santiago, whose office is appointed not by local residents but by the country's president—an office Orrego ran for a few years earlier. Santiago's urban governance is no easy matter: a mix of local, national, and provincial politics blended with laissez-faire neoliberal policy that characterizes the country's post-dictatorship experience. But then again, Sydney's politics are similarly thorny. Jonathan indulges me beyond patience, challenging me to point at any one "of these guys" (making a broad South African–accented gesture toward the dignitaries chatting away loudly at the bar) who "has it easy" in their city. And even more so, to draw a line between the "governors" and the "governed" when it comes to high-powered global urbanists shaping the growth of global cities the world over. He is almost certainly right. If it is fundamental to put an emphasis on the role of leadership in global cities, it is almost impossible to account for the politics of these places, and of the global city-speak I am investigating in this book, without also explicitly acknowledging their systems of governance—that is, of a wider realm of "governing" that happens in the relationship between the formal government of a city and other actors. Perhaps a "bit too much academic lingo," says Jonathan, but a pretty straightforward lesson in global city thinking: do not stop at the often visible mayor, ruler, or *intendente*, and remember that there are deep and continually shifting politics in these cities.

This is most definitely the case if we are to grasp the complex relation between the "mayor" of Sydney in attendance at the event and the other one I have spoken of throughout most of the book. Established by the NSW Parliament with the Greater Sydney Commission Act 2015, the GSC was putatively part of a "shake-up of the metropolitan planning system" sanctioned by then NSW premier Mike Baird.[1] Within the commission's structure, Sydney has been divided into six districts, each nominating a commissioner representing local councils. The GSC's overall direction was embedded in a Statement of Priorities the commission had agreed to with the minister for planning for its inaugural period from 2016 to 2018. Chief among these was to tackle Sydney's housing affordability crisis—for instance, by ensuring that more than 660,000 new homes will be built by 2031. The commission itself, however, has already been an object of governance restructuring. In June 2018 the new NSW premier (Gladys Berejiklian, also from the Liberal Party) announced that she and Lucy Turnbull had agreed on a new set of priorities for the commission, replacing the original Statement of Priorities. According to the state government, the latest changes support the commission's having "a more strategic oversight and assurance role at the center of Government." Key elements of these amendments have been, for example, the requirement for local councils in Greater Sydney to obtain written advice from the commission to support a local strategic planning statement before it is made by the council.

So, does this mean Sydney has acquired a regional government akin to, say, the Greater London Authority? Not so much. With limited experience at hand in the GSC and limited authority for the City of Sydney mayor, Greater Sydney still seems to lack a catalyst for its governance and a productive structure capable of sustaining it in the long term. For instance, new priorities allow the GSC the capacity to speak on planning matters, but this is couched in the form of "voice" rather than given as decision-making powers. One of the priorities gives the GSC "advice and assurance functions," including "directly advising the Minister for Planning," but this is to be done "on request," or with the commission able to make "reasonable requests" for information from state agencies and local councils for the purposes of exercising its role. Likewise, they relieve the commission "of its statutory local plan-making functions." This process has been anything but smooth. Some commentators called it a "bloodless coup" where the NSW premier effectively "usurped" the GSC of tangible powers, drawing decision-making in the city back into the hands of state government.[2] Others, however, argued that the GSC had "won a stronger hand to plan for Sydney's long-term future" via a "direct line" to the premier, with several Sydney academics, the Committee for Sydney, and some national commentators in support of this reading.[3] Either way, the readjustment in priorities, and more widely the story of the setup of the GSC, speaks of the politics of the global city as fundamentally a question of politics of boundaries: not just the relations of power over a defined territory, but the making of the shape, boundaries, and global-local relations of that place—a theme that will echo across this chapter.

This highlights that urban politics are not just a matter of local electoral squabbles, neighborhood fights, or rows over municipal management. Much of the edifice of global city politics is generally a complex interplay of different layers of government within and beyond the boundaries of the city in question, and this is then intertwined with the complexity of public-private relationships and community-driven advocacy. Speaking of leadership requires us to speak of governance: the whole edifice of governing a city, formal ("government"), private, and even informal. Yet, boundary contention aside, the language of global city-speak seems in our cities, at least broadly, to apply across authorities. In fact, it might even present some sort of consensus upon which much of the power struggle over who should rule and what should be ruled in Sydney, Singapore, and Dubai is resolved by the ruling party, monarch, or mayor by appealing to the need for and value of going and building "global." And as per script, upon launching the new GSC priorities, a joint premier–chief commissioner statement agreed that "the new focus for the Commission will ensure Greater Sydney is transformed into a thriving and connected global city."[4]

Governing a Global City

The question of governing global cities is perhaps far more complex than how it might appear to the outsider's eye. The identity of *Sydney* in the popular imagination often hinders a full appreciation of the extreme intricacy of the political geography that underpins it. The ten thousand square kilometers of Sydney's area have for most of recent history lacked a clear metropolitan-wide system of government that features in many other global or world cities such as Singapore and Dubai. Until the GSC (and even then, some would argue), no analogous body existed in the case of Sydney, where the overall conurbation is split into thirty-nine local government authorities with a relatively weak legal position and no identifiable "voice of the city" figure.[5] Perhaps, as per above, the GSC has not exactly filled this gap. As McNeill, Dowling, and Fagan had previously highlighted in 2005, "What characterizes Sydney politics is an inability for one politician to speak for, or to, an identifiable citizenry."[6] Moving out of this mode of governance is no easy fix, especially if the authority in question is anything less than a metropolitan government. Many of the administrative and policy functions are constitutionally devolved to the state level, where in fact the GSC sits, with federal entities playing only minor to nonexistent supporting cast parts. In this sense, establishment of the GSC has in part tried to redress this but, different from other recently set up metropolitan authorities like that of Auckland Council in New Zealand, has gone short of being a regional government. It is more like the *Intendencia* in Santiago than like the Greater London Authority and the office of the Mayor of London.

Certainly, the state government of New South Wales has acted as "animateur" in order to produce metropolitan strategies and orientations.[7] Chiefly through Planning NSW and the Department of State and Regional Development, and now partly via the GSC, the state government has shaped Sydney to become a strategic site in the world urban hierarchy through an increasingly neoliberal agenda oriented toward regulatory flexibility and attempts to attract international elites.[8] Not surprisingly, among the key drivers of the establishment of the GSC we have to account for the Committee for Sydney, the city's peak industry body, which was chaired by Turnbull. In some instances, NSW has even taken the lead against local authorities' own objections. This was for instance the case of the planning for the Sydney Casino in Pyrmont, where the then Council of the City of Sydney and many local communities voiced their complaints to the government and the NSW minister for planning, who was eventually forced to deny wide public participation and centralize the whole process to fast-track the construction.[9] However, the substantial presence of the NSW government in Sydney's decision-making structure should not obscure a much more complex political picture. Sydney's governance can be depicted as crosscutting multiple scales, with many different agents piercing through various political layers, interacting asymmetrically and often bypassing the assumed pecking order of Australian politics.[10] New South Wales and local governments are embedded in a governance where authority is diffuse and hierarchies (beyond constitutional prerogatives) are often dictated by the circumstances and the issue addressed.

After all, the federal government, to date, has had little stake in the development of its core city. This is perhaps one of the most long-lived features of Australian politics, whose tripartite system, based on the federal-state-local government hierarchy, has allowed for a "subnational centralization" at the state scale that, as Chris Aulich noted, "means a relatively small and weak local government level and a limited inclination to engage in significant redistribution of authority across levels, particularly downwards."[11] Besides the Whitlam government's short-lived Department of Urban and Regional Development initiative (1972–75) and the Hawke/Keating "Better Cities" program (1990–96), and more recently in Malcolm Turnbull's government (with a cities "unit" in the prime minister's office), the direct influence of Australia's top decision-making structure in urban affairs has been decisively limited. Where the federal government has had its largest impact is, as McGuirk points out, in the indirect pressure exerted on the fiscal front: a strong federal fiscal conservatism since the 1980s, coupled with a growing emphasis on building a competitive Australian economy, has resulted in a process of aggressive liberalization embodied in tariff reduction and financial deregulation.[12] In this climate, diminishing federal funding for state governments allowed subnational authorities such as the New South Wales state government or LGAs to take the lead role in both the political and physical construction of Sydney as a global city and, conversely, to focus their planning on attracting private capital from abroad with a Harbor City strategy.[13] Overall, this strategy has paved the way to two core trends in the city's organization. First, it has emphasized the increasing interconnectedness of the CBD with global flows not solely of capital but also of culture and mobility. Second, it has promoted the dominance of a globalizing rhetoric at the core of Sydney's development, partly detaching the metropolis from the national dimension and intertwining such discourse with what has since been perceived as a relatively lucrative "green" edge. A "consensus" pinpointed on global city-speak, fostered by the beneficial image of a livable and internationally connected metropolis, provides a de facto agreement on the need to plan a development of Sydney on its sprawling global economic base and its global "livability" aspirations. The lord mayor of the City of Sydney has been key in projecting this abroad with participation in international networks and forums, but Turnbull and the GSC have also taken some relevant stages to reinforce the global Sydney narrative.

What this tells us, then, is that limiting Sydney to state initiatives loses sight of a much more complex picture of urban governance, which is "enriched by attending to its scalar context and its location within dynamic scalar politics."[14] There is, amid this context, an ongoing conversation about the global nature of Sydney not just in the CBD but at the metropolitan scale. Embedded in the development of the *City of Cities* strategy first and then in the *Metropolis of Three Cities* plan championed by the GSC, as well as in the mobilization of the project that sustained these plans, is a complex interaction of actors beyond the constitutionally sanctioned tripartite governmental (federal/state/local) hierarchy. This is a system of links that has progressively surfaced in the "activation" of Sydney planning politics around strategic planning. Indeed, as even New South Wales acknowledged in this planning document, *City of Cities* was nothing but "the start of a process to bring the State Government, local government, stakeholders and the community together to discuss, review and then make decisions to guide the future of Sydney's economy, environment and communities."[15] As a new Greater Sydney Regional Plan (the formal title of these documents), *A Metropolis of Three Cities* has reiterated this more recently, and since the kickoff of the GSC, the plan has emphasized expanding the "polycentric" view to reshape Sydney. Of course, as part of the politics of the boundaries of the city, the shift in priorities of the GSC was seen in relation to this three-city vision, as "consolidates control over big-picture vision of Sydney" in the hands of the premier versus local councils.[16]

To begin with, the lower tier of Australian government represented by LGAs has acquired a key position in the dynamics of strategic planning since the late 1990s. This has been the case of the Parramatta Council, which has progressively been placed center stage by the state's strategic attempt to build a "second CBD" for Sydney's metropolitan region to alleviate congestion and property pressures on North and Central (CBD) Sydney.[17] In this view, local governments have been considered as lower-level implementers (and thus network intermediaries) tasked with carrying out the overall globalizing vision promoted by NSW, or at least conform their planning activities accordingly—a role that has in some instances led to friction between LGAs and the state.[18] Yet, LGAs have not just been "elected" by the state government to an intermediary role for broader interests. The lowest level of Sydney government has often participated proactively in the politics of planning and sought a more influential position in this network. The archetype of this entrepreneurial move is, of course, the City of Sydney, but the new GSC has in part also taken an explicit role in promoting urban entrepreneurialism.

According to many academics, urbanism in Sydney, and its livability focus, is embedded in more and more dominant market logics that are often dissociated from both local dimensions of transnational problems and global efforts to curb them. At a city level, with the rise of the City of Sydney as a core entrepreneurial actor in the complex governance of the metropolis, and with the implementation at the metropolitan level of first the *City of Cities* and then *A Metropolis of Three Cities*, as well as the *Sydney 2030* strategies locally, it seems like the political process underpinning the ascent to global city status has elected the inner city as the catalyst for action. The City of Sydney has, in some sense, been consciously talked into authority by the state government and by its own growing entrepreneurial edge. Yet, the formal, legal, and many of the consuetudinary practices are far from setting this rather limited LGA at the helm of the whole of greater Sydney.

Alongside the changing positions of some LGAs in Sydney planning politics, the role of corporate lobbying in defining the city's strategic orientation has also been a core structural factor of the past decade. Private coalitions are playing an increasingly relevant role in the Harbor City. For example, as Glen Searle noted shortly after the publication of the 2005 strategy: "The development industry vision is writ large across the *City of Cities* strategy and its supporting documents."[19] The Property Council of Australia's *Metro Strategy: A Property Industry Perspective* (published in late 2004) informed much of the 2005 definition of global market-oriented functional areas for Sydney's development, with recommendations for northwest and southwest planning developments flowing almost directly from the council's document to the strategy. Crucially, the key imprint of the business sector on Sydney's strategic planning process since the *City of Cities* approach has been the prioritization of economic development as the core focus and de facto orientation of planning approaches—a tacit feature that has since precluded any other alternative core course of planning.[20] This evidences, as with the drivers of the GSC, that at least central Sydney, but perhaps the whole metropolitan region more widely, has witnessed the increasingly important clout of the property and development sector (or large private actors in general) in determining the leadership of the city.

An often overlooked corollary of this growing centrality has been reflected, despite the general strategic planning, in the increased practice of "planning by exceptionalism," which has consisted of special-purpose concessions allowed by NSW to those developments that have been judged capable of "catapult[ing] the city into global city league tables."[21] The latter, in particular, have also become a customary component of state and private planning documents. First referenced

FIGURE 12. Sydney's "revitalization" and art-based laneway project.

in corporate and public-private documents, global city rankings now occupy a consuetudinary role in state and federal policy plans as well.[22] This evidences that a continual growth has been taking place not solely in the extent of Sydney's global dependences but also in the measure to which Australia's national dependence on its "global marketplace" champion has been accepted by the city itself. As a senior NSW government planner put it: "Sydney has a *national responsibility* to remain competitive with other global cities."[23] And this despite the sustained lack of federal funding and active planning support. In this sense, the private sector has certainly not attempted to undermine the value of state (and LGA) strategies in setting the overall tone for the city's globalization. Instead, the strategic planning process itself becomes, as McGuirk described it, an "institutional site of negotiation of distributional demands."[24] Rather than clustering around NSW, the underlying structure has progressively been networked to enroll rising actors like LGAs and the business sector as in the Committee for Sydney. Moreover, while metropolises like Singapore, Hong Kong, and London have a well-identified catalyst to the pluralist governance process that underpins their entrepreneurship, Sydney is still too dependent on ad hoc strategies, which are mostly the result of state policies. Entrepreneurship, when mainly directed toward its speculative "variety," as University of Melbourne scholars Nick Phelps and Julie Miao put it, can push toward liberalization and demand-oriented branding, while the forces of globalization (and those of neoliberal globalization in particular) pull the city in manifold directions, as inspired by the ever-changing set of global networks and global realignments. Yet there is another variety of entrepreneurialism, noted perhaps more positively by Phelps and Miao, that has progressively become important for the City of Sydney and perhaps even for the GSC—that of "city diplomacy." As I note throughout this book, the City of Sydney has been deeply engaged since 2007 in the workings of international networks of cities like the C40 Cities Climate Leadership Group, gathering ninety-six of the world's largest cities in a climate action-oriented coalition. With a presence by Mayor Moore and her team at major international forums like the Paris Local Leaders Summit ahead of the 2015 Paris Agreement on Climate Change, but also routinely in international working groups on more tangible municipal government matters like walking and cycling, zero emissions vehicles, and low emissions buildings. In many global cities like Sydney, city diplomacy is not an occasional activity: there are today hundreds of formalized city networks exchanging practices, producing joint reports, working on financing and joint procurement, and, in turn, shaping the way they manage their everyday challenges. The City of Sydney, for instance, acquired a $1 million investment in 2016 by the Rockefeller Foundation as part of the 100 Resilient Cities program, which required the city to appoint a chief resiliency officer and develop the *Resilient Sydney* plan—a strategy that has led to thirty-five tangible actions, including district-level vulnerability planning and monitoring social cohesion. The GSC itself has begun undertaking some of these networked approaches—for example, by reengaging with the Metropolis World Association of metropolitan authorities and, as described at the outset of this chapter, with Lucy Turnbull taking the international stage.

The importance of city diplomacy in this part of the story, then, is again embedded in the politics of boundaries of the global city and the bridging role of global city leadership. Engaging on global issues, networking as part of coalitions of cities collaborating internationally, and developing a voice on multilateral stages like those of the United Nations not only enhance the global legitimacy of a place like Sydney in terms of city branding, as some have argued, but also put the city, its administration, and its tangible local development into a network of global connections of capital, ideas, and indeed politics. In turn, the city becomes an actor, or at the very least a presence, in what is generally known as global governance—the international politics of multilateral affairs, treaties, and economies that shape geopolitics on a world scale. As I have argued elsewhere with Melbourne colleagues, we could quite legitimately speak of the urban governance of global cities as "networked governance," as leaders from these places, as much as their municipal officers, are increasingly engaged in more-than-local practices on an everyday basis. This enhances policy mobility between cities like Sydney, Singapore, and Dubai and pushes city leaders to relate with each other. It also internationalizes, at least to some degree, the local character of urban governance, which becomes, as in various iterations of actions of the *Sydney 2030* plan, intertwined with international initiatives for, for instance, climate action, inclusive migration, or sustainable development. After all, the large businesses shaping the management of global cities are often themselves internationally networked entities. Veolia Environmental Solutions, which manages a substantial portion of the City of Sydney's garbage, is in reality a €25 billion French conglomerate with operations across five continents. SUEZ (and its parent company SITA), which manages much of the rest, is equally a €17 billion company. Even something as mundane as engaging in public-private negotiations over waste management in global cities has much to do with networking internationally.

Accounting for Business Interests

Governing global cities does not, however, only mean going abroad. In fact, much of the global political economy on which these cities rest, as Peter Hall intuitively recounted in 1966, is embedded in the everyday of city politics and in the political institutions of the global city. This is an issue that, of course, brings business elites to the fore. Yet it might be misleading that this is in fact something that is antithetical to government.

In Sydney, for instance, the New South Wales state government has for the most part been a strong supporter of this business engagement in the everyday governing of the city. As such, it has been promoting coalition building across local actors and rallying consensus for its initiatives, something that is well rooted in the history of politics in Sydney. Examples include the establishment of the Organizing Committee for the Olympic Games in 1993 and the formation of the 1996 South Sydney Development Corporation, set up to coordinate inner-city industrial transitions. As McGuirk pointed out, New South Wales has been crucial in "producing the capacity to govern in global Sydney" not just by defining the overall ground and financial trend for the global city's expansion but also by allowing a political process that is particularly inclined to encourage public-private partnerships as a core to urban development such as in the cases of the financial and technical support to the Easter Creek Raceway developments in 1989 and the 1995 backing for the construction of Fox Studios.[25]

This twofold role of business coalitions and contemporaneous global markets dependence has been reflected in much of Sydney's planning. In many cases this has resulted in what Penelope Dean has aptly termed "deadline urbanism," which is demand driven, surgical, and oriented toward remedial solutions to adapt existing spaces to changing markets, rather than planning for the long term.[26] Sydney has for many become "the accidental city" where liberalization, laissez-faire policies, and global economic aspirations have driven the design and configuration of the city.[27] The development of growth coalitions to sustain this globalization focus has, many critics argue, regularly trumped localized interests. In turn, this manifests in the governance of the global city as a very explicit politics of boundaries and boundary making—drawing differences, casting coalitions, pushing for distinction. Again, as discussed in chapter 5, this is no novelty but a well-established trajectory. For instance, in 1988 NSW established an ad hoc authority (the Central Sydney Planning Committee) and redefined the boundaries of "Central Sydney" to overcome substantial local community and heritage conservation opposition to the globalizing project for Sydney's CBD.[28]

Private sector coalitions, then, are playing an increasingly relevant role in global cities. Among many, one of the key actors of this kind is the Committee for Sydney. As a policymaking group of business leaders established in 1997, the committee seeks to tackle issues that concern the "whole of Sydney" and in particular lobby at all levels of government in order to promote the city's prosperity. Members of the group range widely across the urban corporate and culture spectrum, with representatives from, for instance, Macquarie Capital Group, Sydney Airport Corporation, Minter Ellison, Coca-Cola, the National Rugby League, and the

Museum of Contemporary Art. As attested by the *Sydney 2020* strategy paper released in 1998, the committee developed a proactive role in Sydney's global positioning because its founding members perceived that the public sector alone was no longer capable of tackling this challenge by itself.[29] Importantly, the committee has been a key driver in the commodification of green features from environmental responses to market qualities. For instance, in its *Global Sydney: Challenges and Opportunities for a Competitive Global City* research paper, "building a sustainable city" appears as only one of the nineteen priorities, listed as a subset among other livability features as an attractive asset of Sydney's reputation.[30] Through this sustainable reorientation, the business sector has pushed for an interpretation of "livability" rooted in internationally recognized development standards and competitiveness priorities—a focus that has promoted an increasing interdependence of "livable" planning with growth strategies. This feature is not unique to Sydney. One could argue that we are witnessing the rise—or return, if we pay homage to the history of politics in the Renaissance's city-states—of a form of urban governance institution that could be termed as business leadership organizations (BLOs). These organizations are designed and deployed to coalesce the capacity of the private sector to promote the prosperity and international engagement of their cities. One such example is Barcelona Global, a private, independent, nonprofit association that gathers key business interests in Barcelona at both the international scale, as with Deloitte, Accenture, or Ernst and Young, and the more embedded indigenous scale, as with SEAT, Saba, or Telefonica. Set up in 2008 as a platform for citizens' ideas and action, Barcelona Global comprises people and companies that care about Barcelona and its future. The association's mission is to actively contribute to making Barcelona one of the most attractive cities in the world, in order to attract and develop talent and foster economic activity. Similarly, the business sector now plays a critical role (and perhaps a paradoxical one, seeing its market bases) in the continuity of urban policy, further embedding these modes of transnational engagement in political-economic lock-ins. In this sense, the Committee for Sydney, originally a lobby group and now an independent think tank champion for "the whole of Sydney," sees itself as key in providing "thought leadership beyond the electoral cycle." The committee, mainly due to a membership that includes major companies such as ANZ, Lendlease, and Sydney Airport, universities, strategically significant local governments (but not all) and state government departments, and key cultural, sporting, and marketing bodies, is a key driver of the "growth coalition" approach, discussed above, which has a much longer life span than most individual local authorities placing longer-term business interests solidly at the heart of policymaking in a global city whose leadership has to confront shorter-term pressures.

Yet none of this says that business interests are at odds with politics. In fact, one could say that at times business actors are actually calling for politics—of a certain kind. Tim Williams, the former chief executive of the Committee for Sydney, argued publicly that "Australian cities are the real orphans of public policy." Williams who led the "cities" practice of global engineering firm Arup, which in itself plays an important strategic planning role in Singapore and Dubai as well as Sydney. However, from this perspective, government is seen in the service of the global nature—or as Hall would term it, "world city functions"—at the basis of the global city. As the council once self-described its role in an annual report, "The City of Sydney has an important role as *caretaker* of Australia's global city."[31] Thanks to the city's privileged location and proactive governance, the local government has been a key driver in setting a tourist-business brand for the whole conurbation and is currently the major actor in the greening of the city.

Governance and the Business Privilege

Here, then, we spot the relationship between city leadership and organized business interests as central in the broader politics of the boundaries of the global city. Authority and strictly defined boundaries, self-evidently, do not ensure independence from market pressures and market-driven actors. While it may be easy to critique Dubai on this front, it is also the case in the context of what might appear as a solidly centralized continuity of Singaporean government. The story of the "casinos debate" might offer some evidence in this regard.

Gambling was, for the most part, legal (and generally tolerated) under British Empire rule in the 1800s, but it was eventually abolished owing to pressure from a petition to the colonial government by Chinese immigrant businessmen in the Federated Malay States in 1905. After Singapore gained its independence, the abolishment was further translated into law by the Common Gaming Houses Act of 1961. The general rejection of gambling was part of a prevalent moral sentiment, fueled by mainland China and Mao's revolution, against what was known as the "yellow culture" (from the Chinese *huangse wenhua*) of decadence (e.g., gambling and corruption). The newly independent government launched a nationwide clampdown on various aspects of Western popular culture that were seen as promoting a decadent or antisocial lifestyle.[32] However, early proposals for allowing the development of confined tourist resort areas were introduced in 1965 and 1967 by none other than the nation's founder, Lee Kuan Yew. These two instances bear a striking resemblance to the contemporary setup Singapore has developed and were eventually shelved not for political or moral reasons but for

FIGURE 13.   Resort goers at Sentosa island—just behind the never-ending scenery of Singapore.

more practical ones. In 1965 the idea of a tourist resort situated on the island (*Pulau* in Malay) of Sejahat seemed impractical owing to the relative remoteness of the island, which lies northeast of Singapore (just above what is now Changi Airport). In 1967 the idea of a comprehensive resort was then associated with the soon-to-be-returned British outpost of Blakang Mati, what is now known as Sentosa, which instead became the base for the Singapore Naval Volunteer Force and various training grounds as well as parklands. The nation-building process, however, soon gave into the desire to attract foreign interests and visitors. A few months after the famed "global city speech" by Rajaratnam, Pulau Blakang Mati was renamed "Sentosa" in 1972 ("tranquility" in Malay) in a public naming contest, and the Sentosa Development Corporation was formed in September 1972.

It is important to note that at this point in Singaporean history, the general moral stance was in fact against the idea of a casino, still seen to embody unwelcome Western debauchery, and this was further fueled by a more modern version of the "yellow culture" rejection embodied by widespread calls for an "Asian Values" debate.[33] This stance even extended to Singapore's Asian neighbors. In 1975 Lee Kuan Yew loudly rejected the proposal by Stanley Ho, the Cantonese "Godfather of Gambling," who had a monopoly on casinos in Macau for nearly four decades until 2002, to expand to Singapore. The term "casino" remained off limits and was closely associated with societal decay in the city-state for over a decade.

Revisions were made to the Common Gaming Houses Act in 1987, but the idea that a casino would be an effective solution to the economic downturn the city-state was suffering at the time was still generally rejected. Yet the tide was soon to turn. After some initial skepticism, newly elected prime minister Lee Hsien Loong, along with his foreign minister George Yeo, pushed forward the idea in 2004. The logic was that, as he put it in his maiden address at the 2004 National Day Rally, "conditions" were changing: China was embarking on a new open-door policy with Den Xiaoping, and Singapore needed to embrace this "new attitude" to take a "deep breath and think about it carefully."[34] This kicked off what became known as the Great Casino Debate, but eventually the government decided in favor of the "integrated resort." At the height of the discussion, a concern with the need to partly "reinvent" the city's global identity, in the words of the prime minister in his 2005 May Day speech, echoed loudly as this and other key developments were slated to "add the buzz and excitement of a 21st century Singapore."[35] In 2006 the Singaporean government passed the Casino Control Act, which eventually led in February 2010 to the launch of Resort World Sentosa on the island. To be sure, some degree of social policing of the resort remains, as with a $100 levy for Singaporean citizens wishing to visit the casino, and societal polarization on the issue is still central in many debates. Once again, the dual nature of the global city is almost explicitly recognized. For example, former deputy prime minister Tharman Shanmugaratnam noted in a 2012 speech the inherent contradiction of going global for the city-state that "can only survive by staying open, but it brings inequality," something that he and many other senior Singaporeans see as a "fact of life as a global city."[36] In this rhetoric, and in practice, business elites are but a simple "fact of life" too. In these global city contexts, entrepreneurialism and the quest for uniqueness allowed for the penetration of often overlooked actors into the definition of the developmental pathways charted by these cities. Hence, planners, architects, and real estate and sustainability consultants have progressively entered the realm of policymaking while bringing with them inherently "globalized" ways to conceive the city.

Appreciation of the workings of international, or "transnational" as some call them, elites in determining the globalization of cities is, then, one of the most common features of global city-speak across all the conversations at the heart of this book. The term is normally referred to either explicitly or in synonyms in over sixty-nine interviews, with no real differentiation on the basis of background or employment sector. Experts in the private sector refer to this almost unanimously, but others working in government, in academia, and across all types of educational backgrounds point at the centrality of the idea of elites in shaping today's global cities. Of course, this does not mean that all experts share direct agreement on what "elite" means and who might be part of it. Yet it still underlines

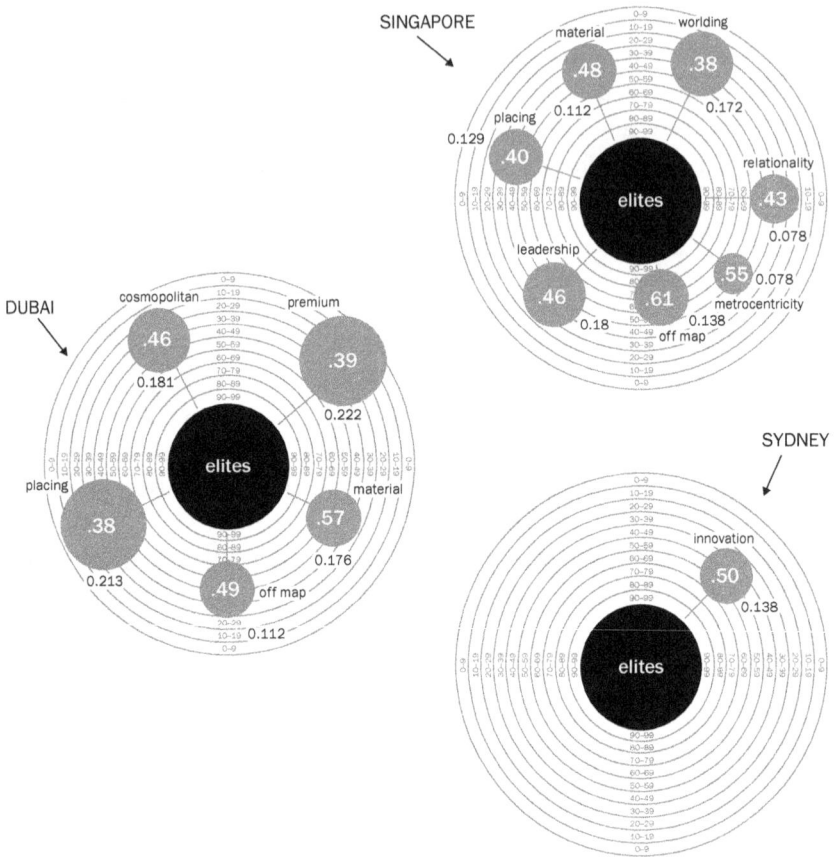

FIGURE 14. Mapping "elites" in global city-speak.

a relative "business privilege," as British planner Yvonne Rydin called it, in the governing of cities in a time of neoliberal global markets.[37] Perhaps the only exception here is experts working in the multilateral sector, with only one mention of transnational elites in twelve interviewees, whereas all the other sectors show common references to this terminology and idea. Another interesting fact emerging from the expert conversations in this book is the correlation between those who mention at least one Global South city and those who mention the idea of the elite: the two seem to go hand in hand, perhaps signaling a sense of the growing importance and historical rootedness of business and other elites in charting the developmental pathways of global hubs in developing countries.

This appreciation echoes, but often does not acknowledge, that the centrality of elites in the governance of global cities is strong evidence of the continuing politics of boundaries that shape its leadership. From this point of view, both the literature on urban politics and the stories above highlight at least five fundamental trends shaping the way cities are governed today. Local authorities have been shifting from a politics of providing to one of commissioning. Since at least the late 1970s, local governments in many countries (developed ones in particular, but with numerous cases in the Global South too) have been shifting from a service provider role to one of contracting or partnering in the delivery of essential citizen services. This has gone hand in hand with the rise of the "entrepreneurial city": urban governance, owing to market pressures but also shifts in politics and political culture, has in many instances moved away from managerialism and local services stewardship toward entrepreneurial approaches to local governments, which see city leaders and officers seeking engagements outside their administrative boundaries and with nongovernmental actors to form "growth coalitions" for their cities. Problematically, perhaps, this entrepreneurial redefinition has had to confront a withdrawal of the state. Central governments (federal or unitary state) have in the vast majority of countries scaled back their involvement in local administration and service delivery. At the same time, we have witnessed a clear rise of nongovernmental actors: private sector (for or not for profit) and community group actors have progressively taken to city hall and driven the expansion of traditional forms of local government into broader processes of "urban governance." This, in turn, has pushed for changing styles and structures of leadership. Entrepreneurial, outgoing, and privately partnered approaches of city leaders are on the rise internationally, but are also coupled with trends in shifting governmental structures underpinning their operations, as with the several metropolitan reforms (e.g., the Greater Sydney Commission) aimed at creating regional urban governance, or the emergence of formalized BLOs (e.g., the Committee for Sydney).

It is important to remember that, at least in Bourdieu's reading of symbolic power, these practices imply a degree of "misrecognition" that drives people to understand the reality (and divisions) stated by those who hold symbolic capital to be "natural," thus in many cases driving the normalization of difference. This is problematic because, as Bourdieu and others in his tradition stressed, it implies a naturalization of inequalities and the stabilization of power relations— something ingrained in most societies from the early stages of education.[38] Dangerously, then, people self-select into or away from opportunities because of the process of internalization of this manifest reality (or *doxa*) hampering their possibilities to advance, shape, or contest the system they live in.[39] As we will see in the next few chapters, this story already points at the central role of global urban ideas and practitioners, be they architects, planners, or indeed academics, not just in upholding this symbolic system but also in recasting the field of possibility embedded in this reality. However, we should not underestimate the power to inscribe what the city is and make manifest, via tangible symbolic "forms," a particular type of understanding of the global city. Control over the way we speak of global cities is exercised not just in the negotiations of governance but also in the written word of strategies and imagination of strategic thinking—the subject of the next chapter.

THE STRATEGIES

InterContinental Carlton: Cannes, 7:00 a.m.

Drinking what is likely the most expensive orange juice I have ever ordered while I enjoy a view of Cannes's famed Boulevard de la Croisette, I am getting the latest on Dubai's flagship logistics development from Roshan, a work acquaintance who was "behind the scenes" just a week before. Construction work on the US$36 billion expansion of the Al Maktoum international airport, designed to be one of the world's biggest hubs with a projected annual capacity of 260 million passengers (more than twice that of Atlanta's airport, currently the largest airport), is on hold. The airport project, as noted in previous chapters, is thought to have an important logistical role for local airline giant Emirates Airlines to consolidate its position as the world's top long-haul carrier. The news is not entirely unexpected among those who follow UAE affairs: the government had already announced in October 2018 a "push back" on the original timeline of five years, forecasting completion in 2030. Dubai World Central, the current airport functioning on the site (along with Dubai's other, larger hub near Deira), which opened to cargo in 2010 and passengers in 2013, is not "clocking the numbers Dubai is used to," my interviewee points out, with obvious reference to record-topping efforts more common across the Emirate. At just over four hundred thousand passengers per year and about fifteen mostly low-cost or regional airlines flying off its tarmac, the current base for the new mega-development above Jebel Ali port is far less than astonishing. My interlocutor, now special adviser to a major global city mayor but a long while back also a PhD graduate just around the time I started my academic career, shrugs. "Don't be fooled though: their strategy is much bigger than that," remarks Roshan, continually glancing back at his iPhone pinging WhatsApp notifications likely from other highfliers of the event we are attending. We are at MIPIM (the acronym for the French *Marché International des Professionnels de l'Immobilier*), almost certainly *the* international property market event. MIPIM is hosted in Cannes, France, each March, with a whopping single admission fee of €1,975 (approximately US$2,300). He is headed to the MIPIM premium event known as the Mayors' Think Tank with the likes of the leaders of Osaka and Warsaw to discuss urban optimization. He takes a brief detour through some gossip on which mayor is lobbying to join which city network but is not getting the access she or he wants. Going back to Dubai, he seeks some degree of shelter in American general-president Dwight Eisenhower's famous quote that "plans are useless, but planning is indispensable." "And that makes for excellent business after all," he smugly admits. But "it also serves an important purpose in the continuity of urban governance in these cities," he quickly corrects, showing that his PhD days are not that far gone.

Even so, it is evident that strategic plans are a now commonly used tool in cities around the world, something that research on over two hundred cities for our book *Leading Cities* confirmed. Strategic urban plans are used by cities around the world to establish leadership priorities and set out what a city and its leaders aim to achieve in a certain time span. They connect leaders to structures and institutions and aim to catalyze action. The process of developing a strategic plan can bring actors together to establish governance priorities. The plans themselves, when completed and adopted by a city, identify an approach to achieve those priorities. In this way, the process of strategic planning and the resulting strategic plan document, as tools, complement the work of city leaders and municipal institutions in cities (global or not) and provide a platform for bridging silos and building coalitions, not least across the often-transitional constituencies that underpin the governance of global cities.

In that, Roshan and I agree that strategies should probably be seen as "a key ingredient" of the making of a global city. Yet Roshan refers to strategy as a "practice," not just a tool or a single document. He is quite right. Strategic planning involves a discursive dimension that goes beyond a branding facade and is linked to a spatial development envisaged by the global city makers in question here.[1] Explicitly, our common understanding builds on more or less academic work on strategy that emerges from business and organization studies. Needless to say, my Oxford Said Business School business card helps a lot in navigating not just this conversation but the halls of MIPIM. The globalization of cities, Roshan continues, is as much the "business of strategies" as it is the "business of strateg*ists*." Global city entrepreneurs, especially those involved either directly in or as supportive of city leadership, become strategic to capture the opportunity to affirm their city on a world stage.

Strategy is an external-internal dialogue: the reification of the bridging role of city leadership I discussed in chapter 7 into a tangible document, process, and set of directions. "The trick," our conversation proceeds, is to drive global cities to be "strategically" global in their orientation. In this context, it is important not to dismiss, as some scholarship has done, the "turn to strategy" as an inherently superficial phenomenon. The forward-looking planning of visions like *Sustainable Sydney 2030* can remind scholars in the global city literature of the importance of comparison in urban policy and research. The strategies illustrated in the previous chapters are in fact informed by substantial comparative reasoning that has the potential to inspire even more multi-case analysis in academia while not subsiding this directly under the sometimes-dispersed lenses of network analysis of globalist accounts of some global city stories. The rationale behind global city plans and urban governance can, in this sense, push for that scholarly shift of comparison from "method to strategy" invoked by Colin McFarlane.[2] As McFarlane points out, there is much to be gained in urban studies from a pervasive development of comparative thinking as a "mode of thought" that can allow theorists to better conceive urbanism.[3] The practice certainly supports this advocacy: almost no issue raised in the previous empirical parts of this book is free from the broader spectrum of comparative consideration. Policymaking, planning, and dwelling alike all bear testimony to the basic relationality embedded in the process of global city making: they refer to other cities and places, relate to their characteristics, confront developmental pathways, and challenge connections. Nonetheless, the inherent comparative outlook of these cities' policymaking is still struggling with producing real reflexivity in the practice of building global cities. The potential reflexivity inherent in comparative considerations such as those that led to the more recent Sydney plans often remains too embedded, if not diluted, in broader discourses of best practices, global economic networks, and "winners and losers" of global city rankings that sidetrack effective self-criticism. Even entrepreneurialism, with its outgoing and innovative ethos, has the capacity to prompt confrontation with the "other" and self-reflective application of this relational reasoning to one's own development. The essential relational mentality of contemporary global urbanism in cities like Dubai, Singapore, and Sydney is, in this sense, skewed by an overemphasis on the competitive element of entrepreneurialism versus the innovative and outgoing components of the move beyond managerialism prompted in the latter part of the twentieth century.

Aspiring to World City Functions

The rise of cities like Dubai, Singapore, and Sydney among the ranks is perhaps best evidenced by their regular appearances in international rankings and the media. Yet, their surge is also testified by the literature and the media increasingly describing them as global next to the likes of London and New York. As we have seen, the three cities have been progressively sanctioned as networked, globalized, and modernized cities, with some less frequent mentions of their global societal problems. As a result of this international recognition, the discussions among urbanists in these three cities have tended to follow similar paths and touch on parallel challenges. A key issue when it comes to globalization and cities, then, is that of convergence: are we seeing a homogenization of urban types across the global cities of our time, or is there some substantial difference in their pathways to becoming global cities? The logic of being a gateway of globalization has no doubt remained a common trait throughout at least the past century (and arguably history) for global cities, and Dubai, Sydney, and Singapore seem to be no exception.

Dubai charted a steep path toward modernization that was seen in early 2000s thinking as unique in the Middle East. Sydney, especially since the 1990s, has aimed at catalyzing visitors of various sorts, from business to tourism and even culture, via its popular livability features. Singapore, ahead of both Dubai and Sydney, embarked on an explicit global city approach pinpointed on the need to survive and thrive amid the ebb and flow of globalization from a viewpoint that is grounded in limited natural resources and complex geopolitical positioning. In light of these orientations, partly different narratives have thus far followed these cities in their strategic positioning.

Beyond the glamour of its skyscrapers, Dubai has put much effort into establishing itself as a modern global hub of commerce, business, and international flows, which is said to be best represented by its iconic developments like the Burj Khalifa but is perhaps even better embodied by the less celebrated logistic successes of its ports and airports. Here we can recognize the strategic importance of less widely celebrated elements of the global city. This is for instance the case of the often forgotten, at least in media reports, of Hall's and Friedmann's original formulations of what accounts for "world city functions" as also critically centered on the city's capacity to articulate mundane flows and everyday connections of goods and people. This of course does not dismiss the importance of other elements of the global city story, whether in Dubai or Singapore. Record-breaking structures, the hybridization of traditional Islam or Chinese culture, and "cosmopolitan" features are core elements in the production of a global city that seeks to cater to the most disparate kinds of visitors and maintain an entrepreneurial and innovative edge on its international competitors. Sydney has instead progressively embraced the productivity of presenting itself as a lifestyle hub where tourists, short-term residents, and business can find the classic social and economic pulls of the global city intertwined with the coastal and buzzing lifestyle embedded in the Sydney-sider experience. Central to this offer, then, are not so much the latest architectural successes or commerce structures but more and more the "quality of life" ingredients such as natural resources, green credentials, or cultural events that put Sydney on the map as a desirable destination and emphasize the "site luck" the city is blessed with.[4] As noted earlier, central in our cases is the importance of the transient elite expatriate and visitor class in shaping the dominant approach to building Sydney, Singapore, and Dubai as truly global cities.

In Sydney, for instance, this has entailed the promotion, as embodied in the 1995 *Cities for the 21st Century* metropolitan strategy issued by New South Wales, of central Sydney (and the City of Sydney in particular) not solely as the corporate headquarters but also as a prime tourist destination. This approach manifested itself as a discursive shift as well as targeted developments that often, at least throughout the 1980s and 1990s, saw a large inference of the state government in planning processes owing to the "strategic nature" of these projects. In the case of Darling Harbor, for example, the once-commercial port was being redeveloped to become a key recreational and pedestrian precinct in central Sydney—a large-scale initiative that was to be replicated in the adjacent Pyrmont/Ultimo harbor front as well.[5] However, the pluralized nature of metropolitan governance in Sydney and the local pressures against this top-down urban management model have pushed New South Wales to accommodate some degree of participatory process, which, nonetheless, has allowed for substantial influence from the business sector and some local authorities.

Similarly, in Dubai, authorities have pushed for progressive development of a multifaceted offer to satisfy a demand for "quality of life" standards or tourist experiences. For instance, while the major developments along Sheikh Zayed Road and Jumeirah were being implemented around oversize shopping hubs and super-tall hotels, the municipality has also pushed for a retrofitting of the old Deira market to advertise the "gold souk" or other developments like Al Seef (discussed in chapter 4), geared toward providing a new face for a bargain jewelry hub in the heart of old Dubai. This renewal was seen as capable of catering to the transient tourist, who can easily access world-class precious goods in the main malls across town, as well as giving a new and more approachable face to the "cheap end of town," where some less branded but potentially lucrative exchanges could be found.[6]

Finally, in Singapore, the development of a now-well-recognized global city has gone hand in hand with a continuous focus on the importance of planning and strategic thinking. As we saw in the previous two chapters, the city-state's founding ethos is essentially entangled with planning thinking and its orientation has very much been aimed at capturing global flows, whether of commerce and logistics or of finance and tourism, with emerging attention to questions of culture and cultural production as well as inherent political, economic, and social tensions. In a way, Singapore has strategically built itself as a city for and of globalization, and in doing so, it recognized that it is constantly exposed to the fluctuations of the global economy. This viewpoint on the world has often been peppered with numerous references to the uniqueness of the Asian city. As recounted in the chapters of *50 Years of Urban Planning in Singapore*, published by a cadre of public service dignitaries gathered by the School of Design and Environment at National University of Singapore in 2016, the over three hundred pages of this collection of short interventions from many of those who shaped planning in the city-state reiterate a common theme: Singapore's conditions are unique. Of course, it is hard to disagree, to some degree. As a small city-state with a peculiar location in Southeast Asia and a complex sociocultural composition, the city seems to have little in common with our other two cases. Yet it still presents us with a particular mix of world city functions recognizable in Sydney and Dubai, it still speaks of a complex governance arrangement that is not free from external pressures and capitalist elite interventions, and, in doing so, it echoes and is echoed in the strategic orientations of Sydney and Dubai.

Global Gateway Strategies

The influence of the business sector can be noticed even more directly in Sydney, although with somewhat less dramatic impacts on the city's landscape than in Dubai, and with an even greater "creative class" emphasis than the shores of the Middle East. For instance, early 2000s research into the drivers behind the location of the IT sector in Northern Sydney, often heralded as "Australia's Silicon Valley," has aptly demonstrated how this positioning has far less to do with the localized benefits of clustering and much more to do with Sydney's attributes and attractiveness for multinational business and with Sydney's strategic interests in maintaining a tight grip on such a core environment for the creative class.[7] Catering to the demands of this ever-present business mantra, most layers of Sydney's governance have adjusted their livable discourse to incorporate this key piece of their global city puzzles. The City of Sydney Council has, in this sense, been a precursor of New South Wales's metropolitan emphasis with its *Positioning Sydney as the Clever City* policy document of 1999 to name but one of many such cases. The approach, now also integrated with the *Sydney 2030* vision, sought to claim a key stake vis-à-vis regional competitors such as Hong Kong or Singapore and thus tap into the creative class's expertise networks and epistemic communities, without which, as the document notes, Sydney "risks wasting enormous opportunities to leap into the top rank of global cities."[8] The centrality of the "livable" nature of Sydney's posture as a global city was again underscored in the publication of the 2030 strategy, highlighting once again the emerging concern noted in chapter 3 that sees a "quality environment" and "world-class" lifestyle features as a core competitive advantage for contemporary postindustrial metropolises.[9] The latest iteration of this logic, as noted in the Greater Sydney Region Plan titled *A Metropolis of Three Cities* (discussed in chapter 8), is aimed to rethink once again the region into three core centers with the idea that most Sydneysider residents should live within thirty minutes of their jobs, education opportunities, and services. These three "cities"—one to the west toward the proposed new airport, one in the new "center" to be based around Parramatta, and one to the east in the current CBD and City of Sydney– dominated area—are once again embodying a logic of spatial differentiation, anchoring around major functions of the greater Sydney conurbation, and valuing of the variety of areas driving Sydney's economy beyond its famed global hub. The three cities, like special areas for development in Singapore and the "cities" built for the internet or finance in Dubai, are not just referential to each other and not just built for the "residents": they also take up fundamental functions that allow these places to be and remain global by articulating flows and allowing for capital to shape their development. In considering this and many other visions, just as with Singapore and Dubai, we encounter the tangible instantiation of the well-established idea of gateway or more generally world city functions that have shaped much global city thinking in academia over the past century. But does this translate into the practice?

Evidence from my conversations in the three cities seems to confirm it does. The idea of global cities being gateways is the second most common (by overall salience, at 0.250) across the entire study underpinning this book. Simply put, just behind the idea of elites and exactly at the same rate of premium connections, Peter Hall's concept of gateway functions that world cities necessarily have to have is common parlance, especially when it comes to indirect mentions (the highest recorded use in synonyms among experts). Of course, experts with a business and economics background understand this terminology well. Yet the idea of gateway functions is not a domain of the social or economic science-minded experts. In fact, those with a background in STEM disciplines seem to understand and speak the language of global connectivity roughly the same way, with high degrees of mentions across STEM-trained experts in all three cities. Overall, across all experts, the twenty-six-to-thirty-nine and the forty-to-fifty-nine age brackets speak more prominently, and generally very supportively, of the influence of gateway functions on the globalization of Sydney, Singapore, and Dubai, with solid representation across all kinds of professional activities, from municipal and national government officers to academics, civil society, and even the multilateral sector.

Correlation analysis gives us further insight into the centrality of this kind of thinking. Not surprisingly, gateway functions are connected to some degree with ideas of relationality and hierarchy between cities, but also with entrepreneurship. These are weak correlations, but they hold true for the three cases. Dubai interviewees in particular are conscious of the centrality of ports and airports, discussed above, standing out as closely correlating with gateway functions and relationality. That, overall, means understanding the global city not just as a port but as a port in a system of ports—a point of connection in the global geography of globalization that is intertwined with many other potentially similar points. Where this stood out particularly clearly in Dubai was in those conversations that were not just boasting about (or criticizing) the Emirate's extreme developments, but rather linked these to the expansion of the city's infrastructural power over a number of other places. This came to the fore very clearly as Dubai's ports company, DP World, progressively came into the international limelight midway through the first decade of the 2000s. Formed in 2005 by the merger of Dubai Ports Authority and Dubai Ports International, which were beyond the logistic expansion of Emirate authorities to Jeddah and Djibouti (two of the region's major hubs) in 2000, DP World is managed by Sultan Ahmed bin Sulayem, whose father was a key adviser to Dubai's ruling Maktoum family and who is well recognized as one of the major business figures of the Emirates. Shortly after taking over the historically British shipping company Peninsular and Oriental Steam Navigation Company (P&O) for a reported £3.9 billion (approximately US$ 5.4 billion), DP World made headlines around the world as US president George W. Bush and the US Treasury expressed concerns as to the Emirati acquiring logistic control of major US port facilities such as New York, New Orleans, or Miami. Outcries in the *Wall Street Journal* lamented the well-planned expansion of Dubai as strategically weaving a web of control over the world's shipping. This eventually led to DP World agreeing to sell P&O's American operations to American International Group's asset management division, Global Investment Group, for an undisclosed sum (reportedly in the billions). But it did not stop Dubai's ascent as a global logistic powerhouse, as a few years later DP World took over construction of the £1.5 billion (approximately US$ 2.1 billion) London Gateway port, opened in 2013, with current links to fifty-one countries and more than ninety ports all over the world, and now housing the DP World London Gateway Logistics Centre. What this story tells us is that we should not think of the impact of global city gateway functions as just localized to their specific place on the map. A well-established and yet much overlooked (by the media at least) characteristic of the Globalization and World Cities analysis has pointed out the reciprocal relations between global cities as nodes in networked geographies. Since the late 1990s, the global flows and connections depicted by GaWC researchers as underpinning the gateway role of cities have also been pointed out as resulting, inevitably, in a continuous relationality between these places and thus co-dependence in how flows shift and change. The growth of a city to global status is measured not just by the height of its skyscrapers or the quantity of flows it articulates, but by the visceral pervasiveness it has on the future of other cities and nations—something strategic thinking in Dubai and Singapore, perhaps much more than in Sydney, has accounted for more effectively.

This shows that when we go beyond the surface of the media and everyday global city talk, we learn that the Emirate's story of globalization is very much a logistics-driven one, not just one of seven-star hotels and impressive record-breaking high-rises. Perhaps somewhat surprisingly, gateway functions, quite commonly mentioned (at a salience of 0.224), do not appear to be clearly correlated with any other term in global city-speak in Singapore, and to some degree in Sydney too. What this tells us (along with an above-normal salience of 0.343) is that world city function thinking in Dubai is very much what skews the account and popularity of this term across the whole study, painting an image of the Emirate that is far deeper than what superficial accounts of its shallow flirt with the idea of a global city might give away. Where Dubai seems to lag behind, though, is in its strategic thinking and strategy-making institutions. No such authority existed in Dubai until very recently, and where a planning council or statutory body (present instead in Abu Dhabi) is still missing and where strategy setting remains in the hands of the Executive Council. But is this changing?

Evolving Global City Strategies

While in Singapore we could clearly speak of a culture of strategic planning thinking, the strategic orientations of both Sydney and Dubai have seen some key realignments in the past few years, with the latter only offering some embryonic institutionalization of planning despite its meteoric rise. As I have already noted, it was not until the 1970s that Dubai even acknowledged the need for some kind of "city planner" to think strategically about urban development. More importantly, the governance of Singapore and Sydney have to some degree, especially in the city-state, formally institutionalized strategic thinking. This is not just an inside-out process based on localized governance realignments:

global drivers are also key. The impact of the global financial crisis on shifting the direction of these strategies is, of course, well demonstrated by Dubai. The Emirate has followed a path that, beginning with commerce, has shifted its focus to business and tourism, followed by real estate, and then pragmatically (or, better, unavoidably) back to commerce and business tempered by a particular appeal to short-term visitors. Dubai is in "search of a new posture," which, as Todd Reisz put it in 2010, is partly aimed at "tempering its bravado" so that the city might still have a shot at being the great metropolis its ruling family envisaged it to be.[10] Yet one of the key lessons of the previous chapter on the Emirate is that of the constant focus on the almost hypermodern approach to building the "next" global city. As illustrated, Dubai has maintained a solid focus on becoming an appealing and efficient hub for the globalization of capital, tourism, and commerce. While the real estate bonanza of the early 2000s has met its limits in terms of sustainability and global competitiveness, the ruling family and the Emirate government have maintained an emphasis on the cutting-edge performances of Dubai's logistic hubs, entertainment offerings, and, perhaps to a lesser extent in the West, emerging centrality in the economy of the Middle East. Yet there remains limited formalization, as with Abu Dhabi's Planning Council or the Urban Redevelopment Authority in Singapore, of a key institution for strategic thinking in Dubai—something that remains mostly in the hands of the Executive Council and dispersed to some degree across the ranks of the sheik's close advisers, often even within his "other" key role in the office of the prime minister. Conscious of this, Dubai embarked in 2013 on delivering the newest iteration of strategic thinking, the *Dubai Plan 2021*, which was set to replace its *2015 Plan* predecessor by giving even greater resonance to themes that, like happiness, the future, or excellence in government, have emerged in the 2010s. Tellingly, the foundational work for the *Dubai Plan 2021* in 2013 and 2014 involved a heavy component of benchmarking carried out by the government in relation to "the world's leading cities" to identify "key metrics to measure Dubai's performance," and embedding relational thinking, at least of the comparative nature, even more directly in its overall narrative.[11] Yet perhaps even more evident is the further emphasis of the *Dubai Plan 2021* toward diversification: Dubai seems very clearly set on not being seen as either a tourist hub or a real estate speculation bubble, but rather as a primary node for global flows. Key to the gateway role of the global city, then is to go beyond superficial usage of the term to a more operational, tangibly infrastructure-based, and often internationalized view of what makes a city global in its positioning in the flows that sustain globalization.

In Sydney, the original focus on commerce has in the past decades been partly replaced by a dominance of the twin business-tourism approach, which has itself been integrated by a growing emphasis on the livable and sustainable features of the Harbor City. These features are not simply a matter of branding, and they step beyond the predominance of the climate change discourse that shapes much of the commonplace understanding of what is "green." In this sense, the sustainability emphasis that both New South Wales, especially in its previous *Metropolitan Strategy 2036*, issued in 2010, and the City of Sydney in its *Sustainable Sydney 2030*, issued in 2013, have been championing is a crosscutting reconfiguration of the city's lifestyle appeal for the global market (as a vibrant, green, and global place) as well as of the city's international leadership in the latest advancement in green urban retrofitting. Here, however, we encounter some important similarities between the two cities in spite of the macro differences in strategic emphasis. All three cities have witnessed, as German American planner Peter Marcuse put it in relation to world cities in general, the impacts of globalization on their metropolitan development in terms of influence on both their processes of urbanization and specific aspects of their built environment.[12] Thus, we can notice concurrent patterns of spatial specialization with, for instance, the diversification of "global" and "regional" parts of the wider Sydney conurbation or with the production of a "new Dubai" and tourist- or commerce-oriented hubs like Dubai Marina or Jebel Ali in the Emirate, alongside a pattern of sprawl in terms of "soft locations" such as CBDs or waterfronts that are "ripe for change" and for a globalizing development.[13] Where these narratives also seem similar is in their strategic reference to other (assumed) global cities. More generically, this external reference and the production of "globalized" locations might seem to hint at potential converging forces in the evolution of Sydney's, Singapore's, and Dubai's built-environment thinking. This is the case of their more and more explicit referring to other global city models worldwide, or the palpable efforts toward developing their built environment in similar directions; aspiring global contenders like Sydney and Dubai might be more or less rationally following an idealized global city model embedded in, as well as championed by, those centers of the contemporary world system such as London or indeed Singapore.

It is important, then, to put the analysis of strategic thinking and planning in our three cities into a wider global context. Do strategic plans in Singapore, Dubai, and Sydney diverge substantially from those of cities the world over? A few lessons from my collaboration with Leonora Grcheva and Elizabeth Rapoport on our *Leading Cities* global review of urban governance in 202 cities may again help us here. Across such a wide spectrum of cases (including Sydney, Singapore, and Dubai), a substantial majority (82 percent) of cities either had some form of strategic plan or were in the process of developing one. In this, our three cities are but part of the wider popularity of strategic thinking in cities, globalizing or not. Interestingly, a large percentage of these plans (45 percent) have endured at least one change in executive leadership, something that has not been the case in Dubai and Singapore. Sydney's election of independent Clover Moore as mayor in 2004 saw the launch of a new strategic planning process and eventually the consolidation of a partly new narrative, that of *Sustainable Sydney 2030*, for the central city. State plans, like *A City of Cities*, have perhaps changed even more frequently, as the Sydney City Council has benefited from the continuing leadership of Moore for the past fifteen years. As we noted in *Leading Cities*, it is also important to take plans seriously as leadership tools that can be used to build links, both within different government sectors, with higher and lower government tiers, and laterally with other actors involved in leading a city. For example, having a strategic plan at the metropolitan scale can help overcome fragmentation between local government jurisdictions and encourage a collaborative approach to managing urban change. This is the case in some major global cities: Hong Kong's *2030 Planning Vision and Strategy* has a chapter on the national dimension of the plan but no evidence of coordination. Yet this is a relatively rare example. In the Strategic Urban Plans we reviewed in that studies very few demonstrated links upward. Only a handful of cities (10 percent), including Christchurch, Bogota, and Adelaide, explicitly referenced plans and strategies from a higher level of government. By contrast, a substantial majority of plans referred to other plans or strategies being implemented from a city government level, with a vast majority (73 percent) referring to tiers of government lower than the city level. Here of course we need to single out Singapore as a city-state, where no clear engagement in discussions of ASEAN emerge in its core strategic plans (the Concept Plan and the Master Plan) and obviously where no formal higher tier of government exists. However, even Sydney and Dubai confirm these limitations. Sydney has limited references to state government, with essentially no engagement with the federal level, which is also largely absent from Dubai's (much more limited in size and detail) strategic plans, like *Dubai Plan 2021*.

Linkages are not the only important issue here: who leads the strategic planning process is also fundamental. The vast majority of the plans (92 percent) were driven by the relevant local government authority (21 percent) or by consultants. However, in many cases, local governments worked with a partner organization to develop their plans. This was a mixture of consultants, multilateral organizations (such as the World Bank or UN-Habitat), and other levels of government. Globally there is ample evidence that other organizations participated in the plan development process but that this is essentially almost always driven by local government and/or consultants. The most common development partners mentioned in plans were the local community and community groups, other levels of government, and the private sector. The local community or community groups were listed as a partner in strategic urban plans where community participation had a relevant role in the process. This is well represented by Sydney and Dubai. The former's process for *Sustainable Sydney 2030* was heavily driven by a partnership between the City of Sydney Council and local consultants SGS Economics & Planning, whose CEO acted as manager of the *Sustainable Sydney 2030* project and convener of the mixed coalition of advisers to the process. In Dubai the still relatively pervasive presence of consultancies is perhaps more explicitly hidden behind the veil of the official Government of Dubai process. Nonetheless, major advisory firms, and typically Western individual consultants, have an important impact on the development and rolling out of strategic thinking in the Emirate. For example, the government signed a long-term contract with American strategy consultancy the Boston Consulting Group for execution of *Dubai Plan 2021* in 2014. Singapore is perhaps the one city of our triad that keeps the reins of strategic thinking closer to its core planning institution, the Urban Redevelopment Authority. This does not mean that companies like Arup, Ramboll, or AECOM have been marginal (in fact, quite the contrary) to Singaporean planning, but it is important to note here that the leadership and the expertise of these processes have often remained predominantly Singaporean versus the case of Dubai and the public-private model of Sydney. What these entanglements with internationally mobile actors like major consultancies reveal, however, is the inherently relational thinking at the basis of global city-speak and planning.

Testifying to a solid currency in both practice and academia, innovation occupies the eighth spot of the twenty global city notions studied here, in terms of salience of mentions in my 170 interviews. It scores well below ideas such as those of elites and of gateway functions, but it does comparatively better than others such as hierarchy between cities and even outperforms the bottom of our "ranking," state rescaling, by a two-to-one margin. Interestingly, for a place whose overall rhetoric and policy veer substantially toward innovation, it does not register any significant correlation in Dubai. It also scores only one, albeit telling, correlation in Sydney—it has a strong correlation with the idea of elites who seem to be inextricably intertwined with innovation-speak in the city. Perhaps more reflective of the overall image of the Southeast Asian city-state, innovation scores two (weaker than in Sydney) correlations in Singapore: logically, owing to the strong outward-focused entrepreneurial governance of the city, with the concept of opportunity, but also interestingly with the notion of rooting globalization in place and grounding it in the Lion State perhaps by favoring innovation-oriented industries, as more ethnographic evidence and indeed the literature seem to confirm. When it comes to backgrounds, innovation was most commonly mentioned in the twenty-six-to-thirty-nine age bracket. Interestingly, innovation is the most discussed notion among planners. Of note is that while this score is higher when considering academics only, it skyrockets to essentially an explicit mention by every other interviewee (an impressive 0.568 salience) when considering participants with a PhD in academia or practice, in line with the common trend of doctorate-carrying interviewees having a far higher explicit or implicit use of global city notions than others.

Perhaps even more interesting is that when it comes to the overall correlations between innovation and the other nineteen notions at stake here across all interviews, only one connection emerges, and, uniquely across all other notions, cases, and correlations, this is a negative correlation—with the concept of materiality (of the global city). It seems, at least according to an overall look at this statistical analysis, that speaking of innovation tends to be antithetical (with a medium-weak correlation) to speaking of the material elements of the global city, and vice versa. When interviewees are divided by age bracket, this negative correlation appears to be driven by two generations: those aged eighteen to twenty-five and, even more strongly, those aged forty to fifty-nine. The eighteen-to-twenty-five-year-olds also display one additional and significant negative correlation between innovation and, curiously, the notion of gateway functions, possibly denoting a generational shift that sees more "material" globalization elements like logistics and finance as disaggregated from newer sectors like that of the creative class.

Relational Plans and Transnational Practices

Strategic thinking in global cities is increasingly about thinking of one's place in relation to other places. This is well demonstrated, for instance, by the lead-up process to the *Sustainable Sydney 2030* strategy. If the final vision document included a number of exemplary case studies like those of Boston or Amsterdam, aimed at representing possible parallels to specific projects proposed in *Sustainable Sydney 2030*, the reference to other globalizing cities was a constant of the whole process that led to this strategic statement. This is well represented, for instance, in the May 2007 *Review of International Strategies*, which produced a "long term vision for Sydney as a sustainable global city" conscious of plans and strategic frameworks currently in place in comparable metropolises.[14] The *Review*, conducted for the City of Sydney by consulting firm SGS Economics and Planning, provided an overview of innovative solutions and complex governance situations as embedded in documents like the 2004 *London Plan* or New York's 2007 *PlanNYC 2030* agenda. In particular, while New York and London were chosen to represent the "global aspirations" of present-day Sydney, the *Review* highlighted how direct and useful comparisons should have instead been drawn with Toronto and Singapore.

In this sense, while the successes and frameworks of the Greater London Authority offered aspirational examples, cases such as Singapore's 2001 Urban Redevelopment Plan *Towards a Thriving World Class City* embodied more direct examples. Practically, the *Review* listed a plethora of globalizing cities such as Vancouver, Copenhagen, Berlin, and Zurich that, although remaining well below the dominant duo of New York and London, represented Sydney's challenges and potential successes far more effectively. As with Dubai and Singapore, lessons and narratives are learned not just from the "highest" echelons of global city hierarchies but also from those growing metropolises that showcase much more "global city pathway" commonality with Sydney. This relational emphasis on strategy making has also progressively driven the attention paid to national rivals. So, if in the 1980s commerce was a core concern, and in the 1990s finance was a predominant discourse alongside considerations of tourism, in the past decade the attention to livability features has become a pivot of both policy and public debate in Sydney. Not surprisingly, the news that the Economist Intelligence Unit had ranked the city sixth in its 2011 *Global Liveability Survey*, with Australian rival Melbourne coming in first, sparked many concerns and policy reactions from both local LGAs (the City of Sydney most of all) and the state government.[15]

While speaking to the necessary interconnectivity among globalizing cities, *Sustainable Sydney 2030* also testifies that strategic relationality in charting the globalization of these cities is not simply a top-down process invoked by the highest authorities in Dubai and Sydney. As with *Sustainable Sydney 2030*'s references to other emerging global cities, charted by a local government authority (the City of Sydney Council), examples of this practice abound across a variety of urban governance scales. If comparative overviews have been carried out at the state and even national levels by New South Wales Planning, as well as by the annual review on the state of Australian cities carried out by the federal Major Cities Unit, relational planning has also been proactively taken up by nongovernmental actors at lower governance layers. For example, in its October 2009 *Global Sydney: Challenges and Opportunities for a Competitive Global City*, the Committee for Sydney set out to provide a benchmarking document capable of capturing the relation of Sydney with other global cities. In particular, and once again in line with that discussed above, the committee recognized that while "New York and London stand apart," it was in the Asia-Pacific region that Sydney was "compet[ing] routinely with cities such as Shanghai, Hong Kong or Singapore" and that competitiveness with similar strategic hubs such as Vancouver or Los Angeles was paramount to Sydney's successful growth.[16]

This process is perhaps even more appreciable in Dubai, where for many years the real estate sprawl of the Emirate testified to the direct influence of other successful global cities. Dubai Marina is but one of many such cases. Developed by

Emaar through a two-phase approach that produced a series of intricate constructed canals just south of the Palm Jumeirah linked to residential developments and several large retail spaces, the marina is a partial replica of False Creek in Vancouver.[17] Now well linked to the CBD via the Dubai metro, as well as to the neighboring Emirates Hills residential and golf spaces and Dubai Media City, the marina has seen a rise in popularity over the past few years.[18] Moreover, at the core of the marina development stands the soon-to-be-completed Infinity Tower, by Cayan Real Estate and architects Skidmore, Owings & Merrill (the planners of the Burj Khalifa), whose 330-meter-tall twisting body is reminiscent of the Turning Torso building in Malmo, designed by star architect Santiago Calatrava. SOM and Cayan have denied any direct linkage, and the tower has been heralded as yet another unique technical achievement for the Emirate. In a somewhat ironic twist of events, an identical tower is slated for construction in Vancouver, as Canadian developers Westbank have commissioned the Danish architects BIG to build a replica of SOM's Infinity.[19] What is then perhaps most interesting is that Sydney's and Dubai's understandings of themselves as global cities is less wedded to the two giants of the New York–London duo and more referential to newly "emerged" global cities like Singapore.

This dynamic in turn conveys, as Bourdieu explains in his 1972 *Outline of a Theory of Practice*, the changing field of what constitutes a "sense of one's place" in the world.[20] This can apply to both individuals and cities alike. It means casting and recasting the boundaries of what, internationally, it means to be a global city and what archetypes, antecedents, and current peer examples might be out there for cities like Sydney and Dubai (and indeed Singapore in its own account) to follow, contest, and relate to. Thus, the symbolic power of the global city discourse is, in this sense, inextricably connected with "boundary work" as a process of drawing and deploying differences but doing so with some measure of graspable commonality. As we saw above, symbolic forms become critical in this process. Repeatable (and much repeated) forms like skyscrapers and airports but also multicultural and innovation districts or the presence of city leaders on world stages are, in this way, building blocks of that understandable alphabet of global city building. If culture is, in Bourdieu's reading, the realm par excellence of symbolic power, then in our story the spread of a now internationally present "genre" of global city thinking (and speaking) might in fact constitute a form of global urban culture in itself. It is a language, made as much of words as of concrete, that constitutes a symbolic system that, while not static and continually an object of some degree of reinvention, has been knitting together and shaping cities for the past century.

THE CITYZENS

Speakers Corner at Hong Lim Park: Singapore, 7:00 p.m.

Sister Sledge's popular tune "We Are Family" is echoing in the background for possibly the tenth time as I attempt the rather impossible task of spotting my friend Siti and her colleague Mark, who, like the roughly twenty thousand people around me, are dressed in pink. I am wearing a more conservative salmon polo, but that does not help us locate each other. The setting is Pink Dot, an annual LGBT rally-come-concert held at Speakers Corner in Hong Lim Park, just a few meters south of the Singaporean tourist mecca of Clarke Quay. Held in the same location since 2009, Singapore's first public pro-LGBT event is now a well-established, and controversial, happening for the Singaporean equal rights campaigners. Pink Dot, whose name originates in the idea of red + white = pink, to riff on the national flag's colors, is attracting much global city attention. The BBC is reporting on it, and large organizations such as Goldman Sachs and BP have signed up as corporate sponsors for the first time this year (2014). This year's theme, "For Family, for Friends, for Love," along with Sister Sledge's song, highlights the LGBT community as an important contributor to the family-oriented nature of Singaporean society. Eventually, thanks to the limited size of the venue, a rather large pink cotton candy machine at the Pink Dot Community Tent, and Mark's rather visible unicorn hat, we locate each other. Our reunion occurs shortly after Janice Koh, member of Parliament, Pink Dot ambassador, and popular actress in the TV legal drama *The Pupil* (but now perhaps better known for her role in *Crazy Rich Asians*), steps off the stage. This is not my first Pink Dot event; three years earlier, as a thank-you for introducing her to Sydney Mardi Gras in 2010, Siti took me to a Pink Dot–themed picnic in Hyde Park organized by Singaporeans in London. I am meeting Siti for the party, but I am also arranging a follow-up with Mark, who works on homelessness in Sydney—a connection that Siti, who is finishing her anthropology PhD in the United States by doing fieldwork on homelessness in her hometown of Singapore, reckons is key for me to get a serious look into the underbelly of the Australian global city.

Yet all that people are talking about at Pink Dot is how the event is "ruffling up feathers the right way" (they say) among those who count in the city-state. As with Google in 2013 and expanding to Apple and Facebook in 2016, major international sponsors are recognizing the opportunity for visibility here. Despite international corporate support, this is a tense year for the event, as Muslim and Christian community organizers hold the counterdemonstration "Wear White" for a "pro-Family, pro-Government, pro-Singapore" against Pink Dot's advocating for cultural acceptance and normalization of nonheterosexual orientations and relationships—perceived by Wear White campaigners as contradicting Singaporean laws and corrupting national values. The opposition is no small affair: pastor Lawrence Khong, founder of the Faith Community Baptist Church, makes a point of this with a telling selfie with an estimated six thousand followers crowding into a packed Suntec Convention Centre. The selfie was posted on Twitter—which became a Pink Dot sponsor the following year.[1] Corporate endorsement aside, the twenty thousand gathered at Speakers Corner, and many others across the island, are still stuck in what Natalie Oswin, who chronicles Pink Dot and the struggles of the LGBT community in her *Global City Futures: Desire and Development in Singapore*, calls a "queer time"—a reality where expressions of nonheterosexual life are out of "sync" with the official way of life that dominates the city. Homosexuality remains relatively tolerated by Singaporean authorities, but laws like section 377A of the Penal Code, which criminalizes sexual acts between members of the same sex, remains in place. The story here, however, is not just one of reaction against LGBT rights claims.

The faith of Pink Dot in the following years is telling not only of the limited steps LGBT advocacy has been allowed to make in Singapore, but also of the dynamics of globalization and local politics we saw playing out in the previous chapters. The global city does not just yield to international interests and pressures, and its governance is a complicated affair. The scholarship on global cities also often, as David Ley pointed out in 2004, tends toward the dangerous "underdevelopment of human agency and everyday life."[2] Overwhelmed by the transnational flows and networks that define the global nature of these cities, the mundane experience of the individual subject in the global city is often sidelined. Yet everyday individual experiences and life on the streets of these cities matter. In 2017, after eight editions of the rally, the Ministry of Home Affairs restricted participation to citizens only and banned foreigners from entering the event. This, perhaps surprisingly in Singapore's affair with international capital, extended to prohibiting organizational roles for foreign companies like Twitter, Facebook, and Apple—with a wealthy cohort of Singaporean businesses now making up for the loss in sponsorship. While subscribing to the dominant symbolic system promoted by the world economy and rising fast in the ranks as a recognized global hub, the successes of Singapore are not trickling down equally across its populace. This surfaces once again a "splintering" reality of alternate privilege in the global city. As both milestones of the global city literature (like that of Sassen) have noted and critics of this scholarship (like Roy) have advocated, the key is to recognize the inherent pitfalls implied in the growth of these places, and the challenges they present to everyday urban dwellers of the global city—not just the transient visitor or the elite.

A "City of Cities"

Mark's suggestion to examine the "underbelly of global Sydney," as he puts it, takes me back to Australia to look more closely into the issue of homelessness and more generally disadvantage in Sydney. The problem of rough sleepers is not a minor one in the Harbor City. According to data from RMIT ABC Fact Check and the Australian Urban Research Infrastructure Network, the percentage of homeless persons in inner Sydney has increased from 1.7 percent to 2.32 percent between 2011 and 2016, and the state of New South Wales, especially in greater Sydney's built areas, is the only one in the country to have seen in this period an increase in the rate of homelessness for children under twelve.[3] Homelessness is not an uncommon problem for global cities, and if places like Sydney and Singapore number in the hundreds of cases, London has repeatedly reported figures ranging from 3,000 to 7,500 rough sleepers on its streets. This is a challenge recognized by the City of Sydney, whose Homelessness Unit has been addressing the issue, especially in hot spots like Woolloomooloo, Wentworth Park, and Belmore Park. Yet homelessness is but a part of a larger problem. The housing rights campaign *Everybody's Home* argues that (as of 2018) over 21 percent of Sydney's households suffer from "rental stress"—meaning that more than 30 percent of household income is spent on rent, potentially putting tenants at risk of duress.[4] So, while the city expands its global clout, key socioeconomic challenges become more and more central.

It might be hard to assign blame for this. The global growth of Sydney is the result of a concerted process of governance by major local actors such as the state of NSW, private sector lobbies, and certain LGAs (City of Sydney *in primis*) that have pushed toward a more entrepreneurial and internationalized take on urban development. Yet, for whom has this global city been built? As we have seen throughout the book thus far, many would argue that much of this has predominantly been driven by international flows and by elites of a "transnational capitalist class" whose consumerist, technical, and corporate fractions have defined the priorities of the Harbor City. The idea of how central elites are to global city making is deeply rooted in the conversation with Sydney experts. It received eight direct mentions across all interviews versus three in Dubai, which has a greater proportion of indirect mentions (eighteen versus Sydney's ten), and was the most cited concept from global city research in my conversations with Sydney experts.

Of course, this orientation raises more than a few eyebrows as the benefits of Sydney's globalization seem to have been spread unevenly across the city. Sydney has progressively been described as a "golden egg" (as the Committee for Sydney put it in 2001) capable of bringing benefits to all Sydneysiders and Australians.[5] However, as Doreen Massey's study of London as a "golden goose" has pointed out, there are important differences between the rhetoric of these localities as global cities and the actual benefit flows that are generated and circulate through them.[6] As journalist Debra Jopson wrote reporting on a National Economics survey in 2002, "Sydney has been described as Australia's only globalized city, but less than 2 percent of the 12,138 square kilometers in the greater metropolitan area really deserve the title."[7] While this might be a little harsh in judgment and narrow in its understanding of what accounts for "global," it still brings up a fundamental challenge as to the centrality of disadvantage in the global city and its inherent separation into different kinds of urban spaces. In this sense, the major problem that is steadily rising to the forefront of the city's landscape is perhaps that of the increase in sociospatial inequality that has followed Sydney's growth in the past decades.

To begin with, Sydney's social structure is facing a dividing tendency. As much of the "dual city" literature tells us, since underlying interests and economic relations underpin metropolitan power geometries, inequality has a propensity to develop both across the conurbation and between the city and other adjacent suburbs and urban centers. Not everyone benefits from the "goose," and the social impacts of globalization are a growing concern for scholars and planners alike, as globalizing cities tend to suffer from a high degree of social polarization. Confirming this assumption, there is today an increasingly worrying trend in Sydney that shows social polarization processes among higher- and low-income groups. For instance, it is particularly significant that Scott Baum was able to partly dismiss this "bimodal distribution" thesis in 1997, but his more recent studies show how Sydney is now "reflecting the polarized nature often associated with global cities."[8] In this latter analysis of metropolitan socioeconomic disadvantage, Baum has found the Harbor City to house some of the most extreme bifurcations among all the Australian capitals, topping a General Deprivation Index in both highest and lowest relative deprivation.[9] If New South Wales embarked first on building a "city of cities" (something echoed internally by the City of Sydney) and then on a "three cities plan" in the name of specialization for the various areas of greater Sydney, some might then also argue that the globalization of the city has been promoting "two Sydneys" split between that of the rich and that of the poor.

This, then, takes us to the idea of the dual city inherent in Sassen's original description of the socioeconomic hourglass effect shaping the population (and labor force) of the global city. The idea is, overall, the fourth most commonly acknowledged in the 170 interviews for this book. With a salience of 0.215 across all my discussions in Sydney (second most common term), it scores above average in all three of our cities, signaling that problems of socioeconomic bifurcation remain at the fore of people's understanding of how cities globalize. The highest scores for dual city are predominantly present in the discussions of those working in civil society, but private sector experts have an equally high degree of engagement with the term—not to detract from the relatively high degree of mentions present across all other backgrounds and professions. Quite clearly, then, this dimension of global city thinking is front and center in a large majority of global city discussions.

Curiously, despite this prominence, correlation analysis shows few connections between this and any of the other nineteen terms; a weak link to the idea of worlding mostly results from a stronger correlation (at 0.49) in Dubai between these two. Of all the concepts underpinning this study, the idea of the dual city is perhaps the most contested one in terms of having a substantial amount of both positive and negative mentions—signaling numerous cases of both experts agreeing and a large number disagreeing on the dual rich-and-poor hourglass nature of the global city. Here, interestingly, it is those with a social science or planning background that reported the lowest (negative) scores when speaking of the dual city, mainly in Dubai or Singapore. These two cities are clearly diverging from Sydney: it seems like the experts engaged in the discussion for this study largely agree that in Dubai and Singapore the implications of globalization have created different socioeconomic conditions from the dual city thesis of the 1990s that saw a polarization between rich elites and the working-class poor. The age group profiles for the term are also quite interesting: while experts in the twenty-six-to-thirty-nine age bracket show both positive and negative scores—marking a divergence of opinions as to whether Singapore, Sydney, and Dubai are in fact polarized cities, something echoed in the forty-to-fifty-nine age bracket—the more recent generations (eighteen-to-twenty-five-year-olds)

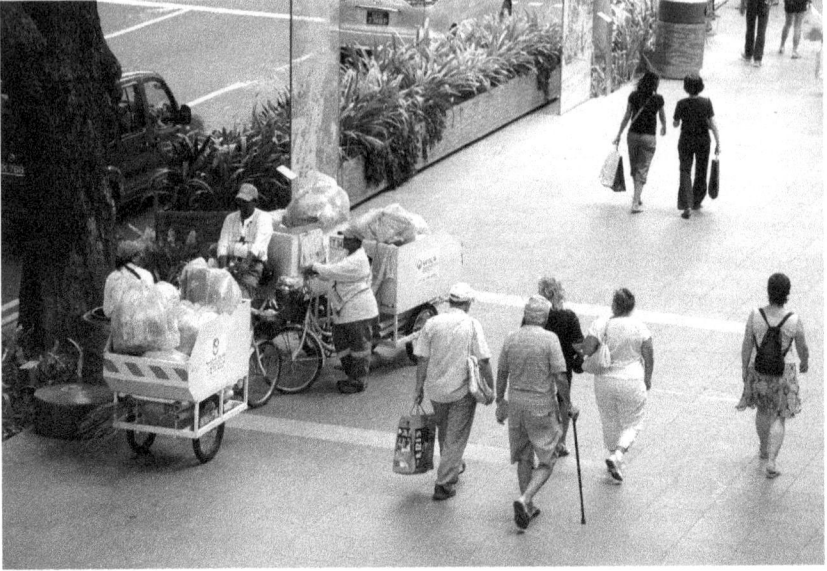

FIGURE 15. Maintenance workers in Singapore's Orchard Road.

report only positive scores for this term, indicating a relative return of the idea of the dual city in global city-speak.

A Metrocentric Bias

The pitfalls of the global city, whether polarizing or splintering, are perhaps made even more acute by a systematic prejudice in the way we speak of global cities. As I noted in chapter 3, Tim Bunnell rightly pointed out in his work that much dominant urban theorizing (if not thinking) tends to fall prey to the bias of "metrocentrism": that "tendency in Anglophone urban theory to look at metropolitan regions—particularly so called global cities—as the leading edge of global urban change."[10] Metrocentrism, noted Julian Go in relation to social sciences, arises because theories, especially of Anglo-European descent, are unproblematically applied everywhere in the world with a premise of universal applicability.[11] This leads, in Bunnell's view, to dismissing the importance of marginal places (like peripheries) and secondary cities, especially in the Global South, and urgently needing an extension of "the range of cities that we study and to diversify the range of ways in which we study them" to practice urban and regional studies in less "metrocentric" ways.[12] A metrocentric bias can occur, in this sense, at multiple scales, with suburban realities obscured by the globalized visibility of CBDs (as with Singapore), but also at regional and national scales (as with Dubai) and all the way up to the global stage (as with London's primacy as a reference point over many southern experiences). An example in metrocentric research is that of Roger Keil's popular work on global "suburbanisms," geared toward promoting a better understanding that the so-called contemporary urban revolution is in fact very much a *sub*-urban revolution and that the growth of global urban centers comes with an even more startling explosion of suburban "constellations" around central cities.[13] Redressing metrocentricity does not mean just accounting for Ras al Khaimah and Ajman as the "lesser" known Emirates in the UAE versus Dubai and Abu Dhabi, but also having a broader sense of the variation of urban experiences and realities across our case studies.

Of our cities, Sydney is perhaps the best embodiment of this challenging bias. Certainly, several have contended that the greater Sydney conurbation is splitting along the dual city lines and that often the poorer "half" is forgotten in global discourse. This "two-Sydneys" thesis is sustained, Australian scholars argue, by a bimodal distribution trend in immigration patterns toward higher-end jobs for skilled migrants and low-income service occupations for others that, as both Grahame Hugo and Ernest Healy and Bob Birrell underlined, tend to enhance Sydney's income structure bifurcation.[14] As they pointed out, polarization is reflected in the physical dissociation of the urban texture of the metropolis, which is effectively splintering as the Harbor City's spatial segregation goes beyond a poor-West / rich-East dichotomy and becomes a "quartered city" with a strong internal hierarchical differentiation that is crowning the City of Sydney at the expense of outer suburbs.[15] As highlighted in a study by Bill Randolph and Darren Holloway (drawing on the Australian Bureau of Statistics Index of Relative Socioeconomic Disadvantage), the city has witnessed a stark sociospatial diversification over the past thirty years, with a progressive "suburbanization of disadvantage" at the expense of the vast west and southwest areas.[16] This disaggregation has also been confirmed in the popular VAMPIRE Index elaborated in 2008 at Griffith University's Urban Research Program by Jago Dodson and Neil Sipe in order to assess household and suburb vulnerability to factors such as mortgage rates, oil prices, and inflation risks. The study found that Sydney displayed a more defined spatial patterning of change and an increase in vulnerability across the 2001–2006 period compared with less "globalized" Australian capitals like Brisbane, again with the major west-central and southwest regions (across Liverpool and Parramatta) registering the worst inflation.[17] As these reports remind us, the problems tied to Sydney's globalization are not just social questions but dynamics reinforced by the physical organization of the city. Yet the contrary is also true: the "globalizing" design of the Harbor City has substantially impacted the city's sociospatial configuration. Despite this conventional planning wisdom, direct imprints that connect urban splintering with the entrepreneurial worlding highlighted above can be traced. For instance, rather than moving toward a "polycentric" organization with multiple CBDs, which is often hinted at in the policy documents issued by local and state authorities, Sydney has progressively embarked on a path toward internal "hierarchical differentiation" with both the City of Sydney and North Sydney playing major roles in attracting global flows, secondary centers organizing the conurbation's physical connectedness to worldwide networks, and outer suburbs (especially in the west) becoming marginalized communities.[18] This is not just the result of an indirect reorganizing prompted by the rise to global city status, but also a conscious project undertaken—at times with different goals—by state government and some LGAs.

So, can we argue that a degree of metrocentrism remains in discussions of the globalization of Sydney? Certainly, some discussions on Sydney's development point at some degree of nonbiased accounts. In 2016 the Australian edition of the *Guardian* spotlighted the "need to talk about our postcode prejudice" in Sydney, and the three-cities plan discussed in chapter 8 surfaced these considerations in 2018.[19] Certainly, the media popularity of current debates as to the split between the more marginalized Western suburbs echoes quite clearly Bunnell's metrocentric critique, but might lead us to think that this bias might not be as bad as global city critics make it. Yet, discussions with experts throughout this study leave much to be desired as to a less metrocentric global city-speak.

Along with notions of rescaling of urban politics, the idea of metrocentric biases in urban thinking is the least commonly mentioned notion across all my discussions with experts in the three cities. The majority of the mentions (sixteen of twenty-eight across 170 interviews) are found in interviews with academics, but it was in the cases of two planners—one in Dubai (working in government) and one in Sydney (working in a multilateral organization), both of whom had a PhD and were in the forty-to-fifty-nine age bracket—that the only two direct mentions of the possibly verbose term "metrocentricity" emerged. In both cases it was in regard to the work of Tim Bunnell on the subject. In terms of correlation, and despite the limited salience across all interviews, it is interesting to see some strong positive connection between those discussions of the idea of leadership, especially when it comes to Dubai (with a correlation coefficient of 0.6). In Singapore, ideas of metrocentricity show strong correlation to the acknowledgment of the role of elites, but also of the hierarchical nature of global cities. A not surprising strong correlation, especially in Singapore (at 0.74, a nearly certain link between the two), also exists between the idea of what is left "off the map" by the global city discourse and its metrocentric bias. Undoubtedly the two ideas are relatively similar, share a quite closely connected postcolonial geography lineage, and, most importantly, gesture toward what is being obscured by globalization-speak, therefore flagging central pitfalls to the global city. This might in practice signal both a more refined reading of the global city's "splintering" rather than "dual" nature and some degree of moving away from thinking of a simple rift between rich and poor to more complicated socioeconomic separations underpinning the development of these global cities. Yet, we still seem far away from embracing more explicitly the need to decentralize global city thinking away from the global "hearts" of Singapore, Sydney, and Dubai, and indeed also with a better appreciation of secondary cities off the map when we refer to these places.

Splintering Rights

The "spectre of splintering urbanism," as Stephen Graham put it at the outset of the twenty-first century, is most certainly still haunting global cities.[20] Of our cases, the sometimes-disorienting urban layout of Dubai embodies this most strikingly. Many commentators have pointed with criticism at how the city is slowly succumbing to a multipolarization that is, rather intentionally, creating separate worlds that are nothing but "transitory spaces" that make the metropolis "a paradise of personal security" for those who can afford it.[21] As Yasser Elsheshtawy described it in his aptly titled *Temporary Cities*, the "ordinary" Dubai often vanishes owing to this very volatile process, which appears almost completely demand driven and highly influenced by global economic fluctuations. Even older zones such as Al Ras in Deira are subject to the perverse logic of splintering urbanism and the dynamics of symbolic power embedded in it. As in the case of the many Chinatowns in the West, these souks are being socially constructed as bounded "places" to be experienced and "consumed" in contrast with the high-income districts of Burj Dubai and Sheikh Zayed.[22] Low-income nationals, a rarity, and even lower-income migrant workers, a significant but silent minority with no leverage on the government's deeds, are migrating to outer dormitory suburbs as rents rise, and foreign expats are given the possibility—almost unique in the region—to own land and develop commercial areas.[23] There is now a "fast-emerging world of premium connections" that is becoming the "ordinary" Dubai for a large contingent of transient visitors who experience the city in a completely different nature than "everyday" residents.[24] The built-in user inscribed in most of Dubai's key developments is more and more the anonymous corporate elitist or the transient tourist. Both of these categories often have little to contribute to the development of a stable local identity and remain transient, while the rights of those low-income classes who have flocked to the Gulf in search of opportunities remain relatively confined even when these are the very people who have built and operate the city for those elites. A key question, then, is that of whose global urban alphabet, or "symbolic forms," is at the heart of global cities today, and whether this works in favor of (or at least in relation to) those whose lives are also intertwined with the city in a less transient, or more vulnerable, way. A classic critique of this by Bourdieu points at symbolic forms and systems as "instruments of domination" produced by the dominant culture and often concealing division (or "distinction") between people. As he puts it, "The culture which unites [also] separates and legitimizes distinctions."[25] Important in the role of those whose work is centered on the practice of symbolic power, like planners, urban developers, and indeed scholars, is the capacity to cast groups drawing who is "in" and "out" of accepted boundaries. Entrepreneurs with sound symbolic capital can play a critical role in, as Loic Wacquant puts it, the "symbolic fabrication of collectives."[26] Global cities, lamented American political scientist Peter Eisinger, are increasingly developed for the "visitor class" rather than their mostly invisible inhabitants, focusing on transitory rights based on what those who can afford mobility want rather than what longer-term residents require.[27]

Practically, this takes the shape of a system of "internalized dispositions" that urban dwellers take for granted as they have undergone in some form a process of naturalization, constituting in (most) people's minds what is to be "taken-for-granted, natural, inevitable state of affairs."[28] In Bourdieu's political reading, then, it becomes essential for those capable of leveraging symbolic capital for the common good to work against the "laissez-faire and complicitous silence" inherent in the symbolic power of those working for a "business privilege" that splinters the realm of possibilities in a city between premium realities and ghettoized spaces—something well understood by at least part of the global city tradition.[29]

To understand the importance of notions of "splintering" for global city thinking, we need to take a closer look at the relevance of two aspects of Graham and Marvin's theorization of the splintered nature of our built environment. Interestingly, the ideas of premium connections and network ghettoes differ substantially in their presence and correlations in my conversations in Singapore, Sydney, and Dubai. To begin with, while premium spaces are a common occurrence in the interviews (as the third most salient term overall), ghettoes receive an almost diametrically opposite level of attention (sixteenth in salience of the twenty terms studied here). The centrality of premium and exclusive spaces in the global city is well acknowledged by architects and planners, but is also surprisingly common among those with a natural scientific STEM background and even lawyers. Ghettoes, on the other hand, receive some moderate attention by planners but are virtually absent in conversations with those with a

STEM or a business and economics background, and are quite limited in their commonality among architects. What is happening here, then, is that premium connections are discussed as a core element of globalization separately from the spatial "ghettoization" consequences they come with. Many of my interlocutors had no problem acknowledging, more or less explicitly, the privileged nature of certain spaces built in (and for) the global city but lacked direct acknowledgment of what happens to those who cannot access these spaces, or indeed the places they inhabit. In fact, if premium connections are regularly cited by scholars (both positively and skeptically), ghettoes remain the third least discussed term even for those working in the academic world, albeit at a higher-than-average salience owing to many social scientists' familiarity with the theory of splintering urbanism.

When looking at correlations between these two terms and other ideas underpinning the global city, we find a similar degree of separation. If notions of spatial ghettoes display only a mild correlation with those of elites, but no particular difference among the three cities in question here, premium connections are another affair altogether, at least in Dubai and Singapore (while Sydney shows no correlations). Mentions of these privileged spaces show some correlation with ideas of putting globalization in place (a link particularly strong in Singapore) and of the materiality of the global city (particularly in Dubai), but are also positively related to discussions where people acknowledged the "cosmopolitan" basis of the global city, perhaps signaling once again the transnational character of the elites often shaping these places. Interestingly, in Singapore, premium connections are negatively correlated with the idea of capturing a global opportunity, possibly highlighting the more external-facing and geopolitical character of conversations centered on the latter rather than the more architectural nature of those on the former. Yet in general it remains clear that, perhaps similarly to the faith of Sassen's discussion of the global city where the polarizing effect of globalization has often been forgotten, conversations that engage to some degree with notions of splintering urbanism do so by bringing up half of its theorization, that of the premium spaces, often lacking more direct engagement with its more concerning socioeconomic implications: that of ghettoized spaces of globalized metropolises. Yet splintering urbanism and the dual city notion do not only work at the small scale. Sydney and Dubai, and to a degree Singapore, are also discussed more generally in the ways that their larger areas and neighborhoods are being divided—another key pitfall of the idea of global cities.

As first step in this direction, I would suggest that by building on "ordinary" and metrocentric critiques of the global city, we could pay greater attention to the lived experience of the global "city-zen" without compromising those ordinary stances. This means to speak more openly of the ways that rights and

responsibilities of residents and visitors are embedded in the politics and governance of the global city, bringing the political back at the heart of our concep-
tualization of the process of globalization in cities. This is even more fundamental
when, as I have highlighted in the case of Sydney's proactive engagement in international coalitions of mayors, "cities" (i.e., city governments) are increasingly speaking *for* their citizens internationally and nationally. Over the course
of their rise, Emirate, Sydneysider, and Singaporean authorities have progressively taken to the international system, whether in UN conferences or visible
international stages like that of the World Economic Forum, and have spoken
of "Singapore" and "Dubai" and Sydney." Thus, in a way, they are representing
those who live and thrive, or indeed often are excluded, in their cities, whether
they have had a voice afforded to them in shaping their globalization or not.

A Question of "Cityzenship"

Situated at the crossroads of manifold worldwide networks, global cities represent unique mixtures of individuals, groups, and rapidly changing affiliations. The
relationship between government, as legitimate authority, and governance, as the
broader processes that govern the city between public and private spheres, is being
questioned by these cities' globalization. This surfaces key questions that pertain
to the "governed": what rights and duties do global city politics inscribe in their
streets and buildings, and for whom? This is not just a function of the growing
business influence that is progressively the central agenda of local governments.
The emergence of metropolises like Dubai and Sydney on a global stage also produces a mounting complexity in the public within these cities that surpasses traditional national boundaries and conventional international structures. This brings
us to a further complication. In the global city, the "local" is not just the French in
Paris and the British in London: foreigners become "localized" through their interplay with a particularly "open" urban, while local cultures and affiliations are
themselves hybridized by the globalizing influence of the city, which questions
many of the traditional boundaries of group affiliation, such as kinship, family,
and ethnicity. Besides, contexts like Dubai, Sydney, and Singapore, just like other
global(izing) cities, are also institutionalizing to some degree the global character
of this city-zenship: nonnationals often partake in local council elections, experiments in city-based working permits and forms of IDs are currently being tested,
and forms of political affiliation in various types of movements, from party electoral politics to housing rights, workers' well-being, and poverty, are afoot across
the world. Crucially for the diverse urban government arrangements we encounter, globalizing cities put in direct confrontation logics of group affiliation with

those political notions of membership (and that of "citizenship" *in primis*), which are more or less formally remodeled, stretched, pierced, and "glocalized" through that open geography with global tendencies represented by these postindustrial metropolises. The challenge of what constitutes citizenship in globally connected cities might after all be one of the most fundamental political challenges of our time, and one that does not lend itself to quick-fix solutions.

At the individual level, by producing endless cosmopolitan encounters, the global city resets the parameters of individuality as they relate to the traditional cultural, religious, and political affiliations that embedded people in the state-centric system of the past centuries. This provokes a social tension whereby, as Ken Booth put it, "identity patterns are becoming more complex, as people assert local loyalties but want to share in global values and lifestyles."[30] The mobility-inspired and heterogeneous nature of global cities provides fertile ground for social confrontation, thus inspiring sociopolitical changes in the parameters of social membership. By putting the "local" in direct contact with the "alien" and opening breaches through the encasements of the national that can offer global gateways to the multitudes, the postindustrial metropolis becomes a strategic terrain for conflict, socialization, and sociocultural hybridization. This of course presents an identity challenge at both individual and city levels. Yet, for the questions of governance at stake here, this sociocultural hybridization also promotes political challenges. As partly incomplete societies that are continually changing, global cities are characterized by a multiplicity of local communities coexisting in the same social milieu, from which many of them derive their distinctiveness. The global city itself thus becomes an object of contention, a "contested terrain of competing definitions" that produces confrontation among indigenous and foreigners, legal residents and illegal migrants, and members of the various "communities" located in the city.[31] Urban governance, defying much of the conventional statecraft logic and admitting countless "external" influences as well as "internal" exclusions, becomes a battleground where multiple and often competing visions of what the global city should be converge. Rights, duties, and benefits of participation in this policymaking dynamic are thus twisted as the globalization of urban planning and the "glocalization" of urban politics redesign the logic of urban governance. The idea of political membership, at the urban scale, assumes novel characteristics and becomes tied to alternative sources of liberties and political involvement. Providers of entitlements and facilitators of political action now range beyond the institutions of the nation-state, with governance spheres above and below it functioning as both guarantors of rights and claimants of duties, and the global city seems to be acting as a core rearticulator of this process. Yet, as the emergence of a "business privilege" in Dubai, Sydney, and London might evidence, not everyone can equally take part in, and benefit

FIGURE 16.   Construction workers in front of Dubai's "seven star" Burj Al Arab.

from, the dynamics of strategic articulation of the global nature of these cities. As Doreen Massey put it in the case of London, "It becomes necessary to ask, when speaking of global cities, *whose city* is at issue here?"[32]

Much of the dominant global city rhetoric, especially ideas like innovation and the creative class or that of capturing a global (economic) opportunity, has to do with appealing to the highly mobile geography of global elites. The "new cosmopolitans" (as Polish sociologist Zygmundt Bauman labeled them) are fundamental in the reiteration and change of the geography of today's world system.[33] The ruling class in cities like Dubai, Sydney, and Singapore has often been persuaded by calls for the appeal of these elites. For instance, in his book *The Global Me*, former *Wall Street Journal* correspondent Pascal Zachary asks public and business leaders to embrace the clout of those who display a mix of rootedness and "wings" that connects them across continents.[34] It is about developing a "competitive edge," even by "picking globalism's winners and losers," as the subtitle of Zachary's book puts it. Nobel Prize–winning economist Robert J. Shiller even argued this might be a new, cosmopolitan social class that is emerging as pinpointed on major global centers like New York and Singapore.[35] Certainly, Dubai has done much to appeal to this elite, but Sydney's lifestyle branding also seeks to enter this sphere. Putatively, these "citizens of the world" are developing loyalties to each other that cross national boundaries. This point of view paints a picture where there is no spokesperson for the cosmopolitan class, no organization that can be blamed for what is happening—the cosmopolitans, Shiller and

Zachary tout in major Western media, tend to be increasingly wealthy, "and their wealth helps mark them as cosmopolitan."[36]

Seen in contrast to the splintering pitfalls I described above for Sydney, Dubai, and to a degree Singapore, such depictions not only may be misleading but also may miss much of what is actually the global "city-zenry" that populates our three metropolises. The idea of "cosmopolitanism" might have been high-jacked by the "new cosmopolitans" when, in fact, it is perhaps even more squarely the domain of lower-income diasporas that have historically (and quite literally) built global cities. One of the main observations from my many conversations is that although many, likely a majority, of my interlocutors would ascribe the term "global city" to the work of Saskia Sassen, few likely read the second half of her book—a marked advocacy for the conditions, rights, and changing socio-economics of the migrant classes servicing, cleaning, constructing, and driving the affluent top of the global city on a daily basis.

Speaking of Berlin, for instance, Wanda Vrasti and Smaran Dayal have out-lined the importance of thinking of cityzenship as derived from the urban dwell-er's engagement and presence (not birthright) with a place or political community (not just nation). As they note, this would in turn allow for better recognition of city-zens in their capacity to access and have a "rightful" (i.e., bearing rights and responsibilities) presence in the city's "urban commons"—the shared resources, places, and practices that make life as a community in a city possible.[37] Political and legal theorists, after all, have been arguing for some time that some degree of explicit "urban citizenship" can be the basis of a more explicitly cosmopolitan society against the inward drivers of nationalism and sovereign divisions.[38]

If still a little complex in academese and sociological-legal jargon, this notion has substantial importance for the discussion at hand. In numbers, a tangible fact is that about 58 percent of the 170 interviewees were not nationals of the UAE, Singapore, or Australia. Recent discussions in urban studies, unfortunately not so tightly connected with the global city debate, have tackled this very issue, arguing quite rightly that "urban" forms of citizenship need to be about expressing, rather than producing, difference.[39] In the wake of increasingly splintering cities, these authors are concerned with the fragmented and fragmenting political worlds in these cities—the splintering of not just infrastructures but also rights and duties.

Of course, the Emirate is perhaps the most startling of the cases here. Certainly, Dubai remains far from being a quintessentially totalitarian state; rather, the Emirate is progressively hybridized with a business and commercial sector that has allowed its staggering growth. In this scenario, the ruling family main-tains a relatively one-tiered authority structure by decree through the two-pronged *kafala* system. As Syed Ali has illustrated, this is effectively a joint ownership system that is common throughout the Gulf and based on necessary visa sponsorship requirements for residency that remain tied to one's employment status and are extremely limited in length and flexibility across all layers of the workforce.[40] Characteristically, the more skills the migrant has, the easier the access and regulations become, with the lower strata of the workforce in the construction, hospitality, and domestic support sectors suffering the harshest conditions and the most brutal consequences of a scheme that can, de facto, trap people in the Emirate or send them home with little justification—a situation that stirred much controversy after the publication of a 2008 Human Rights Watch (HRW) report denouncing these practices in Saudi Arabia.[41] Dubai and the UAE had been the target of HRW for several years, and the dark side of the *kafala* system in Dubai's global city growth was already popularized in 2006 with *Building Towers, Cheating Workers*. This seventy-one-page document reported the serious abuses of construction workers by UAE employers, including the several years of indebtedness to recruitment agencies for fees that resulted in the withholding of employees' passports, the hazardous living conditions, and the dangerous working conditions, with high rates of death and injury.[42] Yet low-wage workers are not the only ones in the tight grip of the central government. The Emirati law also impacts corporate ownership of Dubai-based companies, which are required to maintain a substantial national participation in order to be legally based in the city. This means that in order to be incorporated in Dubai under the Companies Law, the majority (i.e., at least 51 percent) of a company's share capital needs to be held by UAE nationals. In light of this restriction, however, the ruling family and the Dubaian government have once again demonstrated a particularly entrepreneurial (and markedly neoliberal) approach. One of the main benefits provided by the government to foreigners is the establishment of free economic zones that have relaxed the co-ownership scheme. Popular examples include the Jebel Ali Free Zone, the Dubai International Financial Centre (DIFC), and Dubai Media City, along with a variety of other specialized areas inaugurated by Sheikh Mohammed in the past decade. Key to this success has been the possibility of 100 percent foreign control of those companies. Although the zones have driven international business and commerce toward Dubai, the ruling family maintains a firm grip on their operations. For instance, the centerpiece of the DIFC is NASDAQ Dubai, which opened in September 2005 (shortly after the opening of the free zone itself) as Dubai International Financial Exchange (DIFX) with Sheikh Mohammed as president and one of the main promoters of the NASDAQ rebranding in November 2008. Renaming its financial core was not solely a public diplomacy operation but also a statement on the necessary hybridization of local traditional systems of the Gulf with the drivers of the global economy forging the international centrality of Dubai. Borse Dubai, the state-owned majority holder of the DIFX, promoted the rebranding as part of a share-swap deal with exchange giant NASDAQ to begin listing in Dubai and to push almost four thousand of the companies on its platform to consider secondary listings in the Emirate.[43]

Questions of rights, dynamics of governance, and challenges to the contemporary politics of cities go, inevitably, via the relationships between the governors and the governed in cities. Yet as cities change in interconnected ways and geopolitics shifts in both its center of gravity and focus of states, we are seeing the rise of forms of, and claims to, global urban governance that might inevitably bring about a confrontation between cities and states, rural and urban, haves and have-nots. Seeking to bring back more explicit legal and political theory thinking into urban studies and revive the political project of "urban governance" as a field of studies, this chapter highlights the experiments and tensions that relationships of citizenship bring about in cities and draws on current examples from the Global North and South to cast the challenge of "cityzenship" in contemporary affairs.

Certainly, the pull toward this type of political change and reform is far from being on the top of (if anywhere in) the policymaking agendas in Sydney, Dubai, and Singapore. All but a few conversations at the heart of this book, even when acknowledging the challenges of state rescaling as a key notion underpinning the global city, touched explicitly on these matters. Few highlighted whether current political institutions, processes and language are fit for a "world of cities," especially when considering this is a world where these cities are inevitably networked across boundaries and thus political spheres. This is even more concerning because, taking a broader view of not just these three places but their national and regional contexts such as Australia, the UAE and the Gulf, and Southeast and East Asia, we might be left to wonder whether this question cannot in fact be evaded. The early-2000s work of James Holston and Teresa Caldeira on Brazil, perhaps even more relevant today in the wake of populism, had already made a poignant case that it is in fact in cities that the clashes over entitlements and insurgent forms of citizenship are taking place.[44] In speaking of the dual city effects on labor markets in the early 1990s, Sassen noted that global cities may very much be ground zero for reform or collapse of our political system.[45] Yet, the issue of citizenship and its inherent challenges remain silent in the background when we speak of how we are, or should be, building global cities.

THE COMPARISONS

Wen Dao Shi: Singapore, 10:00 a.m.

"You certainly can't deny we are rising through the ranks," my colleague Siu Ji tells me while we are enjoying a meal at the hole-in-the-wall hawker stand called Wen Dao Shi (literally "found food to eat" in Cantonese). The restaurant, which has been selling dim sum "since 1985," is jam packed with locals of Chinese descent. This morning, we are busy debating rankings and the performance of Singapore. Finishing up our second serving of scallop *siew mai*, Siu Ji and I are too deep into an accelerated course on the meteoric rise of the Singaporean higher education institutions to notice the owner is cheekily bringing us a third serving without even asking. Appealing to my relative bias as an alumnus of sorts of the national university here, she is explaining to me why universities are key in the global city aspirations of Singapore. She is certainly not the only one trying to do that, as much of the country's policy shift has been aimed at creating a knowledge and arts city.[1] In this model, as the National Research Foundation puts it, universities are playing a key role in "winning the future."[2] Siu Ji has held senior governmental roles in the city-state and currently holds a similar positions across some of the island's major universities. She recounts how Singapore's university system has mirrored the rapid international success of the city-state. The island now houses a complex higher education system, including six autonomous universities that enjoy a degree of freedom from central government control. At the time of our *siew mai*–fueled conversation, the National University of Singapore (NUS) had risen to 25th (from 28th the year before) and the

Nanyang Technological University (NTU) to 47th (from 58th) in the latest *QS World University Rankings*. I point out that in the *Times Higher Education (THE)* ranking NUS is still in the 40th spot and NTU is 170th and ask why these numbers would matter anyway. Just a few years later, Siu Ji's confidence seems to have paid off: NUS and NTU are joint 11th (ahead of the likes of Princeton, Yale, and Columbia) in the *QS* and, respectively, 25th and 47th in the *THE*, still in rather illustrious company. Our Wen Dao Shi chat is a rather common and regularly repeated one for university administrators and leaders the world over. Yet her point is not one of rankings. The trick, she explains to me, is to think of one's growth as connected to others, and that's when rankings help "and not"— as she hints at the perverse effects of aspirations in interlinked city relations. Relationality is key in this story, and the history of Singapore's university sector is one of mergers and redesigns.

Early higher education and research institutions such as Raffles College and King Edward VII College were established before independence at the outset of the twentieth century. The University of Malaya's Singapore campus opened during the early post–World War II years and was renamed the University of Singapore in 1962. The 1960s also saw the development of a dedicated Chinese university—Nanyang University—founded to provide higher education to Singapore's growing Chinese community. This highlights not only an international "need" for the international basis the city-state was built on, but also some degree of comparative thinking. The University of Singapore and Nanyang University merged in 1980 in an attempt by the city-state to consolidate resources into a globally competitive English-language hub akin to those at the heart of the British or American systems, but also in comparison to the other East Asian gateway, Hong Kong, which had started reaping the benefits of its home institution (the University of Hong Kong, founded in 1911) and a growing higher education system with its own academy for the Chinese community (the Chinese University of Hong Kong, founded in 1963).[3] Hence, we see the birth of the now internationally recognizable NUS. At the same time, the independent Nanyang Technological Institute (NTI) was set up with the goal of training Singaporean engineers and seeking to match the engineering capacity fast expanding in China, Japan, and well rooted in the West. Comparison, and perhaps competition too, was built into the global city-state's DNA, Siu Ji explains to me. A decade later, in 1991, NTI was merged with the long-standing National Institute of Education to form the semiautonomous NTU, which still admitted students via a joint pathway with NUS, but quickly grew into the country's second-largest higher education institution (HEI).

Since the mid-1980s, Singapore's higher education sector has been reshaped by two central imperatives. The first, *massification*, was conceived of as a means to boost the quality of human resources following the 1985 recession.[4] The second, *internationalization*, took shape in 1998 around both the World Class University program, which sought to attract ten globally renowned HEIs to Singapore, and the concerted implementation of the Global Schoolhouse development policy, aimed at opening the territory to global education markets and transforming Singapore into "the Boston of the East."[5] At this point, Siu Ji carefully admits, Singapore had a built-in comparative "imagination" driving its global city goals. Yet it took until 2000, with the establishment of Singapore Management University (SMU), to see the realization of a third university in Singapore (discussed in government since 1996). SMU testifies to the growing embeddedness of Singapore in authoritative circuits of knowledge production, with the university being set up jointly with the University of Pennsylvania to more explicitly follow the American university system. But comparison, and the success in the rankings, is partly misleading here, carries on Siu Ji. You simply cannot see "all the myriad" of "relations" that make the rise of Singapore (and its universities) a "story made of global networks." The link with other universities in the league table is evident and continues to this day, "and yet people forget that," she says to me, because we think of them as distinct entities. The international partnership model has also been repeated in the establishment of Singapore's fourth and fifth autonomous bodies: first, in 2005 with UniSIM as a partnership of Singapore Institute of Management and the Open University; second, in 2009 with MIT playing a key role in the creation of a fifth science-focused institution: Singapore University of Technology and Design (SUTD). The early 2000s also saw the emergence of other international partnerships that set up autonomous institutes centered on NUS, including Duke-NUS Medical School (2005) and Yale-NUS College (2011). During this period, NTU achieved full independent status from NUS (2006), and the Singapore Institute of Technology (SIT) was announced as a university "of applied learning." More recently, UniSIM was redesigned in 2017 as Singapore University of Social Sciences (SUSS) as part of the government's plan to increase the number of publicly funded universities. Finally, and emblematic of the nation's import partnership model and internationalization agenda, the Campus for Research Excellence and Technological Enterprise (CREATE) was approved by the Research, Innovation and Enterprise Council in 2006. It was thought of as an "international collaboratory" (*sic*) for global university research centers working on human, energy, environmental, and urban systems. The first CREATE resident—the Singapore-MIT Alliance for Research and Technology (SMART)—formed in July 2007, and ten years later the campus housed collaborations with ETH Zürich, Technical University of Munich, Hebrew University of Jerusalem, University of California-Berkeley, Shanghai Jiao Tong University, and Cambridge University.

Possibly due to the twin imagination-aspiration of Singapore rising through the "ranks," by all means a common reference point with senior government and business figures well beyond Siu Ji, the city's developmental elites have been increasingly putting an emphasis on linking the city's future to an explicitly internationalist ethos. It has to be, as Prime Minister Lee Hsien Loong put it in CREATE's maiden speech in November 2012, an essentially "international endeavor" that is rooted "in place." This was and is seen as yet another version of the necessary cosmopolitan mix of the city. As the prime minister noted then, "There is no place which is in the first rank and which has scientists all from one city or one country," and a real mix of expertise is needed "to make Singapore the 'Most Liveable City in Asia.'"[6] It would be easy to shrug off these statements, as many do when seeing media reporting on grants. Yet as Siu Ji had told me kindly while settling our dumpling lunch bill (with a quick whip of Cantonese I am nowhere close to grasping), perhaps we often forget that we cannot simply "do away with this comparative imagination." This is a little bit like the tale of *siu mai* (which we totaled at four servings) and their popularity of "yum cha" lunches with Westerners: they only make sense in the eyes of the wider public because they are "a bit of dumpling" but also a "bit different," and that is how you are able to tell what they represent but also appreciate their specific quality. In the comparison (of dumplings, universities, or cities) we construct a global language and a global quality as much as a specialized local flavor. Certainly, this seems to be Siu Ji's reading of why the classic open-top meat-filled *siu mai* is perhaps the most popular, but when gorging on the scallop-filled one we can still tell it is a *siu mai*. She suggests, in an accidental global city-speak reference, that perhaps we may even discover a new culinary place "on the map," as she continues her culinary critique monologue. It is like the well-known variety in the West, which is from the southern provinces of Guangdong and Guangxi, but almost forces us to ask, "Where is this from?" Perhaps there is nothing really wrong with the global element of this language per se. There may in fact be some positive cosmopolitan nature—in its true sense described in the previous chapter, not the media semantics—to these comparative gestures. It is the competitive tenor of the ranked comparison, of "best" and "worst" performers, that the cosmopolitanism and its shared relationality are lost. There, elements of the comparison are pitted against each other for "success," and commonality is abandoned for competition. So, it is in between dumplings, university rankings, and relational thinking that I realize there is some degree of built-in comparative, and thus relational, thinking in the "global" of the "global city." Yet when making these comparisons, we need to be wary of the seduction of choosing which city, or gluttonous scallop morsel, is "best."

The Seduction of Rankings

We would be hard-pressed to argue that rankings are not a thing in today's global media. People are easily seduced by a bit of "sane competition." Benchmarking embodies the growing demand in global cities for urban metrics and internationally oriented comparisons but also city performance measurement. While often making newspaper headlines, benchmarks also inform and influence the practice of everyday city management and drive it toward international thinking. As several colleagues and I argued in recent reviews of this burgeoning "industry" of benchmarking, rankings are not an occasional matter.[7] For instance, in recent analysis by the Business of Cities suggests that over five hundred urban benchmarks have been published worldwide since 2007.[8] The world of comparative city measurement is very diverse and in a period of rapid expansion in terms of both the number of indexes and the breadth of themes they cover. As we noted in our study, almost a quarter of all rankings are now produced by professional services firms like PricewaterhouseCoopers (PwC) and KPMG. The media, so often prone to capturing "winners and losers" stories, also produce benchmarks for their audiences. If the *Economist* is perhaps one of the most well-known rankings producers globally, thanks to its annual livable cities index, today around 15 percent of all rankings are authored by global media and travel groups, with others like *Monocle* magazine or *Foreign Policy* producing their own versions of global city rankings. A smaller but significant number of benchmarks are also developed by real estate and advisory firms (e.g., Jones Lang LaSalle, Savills), financial institutions (e.g., UBS, Mastercard, Deutsche Bank), and industry bodies and IT/telecom companies (e.g., Huawei or Ericsson). Multilateral organizations like the European Union are at it too. The United Nations' own urban agency, UN-Habitat, has been active on this front by promoting the uptake of its City Prosperity Index since 2012.

Planning global cities, then, becomes as much a matter of technical skills as a practice of international comparison. A strong line of continuity between my encounters in Sydney, Singapore, and Dubai has been that of comparing one's own city with those perceived to be in direct competition on an international scale. Local authorities and regional governments often implicitly stress the need to maintain an edge on potential global city rivals by pointing at the vast variety of studies now available on the subject. All sorts of local authority departments, but also major business, in the Emirates, Australia, and Singapore have today a good grasp of the multifaceted offer of lists of "key cities" and "winners" or "losers" at different measurements. Certainly, the authority and global recognition of these charts vary substantially. One could go from the intricate measurement practices of the *Economist* Intelligence Unit (EIU), perhaps the most widely recognized producer of benchmarked comparisons, to occasional efforts that make for a good story in magazines and trivial lists that make an ad hoc appearance as the result of a few hours of googling some basic statistics. Yet academics and researchers should not speak of this world of benchmarking as something "out there." Around 20 percent of benchmarks are produced by research, think tank, and academic organizations. This once again points at the accomplice role that scholars play in shaping the way we think about global cities in practice.

One of the most well-known studies by urban practitioners is the "world according to GaWC" mapping produced by the Globalization and World Cities network since 1998. This study is based on a three-tier network analysis that, departing from traditional approaches focusing on nodes and their interrelations as a net, seeks to diversify the influence of nodes in interconnected systems (like those of financing) by identifying primary nodes and subnodes. Thus, GaWC began ranking the "network connectivity" of cities as they were embedded in a "world city network" of services and firms.[9] Developing this initial approach, researchers at (and associated with) GaWC carried out a series of data collection exercises in 2000, 2004, and 2008 and recently updated their results by looking at the post-financial-crisis scenario in 2010. GaWC follows this approach by scrutinizing the centrality of cities on the basis of concentrations of advanced producer services such as accountancy, advertising, finance, or law, which are then aggregated through a service values matrix to investigate different network connectivity. This is done not solely to evaluate the networked integration and central positioning of particular cities (London originally and then a progressively large pool of cases) but also to measure their particular orientation in a complex world of flows.[10] Originally a by-product of this analysis, GaWC's ranking of global cities into three major categories based on their economic interconnectedness has time and again been referred to in major strategic plans, visions, and documentation produced by local governments (but also multilateral agencies and the private sector) and stands as a testament to the capacity of scholarly analysis to inform global city practice. The original methodology,[11] eventually updated to the more sophisticated "interlocking network model,"[12] continues to be updated biennially by the group and shapes the global imaginary. Yet GaWC also reminds us of the need for caution and for proactive engagement: the ranking of alpha, beta, and gamma has historically been only a small part of what the model does, and yet, owing to the appeal of "best" and "worst" lists to both policy and media, it has often been represented as *the* output of GaWC, requiring considerable explaining and advocating to go beyond the headlines to understand its valuable empirical complexity.

The growing impact of GaWC's work in Sydney's strategic planning, if relatively marginal in its first version, might now be seen by many, along with the

EIU, as an "official atlas of global cities."[13] This is evidenced by the pervasive-ness of GaWC's map in successive versions of the 2036 plan process. The rank-ing was used in the final December 2005 *City of Cities* strategy to justify Sydney as "a key player in global supply chains and major hub in the Asia-Pacific re-gion" and occupied much of the background information throughout NSW Planning's drafting process.[14] In the successive edition of the strategic plan elab-orated by the state government, the 2036 strategy, GaWC's revised study still appeared prominently but alongside seven other charts such as the Mori Foun-dation Global Power City index and the Anholt City Branding Index. In this con-text, rankings were again used to illustrate Sydney's central positioning among the most important global cities, to note what had changed since the 2005 strat-egy, and to highlight the main challenges faced by the Harbor City when con-sidered "from above" in international city comparisons. In this sense, city rankings such as those of GaWC have been mobilized to sanction the centrality and complexity of Sydney's geographical positioning through the authoritative "array of sophisticated indicators" supporting these studies. NSW planners, of course, took the lists with a grain of salt but still provide conscious evidence of their growing importance: "Whilst these rankings cannot provide a complete understanding of the relative importance of cities, they are increasingly influ-ential as the competition between cities increases and governments, corpora-tions and citizens seek to work together to gain advantages for their city."[15]

This emphasis has once again appeared on the pages of global city strategizing in the latest effort by New South Wales toward a review of *Metropolitan Strategy 2036*: as the *Sydney over the Next 20 Years* discussion paper issued by NSW once again stresses, much of the success is well demonstrated by its "alpha+" position-ing just below New York and London and right next to cities like Singapore and Paris.[16] What the document once again points out is that a key factor in maintain-ing Sydney as a global city is the successful development of an advanced con-sumer service industry that is competitive in the global marketplace.

Benchmarking has become more and more of a business, and in doing so, it has shaped the language of the global city. First and foremost, it is a common reference point in global city-speak. Fifty-nine interviewees mentioned rank-ings (forty-nine times) or indexes (ten times) in their reflections on Singapore, Sydney, and Dubai. The Emirate takes the lion's share of these mentions, twenty-five in total (nearly one in two interviewees), with Singapore (nineteen) and Sydney (fifteen) following behind. This immediately tells us that rankings and indexes are entrenched in much of the discourse about the global city. But how does bringing questions of rankings into the discussion change the way we speak of global cities? If we compare the overall language of the 170 interviews at the base of this study against that of those who have mentioned indexes and

TABLE 2 The incidence (increased salience scores) of rankings on global city-speak

Full dataset	0.159	0.168	0.250	0.103	0.176	0.171	0.088
Rankings	0.194	0.235	0.337	0.112	0.327	0.153	0.143
Concept	History	Entrepreneurship	Gateway	Control	Leaders	In place	Metrocentric
Full dataset	0.141	0.138	0.250	0.147	0.088	0.147	0.138
Rankings	0.265	0.092	0.265	0.184	0.153	0.173	0.245
Concept	Hierarchy	Worlding	Premium	Material	Rescaling	Cosmopolitan	Off the map
Full dataset	0.180	0.100	0.126	0.265	0.118	0.162	0.156
Rankings	0.173	0.133	0.163	0.347	0.092	0.184	0.198
Concept	Dual city	Relational	Opportunity	Elite	Splintering	Innovation	Overall

Left diagram:

Singapore

Sydney

Beijing (1)
Bilbao (1)
Bogota (1)
Buenos Aires (1)
Jakarta (1)
Milan (1)
San Francisco (1)
Venice (1)

Brisbane (3)
Los Angeles (2)
Shanghai (2)
Tokyo (2)
Vancouver (2)
San Francisco (5)

Barcelona (1)
Boston (1)
Dubai (1)
Ho Chi Minh (1)
Toronto (1)

London (14)
Sydney (3)
Doha (2)

Singapore (12)
Melbourne (2)

Abu Dhabi (5)
Bangkok (1)
Cairo (1)
Copenhagen (1)
Glasgow (1)
Hong Kong (1)
Kuala Lumpur (1)

Kuwait City (1)
Mumbai (1)
New York (1)
Sharjah (1)
Teheran (1)
Tel Aviv (1)

Dubai

Right diagram:

Singapore

Dubai (8)
Tokyo (7)
Brisbane (5)
San Francisco (5)

Sydney

Bilbao (1)
Buenos Aires (1)
Hanoi (1)
Milan (1)
Rio de Janeiro (1)
Santiago (1)
Venice (1)

Paris (4) Vancouver (3)
Beijing (3)   Beirut (2)
Jakarta (3) Berlin (2)
Toronto (3) Boston (2)

Adelaide (1)
Cape Town (1)
Ho Chi Minh (1)
Perth (1)

London (42)
Melbourne (13)
Los Angeles (11)
Shanghai (11)

Sydney (10)   Chicago (6)
Doha (7)   New York (5) Singapore (26)
Auckland (4)   Barcelona (4) Hong Kong (4)
Kuala Lumpur (4)   Bogota (3)   Bangkok (2)
Mumbai (3)

Abu Dhabi (9)
Cairo (3)
Sharjah (2)
Bristol (1)
Copenhagen (1)
Glasgow (1)
Istanbul (1)

Kuwait City (1)
Medellin (1)
Riyadh (1)
Rome (1)
Stockholm (1)
Teheran (1)
Tel Aviv (1)

Dubai

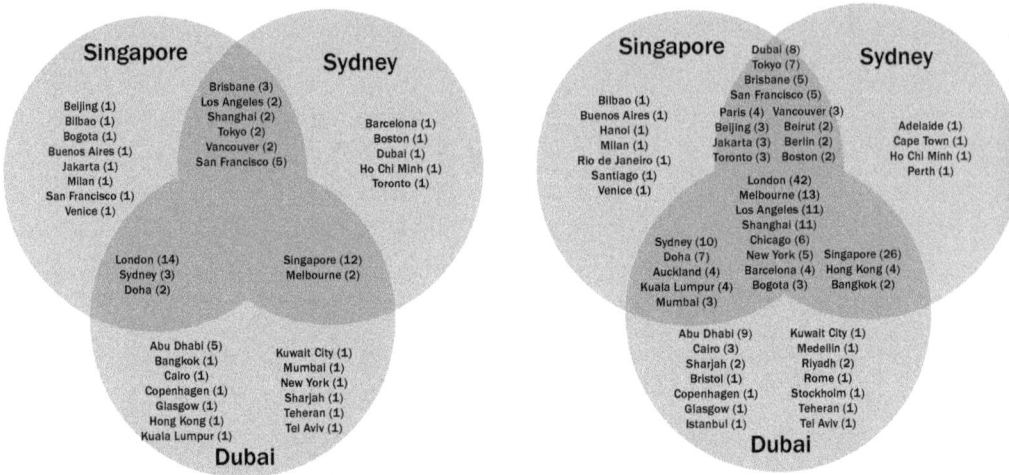

FIGURE 17. Comparing comparative gestures in each city: all interviews (*right*) and when mentioning rankings (*left*).

rankings specifically, some interesting facts emerge. To begin with, there seems to be a relatively positive correlation between mentioning rankings and acknowledging more explicitly the ideas underpinning global city-speak. Twelve of our twenty terms have much greater salience (i.e., they are mentioned more explicitly) in the interviews that mention rankings than in the overall data set, with an additional three terms also scoring marginally higher. Overall, the global city discourse scores an average salience of 0.198 mentioning rankings versus 0.156 more generally. Ideas of entrepreneurship, premium connections, gateway functions, and elites all show as more prominent when rankings emerge in the conversation. Even more significantly, leadership (0.327 vs. 0.176), and interestingly both rescaling (0.153 vs. 0.088) and metrocentricity (0.143 vs. 0.088), nearly doubles its relevance in interviews mentioning rankings. Although we cannot really say which way the casual relationship goes (if in any direction)—that is, if mentioning rankings heightens global city-speak or vice versa—it remains important to highlight this mutual occurrence. It is also relevant to underline that, when rankings are mentioned, ideas like worlding and of the "splintering" nature of the global city see a significant drop in mentions (down to 0.092 from 0.138 and 0.118, respectively), with concepts of putting globalization "in place" and the "dual" polarization of the city witnessing some decline. Data aside, what this observation tells us is that ranking (and some competitive index-oriented thinking) relates to an even stronger global city-speak.[17] Who controls and shapes this emphasis, then, becomes of even greater concern for our story. Symbolic power is often an apt form of influence for the entrepreneur because, as Bourdieu and others put it, it takes the shape of a "gentle" form of power as a process of describing reality and persuading others to act on it—which is different from overt oppression and coercion. Misused, it becomes a "gentle" where not "invisible" or "disguised form of domination" no less violent at times than coercion itself.[18]

Not surprisingly, the private sector has since the early 2000s produced a growing quantity of reports that analyze alternative global city hierarchies and specific global metropolitan features. Seeking to capture the growing importance of cities in the global marketplace and in the location of multinational service providers, a plethora of private consultancies and leading sectoral firms have developed their own rankings and charts. In Sydney, PwC, the largest professional services firm in the world, has long held a particular position in consulting on this matter to both the government and business sectors. Numerous key New South Wales and City of Sydney documents cited in the chapters thus far have had substantial PwC input, if not direction. In a perhaps more subtle fashion, or according to many in a far less transparent manner, key consultancies have also had substantial stakes in Dubai's and Singapore's strategic planning—although in most cases this has had a more direct inference on specific developments like Dubai Marina or Emirates Hills, and a less direct one on the city's overall master plans. Central to this problem is the progressive embedding of competitive thinking, linking a city's fortunes not just to global markets but also to a rank within this, thus skewing perhaps more subtle comparative views of a city's place within the global map. This has heightened the emphasis on the hierarchical element of global city thinking: as I noted above, if this is an important but not dominant element of the global city "genre" (falling among the low tiers of salience in my interviews), it is also heavily heightened by appearing in conversations about rankings and indexes (going from a salience of 0.141 to a rather high 0.265). The challenge, then, is one of competitive relational thinking, not just of benchmarking per se. By some account, over 85 percent of all international benchmarking exercises involve an explicit attempt to rank cities in the traditional sense of the word. This produces hierarchically organized lists of "best" to "worst," which are prone to more news coverage, making for an easy sports-related headline ("Singapore beats London at greenest city in the world") that in turn fuels the global demand for more rankings. Therein lies much of the problem with city rankings in perpetuating uneven geographies and power imbalances. It further pits cities against each other, while, as Siu Ji's story of the rise of Singapore's universities (or of *siew mai*) tells us, much of the construction of the "global" and even of the inherent success of a "globalizing" place like Singapore is about a continuous interconnection between places that are accomplices in each other's success. This emphasis on hierarchy and competition, in turn, might therefore be a driver of losing a series of other key terms: not only the cosmopolitan relationship between diverse global cities but also the necessity of specialization (the search for "difference" in chapter 4) where in fact the best "game" in the race for success might be playing a different and novel one rather than being "better" or "best" at the same—something few, if any, rankings could easily capture. What is fundamentally lost here, then, is perhaps the necessary relations that connected cities and that we might often underplay or miss altogether.

Relationality Lost

Certainly, the business of city ranking has moved from a perhaps crude view of competition embedded in the early 1990s and 2000s rankings to a more complex way to index cities. From this point of view, many rankings are to some degree becoming subtler. If simplistic lists like those accounting for the number of Starbucks in a city are still common, rankings by major consultancy players like PwC have evolved in relatively more refined analyses of the multiplicity of factors that drive business to specific centers. While some like the Global Financial Centers index have emphasized particular features and dug deeper into financial, commerce, or trade indicators, others like PwC *Cities of Opportunity* or Knight Frank's *World City Survey* (part of this property consultancy giant's annual Wealth Report) have cut across a varied set of issues such as politics, institutional support, or sustainability. This, however, seems to have led to a series of dangerous abstractions. On the one hand, since the cities listed on these charts tend to remain fairly constant, there tends to be an unproblematic acceptance, and subsequent widespread replication, of the top echelons of this world urban hierarchy. To identify potential competitors, city planners generally rely on readily available global surveys rather than carrying out open-ended analyses themselves. This is of course a reflection of the relatively limited resources and critical scrutiny that characterize strategic urban plans. Likewise, there is still very little consideration of the inherent relationality of some of the more academic rankings in question. Projects like that of GaWC were in fact born out of human and political geography scholarship deeply wary of interconnectedness among cities. Mapping and (eventually) ranking global city connections, in this view, allowed for a step beyond the dialectic of structure and agency that has long dominated much of the social sciences: city-network was intended as a reciprocal relation, where the two are not separated elements of the global scenario but mutually constitutive facets in the worldwide processes of globalization. In such a networked geography, cities were seen as inherently related to each other, and the main task of the mapping effort was geared toward understanding the variations and hierarchizations of such relationality. Metrics for the evaluation of a city's networked performance, in GaWC's view, were not factors of success and globalization shopping lists, but a response to a perceived need to redress a bias in the global city literature, which was character- ized by "theoretical sophistication and empirical poverty."[19] Finally, the popularity of rankings has had the indirect effect of shifting the discourse on global cities to a higher ground than the mundane materiality of planning and urban public policy. By abstracting the urban determinants of globalization and livability to represen- tative metrics and comparable features, such as the number of corporate head- quarters or the air pollution levels, the readers' attention is abstracted to an international dimension of city-to-city competition where urban redevelopments and local government initiatives become elements of scorecards, and where cities confront each other on planetary hierarchies across recurring global city determi- nants. While not negative per se, the influence of this abstraction on planners is that of an even greater emphasis on the competitive dimension of entrepreneurial- ism and on flagship projects and citywide initiatives, often at the expense of less glamorous and yet fundamental services such as waste management.

Here, however, the rankings rationale embedded in many urban aspirations might show some crucial limitations. The story of Singapore's universities re- counted by my friend Siu Ji teaches us the importance of thinking of one's posi- tion as a factor not just of one's own value but of one's relationship with others. Simply put, whether we subscribe to the hierarchical thinking about rankings or not, a global city's fortunes depend as much on that city as they do on the others it is networked with. Growth and development come as a function of how globalized cities engage with each other, but to some degree they are also affected by how other cities relate even independently from the place we are looking at. This is not complex academic thought: anyone who follows competitive sports— say, football—understands that a team's standing in a given season is as much the outcome of that team's direct encounters with other teams as the result of other teams encountering each other independently of our favorite squad. Yet equally this does not have to be competitive thinking—as it perhaps has been the case with Singaporean universities as well as our three global cities.

However, this relational thinking remains relatively sparse in global city- speak and the urban aspirations of many of the developmental elites shaping emerging centers like Singapore, Sydney, and Dubai. Similar to state rescaling or metrocentricity, the idea that cities are relational in networks shows very limited currency in the expert conversations at the base of this study. This, for an aca- demic, is perhaps even more surprising because relationality has been very much embedded in the study of global and world cities throughout the 1990s and 2000s. If it seems obvious to most global city scholars that a city's globalization happens necessarily in relation to other cities—something best depicted by the "world city network" mapping generated by the GaWC program—practitioners and even many scholars still seem to disregard this dimension of the global city. With one of the lowest degrees of salience across all terms investigated in this study, the networked relationality of cities shows surprisingly little currency among those with a business and economics background, but also among experts working in civil society. This is perhaps even more startling because of the widespread understanding of the idea that global cities are centered on gateway functions like global logistics, people mobility and tourism, or corporate headquarter locations. Business and economics backgrounds, for instance, are some of the best-versed ones in the idea of "gateway cities," and yet struggle to understand that this comes with reciprocal relationships between cities where their aspirations and imaginations are unequivocally subject to reciprocal influences.

This lack of appreciation of the intertwined relation between cities is also central to unveil the limited explicit understanding of how symbolic power operates in determining the fortunes of global cities. This is a common limit of the practitioner engagement with the vast scholarship on global urban systems and the networked dimension of the global city. For example, the complexity of the methodological bases of study, such as GaWC's world city network, and even more importantly its analytical premises, is often overlooked. The basic argument sustaining the analyses provided by GaWC has been heavily influenced by Taylor's geographical approach and his reading of Jane Jacobs's understanding of cities as interactive contexts: cities are understood in an inherently relational sense as they "need each other, come in groups and relate as networks."[20] The evidence illustrated in this book points at a simplification of this approach. The practice represented in the metropolitan strategies of Dubai, Singapore, and Sydney has maintained a relatively superficial comprehension of this complex idea. Documents like the *City of Cities* plan as well as complex rankings by firms like PwC have focused on the hierarchical nature of these networks and on the classification of network hubs and have sidelined that the intrinsic property of the system of flows that world cities are embedded in is that of mutuality and crosscutting connectivity. Global cities are often represented inside out as absolutely separate entities offering diverse mixes and quantities of globalizing "ingredients" like financial hubs, institutional structures, or livable suburbs in a global market where they compete for primacy. While not wrong per se, this view overlooks the mutuality of cities in this economic geography and, conversely, the influence of the global market itself as a force shaping these metropolises. Moreover, the (limited) appreciation of this interconnectedness is at times skewed toward the material and the financial. Representing core mobility hubs for goods, tourists, or capital, the "immaterial" connectivity between cities such as Dubai and Sydney and the rest of the world remains vastly overlooked. However, there is much more that travels to, through, and from these metropolises.

When it is recognized, however, the idea of relationality shows important correlations with other key elements of global city thinking. Importantly, across all interviews, relationality displays some connection with both the centrality of elites in global city making and the cosmopolitan character of these cities—confirming these two features of the global city are inherently international in their nature. Perhaps even more interesting is that there is also some very thin but perhaps telling correlation between those few acknowledgments of relationality and their discussion of the material or gateway dimensions of the global city. Unsurprisingly these latter are key ways in which cities are built (logistically as much as physically) in relation with each other. So, if perhaps still not well understood, we could argue that those who grasp the connectivity of the global city do so in complex ways, and perhaps academia should do more to encourage this complex view of how cities network. From this viewpoint, perhaps the strongest correlation with relationality is, encouragingly, with the idea of what is left "off the map" by global city-speak. In Singapore in particular this connection is blatant: perhaps because of the inherent "Singapore story" that sets the rise of the city-state in relatively explicit connection with other global cities, this correlation is deeply entrenched in the Southeast Asian metropolis, along with (at an equally strong correlation) the link between relationality and leadership. Many Singaporean leaders, perhaps somewhat different from Sydney's leaders (aside from Mayor Clover Moore), have generally focused on their local context rather than global discussions and have spoken of their place in dialogue, engagement, and often competition with other places. Yet while recognizing this factor, we also have to be cognizant of the reality that the global city "atlas" might also be changing owing to new comparative gestures and new cities having moved "on the map." This point might hold much promise in pushing toward a more cosmopolitan global city thinking than many rankings give away. Yet, one more fundamental factor highlighted in the rankings of the current global city genre needs to be unpacked here—numbers matter fundamentally.

In Numbers We Trust (and Compete)

The twin growth of comparative referencing and entrepreneurialism has, as I have highlighted thus far, meant an increasingly central focus on competitiveness. Since the 1990s, the governance process underpinning Sydney politics has been inspired by a "global imperative of looking, acting and being governed as a competitive city."[21] The growing salience of global networks, the increasing importance of the advanced producer services industry, and the key role of business elites in shaping the form and orientation of the city have all been essential factors in pushing toward the antagonistic element of entrepreneurialism, thus subjugating its other features (such as innovation and connection with other cities) to competitiveness. This shift has been fed by the heightened interest in city rankings—with a sprawl in urban measurements and up-to-date monitoring of urban performances that have provided even more justification for an emphasis on intercity rivalry.[22] Yet they also underscore a bigger trend in global city thinking: "If you can't measure it you can't manage it."[23] Whether it was in his role as mayor of New York, chair of the C40 Climate Leadership Group, or UN special envoy on cities and climate change, Michael Bloomberg has long reiterated his support for data-driven urban policy, and in this he is not alone. Calls for the use of urban data in policymaking, but also more broadly evidence-driven strategies and knowledge exchange in and between cities, have echoed loudly and repeatedly in many contexts over the past few years.[24] If we have entered into a "data revolution," twenty-first-century cities are at the very heart of it and are often portrayed as central engines of data production and use in ongoing "smart cities" discourses.[25]

To be clear, this is not simply a fad. The size of this challenge is no small matter. Every day we create 2.5 quintillion bytes of data, and every minute 100,000 tweets are sent globally. Cities are embedded in this data-intensive world like never before. And the cities themselves are also speaking: in Norway, more than forty thousand bus stops are tweeting, allowing passengers to share their experiences. As of 2020, a quarter of a billion vehicles are connected to the internet, creating unthinkable options for in-vehicle services and automated driving. The scale of information sharing and knowledge production within cities is enormous. Data exchanges in and for cities will continue to grow and become even more vast in the future. What this entails can already be observed by looking at how cities are currently managing data and information: cities such as London, Chicago, and Seoul have made thousands of discrete data sets available for anyone's benefit. Cities are also increasing the number of reports with information about their current state and future aspirations. The city of Melbourne made five such reports available online in 2010, with a quintupled increase within just five years. Importantly, cities recognize that information is not just about digital data on an online server but also about knowledge dissemination between people. The significance of "informed cities" thinking on urban governance can be seen clearly today with mayors ensuring their already packed agendas allow time to participate in knowledge-sharing events both locally and globally—for example, the mayor of Johannesburg delivered more than twenty speeches at various conferences and summits throughout 2015.

Our case studies are not immune from this data-driven shift in city leadership. Symptomatically, for instance, the *City of Cities* strategy makes direct reference to the idea of a "global Sydney maintaining a competitive edge," even reporting GaWC's 2004 urban ranking and signaling ways to improve the Harbor City's positioning.[26] This has reflected on Sydney's planning rather substantially, resulting in what Penelope Dean has aptly termed "deadline urbanism," which is demand driven, surgical, and oriented toward remedial solutions to adapt existing spaces to changing markets, rather than planning for the long term.[27] For much of the local (social scientific) academic community, Sydney has become "the accidental city" where liberalization, laissez-faire policies, and global economic aspirations have driven the design and configuration of the city.[28] Many have argued that even the greening of the conurbation has increasingly become a matter of market competition: the *Sydney 2030* strategy, for example, is a foremost attempt to, in the words of Lord Mayor Clover Moore, "position Sydney as one of the leading green cities in the race to address global warming and to become a city with strong green credentials to attract future business and investment."[29]

In this organization, the plan remained complacent about the underlying global city consensus that prompted it in the first place. However, the overall planning direction was not coupled with more targeted master planning, thus providing a general vision but lacking specific indications on the implementation, relegated to "sub-regional" plans. This had been encouraged in several cases by the corporate sector, which had been pushing for a laissez-faire approach since the early days of the strategy's drafting. For instance, the Property Council of Australia, an advocacy and public relations provider for more than 2,200 companies, has lobbied against detailed large-scale blue-printing, calling for a more flexible and demand-oriented planning approach conscious of the dynamic uncertainty of a global city.[30] To this extent, New South Wales has arguably played the part of the key mediator in developing a network pinpointed on managing the globalization of Sydney and capable of locking allies into place on the obligatory passage point of the Harbor City strategy. However, this mediation role needs to be conceived as intertwined with the participation of two types of key intermediaries, LGAs and private actors, which have played increasingly central roles in the formulation of strategic plans as well as of complementary planning instruments, therefore progressively becoming an integral part of this structure. Increasingly essential in all of these discourses has been the relative political consensus, whether between left-leaning, centrist, or right-wing politicians (and governmental executives), on the importance of indexes, rankings, and benchmarks in general to governing Australia's cities.

This belief in competitive metrics has also been underscored in recent years by the federal government in one of perhaps a handful of its more explicit efforts to engage cities programmatically. In December 2017, after several months of testing but also engagement with key consultants from the United Kingdom, the Australian government launched the first National Cities Performance Framework. The framework was designed by the Turnbull government to provide a "snapshot of the productivity and progress" of Australia's twenty-one largest cities (Sydney included) and produced as a website to offer an easily accessible resource where people "can track the performance of cities." The framework indexes, and compares, Sydney and other Australian capitals across a number of measures such as infrastructure and investment, livability, innovation, governance and planning, and housing. This type of index is not unique to Sydney or Australia. Perhaps even more explicitly, Singapore has regularly emphasized measurement of its performance and trajectory, even projecting into the future. Dubai has also expended considerable effort to put data at the heart of much of its work. This has revolved around the Smart Dubai Office, launched in the early 2010s, and more specifically its Dubai Data Establishment. In the "race for excellence," to borrow Sheik Mohammed's tagline, rankings matter as a measure of progress and benchmarking against, or at the very least in relation to, other global city competitors. The number-based hierarchical tendency embedded in thinking about ranking global cities, then, has compounded the competitive basis that afflicts much of the contemporary discourse. It has fueled a growing demand for comparability (benchmarking) from both local governments and other pivotal international urban stakeholders in the private and multilateral sectors, including the OECD, major businesses like JP Morgan and Knight Frank, and academia and UN agencies. In sum, then, what seems lost in this data-based ranking-fueled shift to a more explicitly competitive entrepreneurial global city thinking is the inherent relationality that cities are embedded in. Hierarchically ordered lists of global cities, when lacking in nuance and especially when simply translated via news reports, continue to promote a zero-sum view of the map of global cities where one's gain is someone else's loss, just like in sports. Yet, this might paradoxically be a unique entry point for those global city scholars who have seen their academic efforts perverted into a dangerous trope of "global" cities and lost the substance of over one hundred years of scholarship. To engage meaningfully in this sphere of powerful global city imagination and aspirations, however, we need to recognize one last piece of the puzzle that emerges from my inquiries in Dubai, Sydney, and Singapore: the role of what we might call "symbolic entrepreneurs."

SYMBOLIC ENTREPRENEURS

Sin Hoe Huat Café: Singapore, 8:30 a.m.

"There is something in the way Singapore *feels* that is 'global,' right? An entrepreneurial spirit maybe." I am out to chat about this spirit with my former colleague Kiara, who is Indian born and a longtime senior urbanist figure in a major multilateral agency. We are in a *kopitiam* (loosely translated for Westerners as "coffee shop") just north of Little India and off Farrar Park MRT station. Kiara promised me that the kopitiam is really where Singapore's "cosmopolitan" and "entrepreneurial" spirit "is brewed." I have had my fair share of traditional coffees and *kaya* (coconut jam) toast in my doctoral student days visiting NUS, but I go along with the experience as she has proved time and again a source of insight into the global urbanist circuit and a regular promoter of the global city idea. Our chat echoes a bit that of two political philosophers, Canadian Daniel A. Bell and Israeli Avner de-Shalit, who wrote in a 2012 study titled *The Spirit of Cities* that we need to revive the classical idea that a city expresses its own distinctive ethos or values.[1] They wrote of the nation-building spirit embedded in Singapore, the ambition that characterizes New Yorkers, and the materialism of the Cantonese in Hong Kong. Perhaps as a common thread throughout our cases, the spirit of the global city seems to be a very much entrepreneurial one, whether we speak of elites molding the cities as global hubs or everyday urban dwellers devising strategies to open up the opportunities the metropolis holds in its world city nature. Yet bottom up contestations to the seemingly incessant advance of neoliberal globalization in my case study of cities seem to contrast that and refute that there is

FIGURE 18. The Singaporean hawker center.

"a" spirit in "the" city but rather, as splintering urbanism teaches us, many cities folded in one at the same time, and many social justice problems embedded in that ethos. We do not start our chat from urban development, global connections, or elite conferences where we often meet. This time, it is about understanding the global city in a coffee cup.

Like the famous "hawker centers" (food courts), the kopitiam in Singapore embodies some of the spirit of this global city as much as its splintering contradictions. It is, as NUS scholar Lai Ah Eng notes, a "miniature society and metaphor for Singapore."[2] The name itself hints at the junction point nature of Singapore: *kopi* is the Malay word for "coffee," and *tiam* is the Hokkien (or, more precisely, Fujianese) word for "shop." The kopitiam emerged in the preindependence years as an early sign of Singapore's entrepreneurial nature, but also of its place as a nexus of international flows of goods and habits. It saw its heyday when Chinese migrants (mostly men) hired by colonial settlers to cook in their households began leaving these jobs to open their own food stalls and coffee shops, targeting the growing working class on the island with the offer of cheap meals and accessible eateries. The kopitiam, just like the hawker center stall, has to be inherently entrepreneurial in a changing "reference system" that is at the same time fast evolving locally and internationally, begging for novelty and upgrade, while being continually referential to places other than Singapore and times other than the present, suggests Kiara. The practices of global urbanism are here steeped in a symbolic system of meanings (or "forms" as I described them earlier) forged at the intersection of multiple cultures. The language of global city making, beyond static ideas and circulating global forms, is very much a language of the "frontier", Kiara reminds me. Things are afoot and changing and bumping against each other, often uncomfortably, but also highlighting the power of possibility in these turnstiles of globalization that both rich elites and low-wage migrants recognize when getting on a plane to seek their fortunes in these urban centers.

A relatively common preindependence entity, the kopitiam began evolving in its current direction in the 1970s and 1980s, as Singapore pushed into the island's "heartlands" with new housing developments. Kopitiams began to appear as commonplace features of Housing Development Board (HDB) estates alongside rows of essential shops and more and more common hawker centers. In this context, as Singaporean researchers have noted, this type of coffee shop became an important node of multiculturalism on the island, providing broader ethnic food choices rather than just traditional dishes for a Chinese or Malay clientele.

Nothing speaks of this better than, Kiara says, the staple product of the kopitiam. *Kopi* (coffee with sugar or more often condensed milk), in all its variety from simple black Western coffee (*kopi o*) to kopi over ice (*kopi peng*) to coffee with no sugar (*kopi kosong* from the Malay word for "zero"), is a good representation of the cultural appropriation and transformation of globally mobile techniques. Because the original Chinese kopitiam entrepreneurs of the colonial era could not afford the high-end coffee bean imports, they often settled for cheap alternatives but enhanced their aroma by frying the roasted beans in a wok with butter, lard, or sugar before grinding them for use in the traditional sock-like filters still used in most kopitiams on the island. Frontiers, in Kiara's view, need to be seen as places of entrepreneurship and profit, often very unequal ones, where much innovation is possible but also where much is dictated by the power of the markets that connect the frontiers to the rest of the world.

In recent years, the Singaporean kopitiam entrepreneur has had to adapt and confront the increasing encroachment of national and global market pulls. For instance, Ya Kun and Killiney Kopitiam, which date back to 1944 and 1919, respectively, are kopitiam chains with dozens of locations across the country. Killiney, named after the central street of its first location (just off Orchard Road), branched out across the island to become a recognizable destination for those seeking a more modern rendition of the kopitiam. In its overseas locations, it promises its international customers "a walk back to the 'good old days,' where you have a chance to enjoy food and beverages prepared in the traditional [Singaporean] way," by stepping into one of its outlets on Bourke Street in Melbourne, Australia, or on the town square in Surabaya, Indonesia. Killiney chain kopitiams

re-create the atmosphere of the old Hainanese coffee shop with period furnish-
ings, décor, and historical memorabilia. Its mission is "to keep the 'Kopitiam'
tradition going for this generation and for the many generations to come."
These kopitiam chains, however, embody not just the commodification and forging of a Singaporean identity but also the rise of a markedly neoliberal mentality
in most of the more recent generation of young Singaporeans. For example, Ya
Kun Kaya Toast (originally Ya Kun coffee stall) was for well over a half century
a single store in Telok Ayer Market until its founder's son decided to open a
second store at Tanjong Pagar and then, in 2000, franchise the brand to over forty
stores in Singapore and thirty overseas. Today one can enjoy food or beverages
from this kopitiam while walking around Ibn Battuta Mall in Dubai's Jebel Ali.
Much like Killiney, Ya Kun bets on sepia pictures of its founders, branding quintessential Singaporean offers like kaya toast, and promising the snack "can
bind kinship, friendship & partnership." Recounting this story with a dose of
healthy skepticism, Kiara tells me that in Singapore, the kopitiam—especially
in its more traditional form rather than its mall-based rendition—becomes a particular site of a local-global nexus embodying the cosmopolitan crossway of the
global city. It is a place where diverse classes mingle and where local distinctiveness is forged by developing variations on overseas dishes. The essential role, if
not the spirit, of kopi entrepreneurs is one of bridging cultures and countries
while demonstrating a (hi)story of their own. Kiara refers to them as "T individuals" with deep expertise on a specialist matter and a breadth of reach across
a vast variety of peoples and the places customers come from.[3] It is in the mix
of the two, she tells me, that their global city entrepreneurship really works.

The "market," be that of global flows or the very localized hawker center, looms
large behind this conversation. The branching out of the kopitiam—from a
single-store, immigrant-owned cheap food stop in government housing (HDBs)
complexes to a series of mall-based chains selling the Singaporean tradition—
speaks to the lucrative and powerful market dynamics that intervene in the development of the global city. Kopitiams, just like hawker centers, now feature
regularly on tourist must-do lists, like those of Lonely Planet, as characteristic
local experiences.

The term "kopitiam" itself was the object of a bitter dispute at the end of the
1980s. The legal scuffle between Kopitiam Singapore Restaurant and Kopitiam
Pte Ltd over the exclusive use of the name Kopitiam resulted in the latter's favor
as it was ruled that the term is generic and could be used by anyone. This was
important not so much for the legal resolution of a business dispute but for the
reaffirmation of the cultural heritage of a Singaporean experience the city-state
has learned to advertise to its global audiences as significant of a uniquely

"brewed," not simply imported and replicated, local global city identity. Yet this does not mean the lucrative nature of this (and many other) key Singaporean signifier is protected once and for all from the ebb and flow of the market. In 2018, Kopitiam Pte Ltd was slated to be acquired by the enterprise arm of the sole national trade union center of Singapore (the National Trades Union Congress), possibly paving the way to further commercialization of this model across the island, if not beyond.[4] Yet this speaks to a broader issue that emerges throughout the book: the central role of internationally mobile urban entrepreneurs. The effects are apparent just under our feet, and Kiara is keen to prove that I, in a way, am an accomplice to this.

Much of today's spatial layout of Singapore, Kiara reminds me, is a legacy of the 1971 Concept Plan, or "Ring Plan," which was first proposed by a set of experts contracted by the United Nations Development Programme. The UNDP had been central in pushing the country to embark on a new land use plan conceiving the development of new towns (a "ring") around the central area of Singapore (to be key to its global connectivity aspirations), linked by a set of expressways and pushing for more rationalized industrialization and economic growth. She mentions the plan not to boast of her historical knowledge but to drive a point home for me. The plan was heavily influenced by firsthand input by a set of three foreign urban experts—Charles Abrams, Susumu Kobe, and Otto Koenigsberger—in 1963. She spells out Koenigsberger's name slowly to strike at the heart of where I am (at the time) coming from: London, and more specifically, the global urbanist community of University College London (UCL). Polish American housing expert Abrams was behind the establishment of the New York City Housing and Development Administration in the 1960s. Kobe was a Japanese transport specialist for the United Nations Development Program. German architect Koenigsberger was at the helm of the Department of Development and Tropical Studies at the Architectural Association, which in 1971 became the Development Planning Unit (DPU) of UCL—one of the world's leading voices in Global South planning and urban development, home to many of the academics offering an alternative ("ordinary" some would say, as per chapter 3 in this book) take on global city questions. At perhaps the opposite end of the spectrum, Kiara suggests, we can easily spot the fingerprints of another UCL urbanist on Singapore's development—Peter Hall. Recalling one of my questions, Kiara goes back to how Rajaratnam, in his much-recalled 1972 global city speech, called on Singapore to embrace its embeddedness in the global (economic) system. What follows in the speech, she reminds me in a symbolic but not unique testimony of how ingrained global city thinking is in the minds of Singaporean leaders, is a quite detailed outline of "world city functions" and

FIGURE 19.   Singapore's classic HDB housing landscape (*front*) and new condo developments (*back*).

Singapore's possibilities within them. Not surprisingly, these notions have since the 1970s become progressively entrenched in Singapore's outlook on the world. Hall was a member of the Nominating Committee of the Lee Kuan Yew World City Prize and had also been a member of the Urban Redevelopment Authority's International Panel of Experts from 2001 to 2013, but his legacy on Singapore's development echoes more deeply, as Rajaratnam's speech demonstrates and as many senior Singaporean planners reverential stance toward any mention of his name testify to.

Just like Hall, the likes of Abrams, Kobe, and Koenigsberger are part of the long-lived tradition of external influencers shaping the direction of Singapore's global city thinking. In short, Singapore's development speaks volumes to its interdependency with a broader system of circulation of global urban expertise and urban ideas from its very origins. As chapters 4, 5, and 9 already noted, this is not an exception and is in fact something that is well echoed in Dubai, for instance, with John Harris's master plans for the Emirate, and in today's bustling conference circuit of cities-themed events, where my Kiara and I tend to spend a substantial amount of time. Are we, I wonder, symbolic entrepreneurs of our own right? The answer to that depends very much on understanding who the entrepreneurs are.

Global City Builders

At this point in the book, it should be clear that I believe ideas make cities global as much as their airline connections and gateway functions. In the business of global urban imagination, the figure of the architect is perhaps one of the most commonly touted by the media as well as academia, presenting a handy example of how shaping global city imaginations and aspirations is a commonplace practice as well as one that often connects words to deeds and, importantly for our story here, discourse to materiality. Architects and designers, creative class participants themselves, are seen as prime actors in supporting the planner in developing this globalized (or globaliz*able*) environment. Cities such as Sydney, Singapore, and Dubai quite blatantly looked overseas in the past decade for the latest architectural trends and the dominant design or planning credos when it came to producing global spaces capable of maintaining and enhancing their international positioning. As Paul Knox, Donald McNeill, or Davide Ponzini have already underlined, this process has allowed the emergence of "starchitects" who can cast their influence on city planning from the confined structures of iconic buildings to shaping large parts of or even entire master plans.[5] For instance, Dutch starchitect Rem Koolhaas's OMA was commissioned an entire neighborhood of Dubai for Nakheel's futuristic Waterfront City that may never see the light of day in the Dubai Waterfront. Likewise, Norman Foster's role in producing another signature space at 126 Phillip Street in Sydney boosted the impact of planning and construction to a public event monitored (and publicized) via newsletters, real-time webcams, and media reports. The overall perception, in both Sydney and Dubai, is that mobilizing major architectural firms will be equally beneficial in terms of the "Bilbao effect" as well as design quality: in a somewhat analogous reasoning with that underlying the interest in city rankings like GaWC's or Mercer's, many city policymakers seem to view starchitects as synonyms of authoritative and well-substantiated urbanist practice. Sydney, of course, was one of the very first emerging metropolitan centers beyond the West to appreciate the power of signature design. Planned as early as 1957, the music hall forever changed the shape and global recognizability of Sydney Harbor. This signature trend continued in the following decades, especially in the "global Sydney" heart of the conurbation that has catalyzed international architectural and property interest around both its CBD and major natural attractions of the bay. As several authors have underlined much more at length than I can dwell on here, the emphasis on signature design as a quintessential element of the modern global city has in turn sustained and extended the production of an international circuit of urban design firms.

Spotting this in architectural and planning practice is easy enough. To confirm the inherent interconnectedness in designed spaces we can easily look for familiar "faces" that have crossed from Sydney and Singapore into the Emirate, and vice versa. One such case is the Index Tower, designed by Foster and Partners. The building was the recipient of the 2011 Best Tall Building Middle East & Africa award by the Council on Tall Buildings and Urban Habitat. The Index partakes in the promotion of design principles similar to those championed by Piano and Foster's buildings in Sydney (such as Aurora Place, discussed below), having been designed according to an environmental strategy aimed at reducing the energy costs for its tenants.[6] Besides, in a context of crosscutting austerity such as that introduced by the 2008 financial crisis, green design elements have progressively been intertwined with economic considerations.

Conversely, the creation of a global architectural market shapes the development of these metropolises in that it further promotes the transfer of similar forms and concepts across cities. The problematic issue is that the drivers of iconicity, as Leslie Sklair noted, now tend to be in the corporate sector, whereas iconic buildings historically tended to be driven by the state and/or religious institutions.[7] This was the case of the RBS Tower building in Sydney, more commonly known as Aurora Place, which took the place of the well-received thirty-two-story State Government Office Block designed in 1967 by Ken Woolley. First presented to the Central Sydney Planning Committee in 1996 by a joint initiative of Mark Carroll, Shunji Ishida, and Renzo Piano and subsequently developed by Lendlease, the plan for Aurora Place embodied cutting-edge design principles. For instance, the sail-shaped white fritted glass that makes up the primary component of the building was designed as double-skinned not just to make an iconic statement separating the edifice from its neighboring high-rises but also to act as a thermoregulator agent for the whole development. Piano also paid much attention to maintaining a narrative consistent with Sydney's growingly popular international image. The sail facade, for example, was meant to maintain direct continuity with the tiling of the Sydney Opera House, located a few hundred meters north on Philip Street and directly visible from most of the upper floors. The building was sold in January 2001 for AUD$ 485 million. This starchitect contribution to the Sydney CBD skyline has also been sanctioned by the increasingly influential business community, which from the early days supported the project as a flagship development. For instance, for its technical and financial (read: property) qualities, the building received the Rider Hunt Award in 2002 from the Property Council of Australia. Cases such as Aurora Place speak to the changing nature of planning in these globalizing cities. Many of the office block buildings from the 1960s and 1970s have since been demolished or converted to apartments as the real estate market changed course and inner-city apartment dwelling suddenly became fashionable for both owner-occupiers and investors. Critically, these projects have had a stake in redefining who the global city is for. As McGuirk and O'Neill note on Sydney,

"These developments are creating a new public—albeit, and this is a critical point, one that is exclusive to the CBD and its elite service workers."[8]

The function of the starchitect, in this sense, goes beyond the symbolic and planned sides of global city making: signature architects like Piano and Foster are also (indirectly, for the most part) capable of catalyzing substantial governance consensus behind key flagship projects. In this sense, as McNeill points out on Sydney, the enrollment of Danish architect Jan Gehl into the production of the *Sustainable Sydney 2030* strategy was "a shrewd attempt to build a public coalition around the vision, as he was in strong demand from city center stakeholders in major cities such as New York."[9] This is of course not a feature of just Sydney or Dubai alone. For instance, the recruitment of Renzo Piano Building Workshop to lead the development of the London Shard in place of the less well-known Broadway Malayan was crucial in defining the confines and flexibility of planning permissions on the site. As a former City of Sydney officer noted by comparing Gehl's role with that of Piano and Foster, "This time we actually brought the architect into the room. . . . It is no longer consultancy, but not quite decision-making either."[10] This catalytic role merges even further the public and private as well as the role of the planner with the indispensable clout of the architect and developer. As with Gehl, McNeill also noted this process in relation to Piano and Foster's role in developing central Sydney, pointing out how starchitect design makes a real difference not only by "lubricating the planning-approval process in sensitive urban contexts" but also by producing added value to the development and enhancing its appeal to prospective commercial tenants.[11] Some might argue that until we step onto the streets, the roles of the architect, the planner, and the designer remain relatively technocratic and ceremonial. But are they?

In 2001 Kris Olds defined these entrepreneurial and internationally mobile practitioners as "intelligence corps": "the very small number of elite architectural and planning firms that aspire for prestigious commissions in cities around the world," whose unique status gives them substantial influence on the development of emerging and emerged global cities around the planet.[12] As of 2020, the corps and the circuit upon which they depend might have enlarged substantially. Rapoport encourages us to think of the model that the "intelligence corps" more narrowly, but global urbanists more generally, are "taking around the world" as a "bundle or menu of options."[13] There seems to be a conviction that certain elements, when carefully combined, constitute the recipe for global significance. While some ingredients and tools may vary, some specific features are recurrent in both literature and practice, whether we find ourselves in the long-lived boroughs of London, on the urbanizing bays of Sydney, or in the sprawling conurbations of Dubai. As both cases tell us, cities look "out" to what are seen to represent winners and losers in the quest for global primacy.

New York, London, Tokyo, and Paris all present newcomers to the international stage, like Dubai and Sydney, with extensive inventories of appealing global features. Yet, as I have already noted, there is also a willing divergence from standardized global city models toward a particular specialization that defines these cities as different from other international competitors. Dubai is the hypermodern hub that offers attractive business and tourist lures and seeks to play a substantial role in shaping the geographies of commerce and trade not only in the Middle East but globally through its Guinness-record-breaking ports, free zones, and airports. Sydney, on the other hand, is the livable metropolis that attracts visitors and international residents through its Harbor City lifestyle, green credentials, cultural drivers, and the quintessentially cosmopolitan composition of its populace. While Dubai has placed much emphasis on the production of world-class icons such as the Burj Khalifa and Burj al Arab as symbols of its stake to global city status, Sydney's iconicity seems to be of a different nature. The city has opted for a lifestyle branding that, while still dependent on a few landmarks such as the Opera House or the Sydney Harbor Bridge, is rooted mostly in an imagery that equates Sydney with its natural amenities (green parks, beaches, and coastal landscapes) and Sydneysider vignettes (surfing, cafés, museums, and social happenings) rather than purely with its built environment. In these terms Dubai and Sydney showcase similar strategies despite the surface diversity on the thematic orientation of this iconicity. So, if Sydney has pushed extensively in the "livability" direction by prompting green, sustainable developments, and Dubai has instead focused on hypermodern structures depicting the rise of the ultimate mobility hub in the Middle East, the global city pathways charted by both are quite similar. The two cities have sought to master the handling of a symbolic power that is at the same time global and unique.

The risk, as the initial experiences of Dubai in the 1990s and early 2000s tell us, is that this orientation can be easily hijacked by a quest for globalized ingredients of the global city recipe, creating homologous spaces that reiterate similar power structures across major metropolises and grant benefits only to those who can access such technologies. What appeared to be lacking in the Emirate in that period was an understanding that the "seduction of place" in the vast majority of today's world cities is not simply a product of symbolic power or a function of a meticulously planned locality.[14] Instead of following the now much-cited path of Singapore, the Emirate was in the early 2000s on a route toward turning into an immense, glittery, "Disneyzated," and hypermodern metropolis much closer to a theme park than an amalgamated cosmopolitan hub.[15] The financial crisis was, in this instance, a wake-up call to focus less on the symbolic fortunes of the global city and more on the pragmatic approaches for sustaining the globalization of these cities.

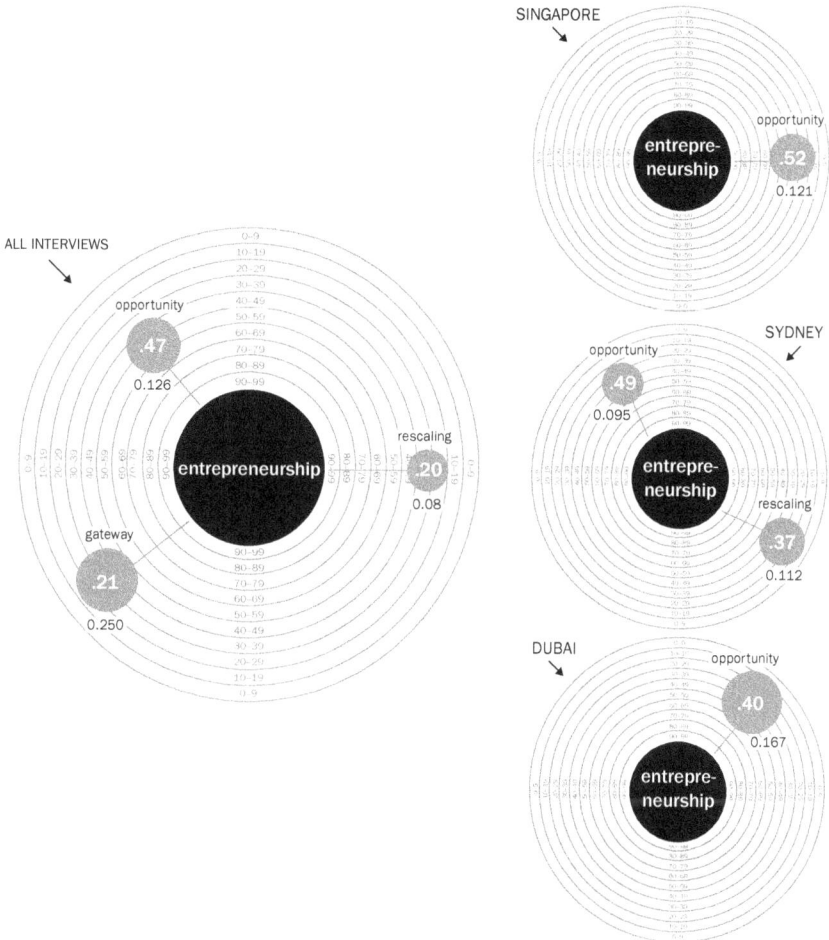

FIGURE 20. Mapping "entrepreneurship" in global city-speak.

The story here tells us that these actors are nowadays quite wary of the practices of symbolic power depicted in the book. At the same time, all evidence points to the fact that this is but the tip (self-professed, perhaps) of an iceberg of global urban expertise rarely discussed by scholars—whereas it is everyday business for the private sector and the circulation of talent across global cities. Before we jump into this key dynamic for urban politics, let me pause to contemplate whether entrepreneurs and entrepreneurship are understood in global city-speak in our cases. Despite its blatant popularity among practitioners and scholarly resurgence in management, geography, and policy debates, entrepreneurship is surprisingly not at the top of salience scores in my interviews, but still occupies a significant seventh place overall among the twenty global city notions investigated here, above innovation by a very small margin and below leadership by a similarly low differential. Not surprisingly, in Dubai and Sydney and even more so in Singapore, it shows strong correlations with the notion of opportunity. This is, however, the only significant connection with the other concepts present in the 170 interviews of this study, apart from a solid correlation with the idea of rescaling in Sydney. This shows how the two ideas have been tightly intertwined in the way they push urban governance beyond its limits, outward and globally in our cases more specifically, and how discussions of entrepreneurship and opportunity are common parlance between practitioners. Unsurprisingly, those with a business and economics background are the category of interviewees most acquainted with and conversant in entrepreneurship. The same goes for those working in the private sector, whereas only three local government employees in all of the interview sample made reference (indirectly via synonyms) to this notion. Generationally, the twenty-six-to-thirty-nine age bracket of my interviewees seems the most acquainted with entrepreneurship, but it is worth noting extremely high (as in well above the average noted above) levels of correlations between this term and opportunity in the forty-to-fifty-nine age bracket and a near-certain correlation (0.82) in the sixty-plus age bracket. What is more, then, is that the variety of the types of urban entrepreneurs is widening and ever expanding, but so are their reference points.

Changing Reference Points?

More cities from more countries emerge today on the map of global city-speak and the horizons of its global urban imagination. There are easily spotted markers of this expansion in the worldviews represented by the words, ambitions, and imaginaries that go hand in hand with our twenty concepts. For instance, as I noted with colleagues in a few research pieces on urban benchmarking, the total of all city mentions in city rankings increased nearly threefold between 2014 and 2018, with most of the increase concentrated in the European Union, eastern Europe, central Asia, and North America. At the same time, more cities are being measured as new types of comparative benchmarking come to the fore.[16] For example, the original *Sustainable Sydney 2030* vision published in 2008 by the Sydney City Council contained numerous references of how other key "global" cities' initiatives could inspire the delivery of the 2030 plan. This included vignettes and case studies from Boston, Amsterdam, San Francisco, and, of course, London on matters such as railway infrastructure, harbor-side renewal, or traffic alleviation. From the British capital, the vision took into account the mayor of London's 2007 housing strategy and in particular the question of how the Greater London Authority was tackling problems of providing affordable housing while retaining diversity in the city.[17] The reference was not purely cosmetic. Rather, the City of Sydney (once again more proactive than New South Wales) was at the time in the process of issuing a new Affordable Housing Strategy linked not only to the 2030 vision but also to other local social policy instruments such as the council's *Homeless Strategy* and *Social Plan*, as well as to other governmental layer policies such as the *National Framework for National Action on Affordable Housing* or the *Commonwealth State Housing Agreement*. In producing these new planning tools, the City of Sydney has maintained a strong reference to other global cities' experiences. So, for example, the research for this strategy scrutinized housing initiatives by other councils in the Sydney metropolitan area such as the Waverley City Council (just southeast of Sydney), national rivals such as Brisbane and Melbourne, and, more importantly, other global cities such as Vancouver and London.[18] This lessons-learned approach is not simply driven by city authorities. Nongovernmental, think tank, and private sector actors also reinforce this relationally. For instance, reporting on Sydney's housing issues, the McKell Institute made large reference to affordability ratios in New York and London as a critique of the systemic challenges faced by a global city.[19] In a similar fashion, when compiling a study on Sydney's performance as a global city in 2009, the Committee for Sydney selected London, New York, and Tokyo as "cities that define Sydney's global aspirations and standing," Singapore, Hong Kong, and Shanghai as "cities that are direct competitors," and Vancouver, San Francisco, and Los Angeles as "cities that have similar urban characteristics and challenges."[20]

The narratives developed in strategic plans like *Dubai 2015* or *City of Cities* are similar in their reference to what are assumed to be exemplary cases of global cities—Singapore, Vancouver, and London being cases in point. More generically, this external reference and the production of "globalized" locations might seem to hint at a potential convergence in the evolution of Sydney's and Dubai's built environments. If we think of this in relation to their local specialization as "hypermodern" and "livable" global cities along similar trajectories, we might therefore be prompted to think that there are inherent processes of hybridization in place in these metropolises, which might be pushing toward the creation of homologous spatial alignments. These considerations might therefore lead to a logical conclusion that, by hybridizing their characteristic locality for an international audience, referring to other "global city" models worldwide, and developing their built environment in similar directions, aspiring global contenders like Sydney and Dubai might be more or less rationally following an idealized global city model embedded in, as well as championed by, those centers of the contemporary world system, such as London. To consider whether this is really the case, it is necessary to relate these cities' pathways to that of the British capital.

Recognizing the potential of alternative global city paths to those of the dominant NY-LON duo and classic referents like Paris and Tokyo, Dubai and Sydney have in many cases turned to rising successes like Singapore or Vancouver to legitimize their emergence as alternative hubs to the well-established geographies the Londons and New Yorks of our time depend on. A similar reasoning can be found in Sydney, although with the almost opposite appropriation of the Western sphere. This "second tier" or "alpha+" relationality is well demonstrated, for instance, in the lead-up process for the *Sustainable Sydney 2030* strategy. If the final vision document included a number of exemplary case studies like those of Boston or Amsterdam, aimed at representing possible parallels to specific projects proposed in *Sustainable Sydney 2030*, the reference to other globalizing cities was a constant of the whole process that led to this strategic statement. Practically, the review ended up listing a plethora of globalizing cities such as Vancouver, Copenhagen, Berlin, and Zurich that, while remaining well below the dominant NY-LON duo, represented Sydney's challenges and potential successes in a far more effective way. As with Dubai, lessons and narratives are learned here not just from London but also from those growing metropolises that seem to showcase much more "global city pathway" commonality with Sydney.

Not all of the 170 interviewees I spoke to for this study mentioned other cities. In fact, 22 percent of the conversations in Singapore, Sydney, and Dubai (thirty-nine interviewees) were entirely focused on their own city, with little to no explicit outlook to other places. This tells us that the vast majority of the discussions of what makes a city global (just over 77 percent in our case) are inherently relational to cities other than the one in question. Or, to put it simply, global city thinking is by and large embedded in a globally comparative imagination.

Evidently, though, this outlook on what the world looks like from the global city is slightly different depending on the job, background, and position one has. When differentiated by current employment, elite interviewees engaged in this study present us with differing maps of comparative gestures toward cities other than their own. For instance, those who work in national government and other governmental institutions "above" the city level predominantly referred to European cities as the most common comparators, with London as the most commonly named city, and with minimal reference to Middle Eastern cities (other than Dubai) or South/East Asian cities (other than Singapore). This paints a quite different profile from the map of the world as seen from the private sector. Here, my interlocutors regularly pointed at Middle Eastern and South/East Asian cities like Abu Dhabi or Kuala Lumpur, and the degree of explicit mention of Latin

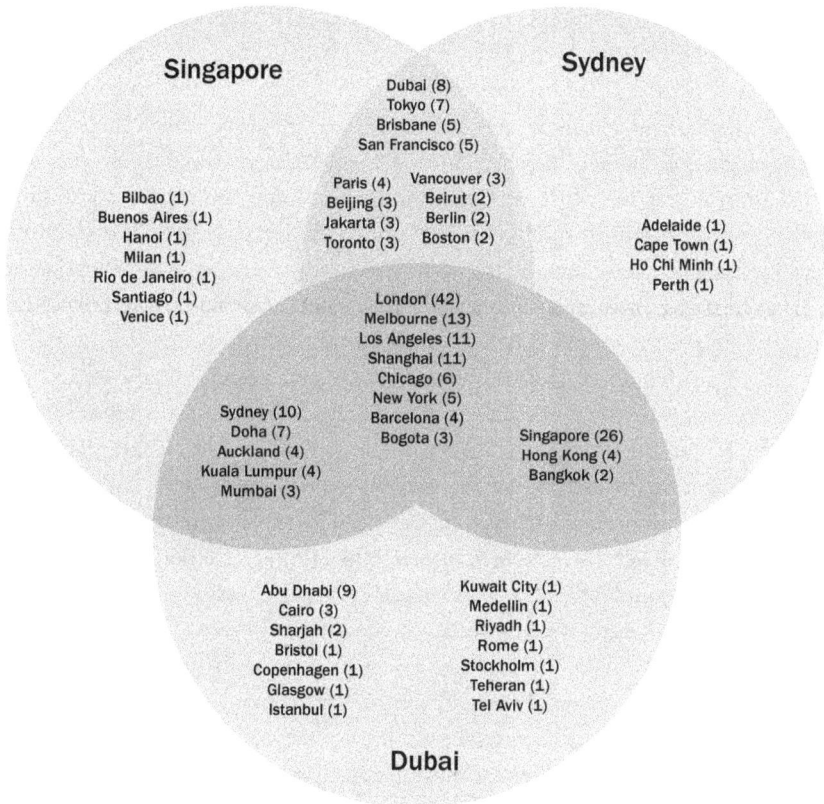

Singapore

Dubai (8)
Tokyo (7)
Brisbane (5)
San Francisco (5)

Sydney

Bilbao (1)
Buenos Aires (1)
Hanoi (1)
Milan (1)
Rio de Janeiro (1)
Santiago (1)
Venice (1)

Paris (4)   Vancouver (3)
Beijing (3)   Beirut (2)
Jakarta (3)   Berlin (2)
Toronto (3)   Boston (2)

Adelaide (1)
Cape Town (1)
Ho Chi Minh (1)
Perth (1)

London (42)
Melbourne (13)
Los Angeles (11)
Shanghai (11)
Chicago (6)
New York (5)
Barcelona (4)
Bogota (3)

Sydney (10)
Doha (7)
Auckland (4)
Kuala Lumpur (4)
Mumbai (3)

Singapore (26)
Hong Kong (4)
Bangkok (2)

Abu Dhabi (9)
Cairo (3)
Sharjah (2)
Bristol (1)
Copenhagen (1)
Glasgow (1)
Istanbul (1)

Kuwait City (1)
Medellin (1)
Riyadh (1)
Rome (1)
Stockholm (1)
Teheran (1)
Tel Aviv (1)

Dubai

FIGURE 21.   Key comparative gestures in each case city.

American cities is slightly higher than that of people employed in other sectors. Interestingly, North American cities are not common here. London is once again the dominant reference, having been mentioned by all ages interviewed for this study. Following the British capital, my interlocutors in the twenty-six-to-thirty-nine and forty-to-fifty-nine age brackets had the greatest number of mentions, as well as the most variety, of European cities, such as Milan, Venice, Berlin, and Barcelona. Those in the sixty-plus and the forty-to-fifty-nine age brackets mentioned Singapore, Tokyo, and the Chinese cities Shanghai, Beijing, and Hong Kong. However, this imaginary of the "global" city in Asia expands in the eighteen-to-twenty-five and twenty-six-to-thirty-nine age groups, who tended to mention these cities as well as other South and Southeast Asian cities such as Ho Chi Minh, Mumbai, Jakarta, and Kuala Lumpur. Equally, only the twenty-six-to-thirty-nine age group (except one interviewee in the eighteen-to-twenty-five age group) mentioned Latin American cities as comparators. While Singapore and

Sydney gathered some regular mentions in cities other than themselves, Dubai presents a slightly different profile: it was not mentioned by those aged sixty and older, whereas its regional neighbors like Doha and Abu Dhabi were more regularly discussed (and dominant in those interviewed in Dubai in that age bracket). Yet mentions of Dubai and other cities in the Middle East and Asia appeared much more commonly with younger interviewees in the eighteen-to-twenty-five and twenty-six-to-thirty-nine groups. Those in the sixty-plus and the forty-to-fifty-nine age brackets were the only ones who, in my conversations, mentioned North American cities, especially in relation to New York and Los Angeles. The younger eighteen-to-twenty-five and twenty-six-to-thirty-nine age brackets also included Canadian cities in their American reference points. Of course, 170 interviewees are perhaps nowhere near representative of the entirety of the elites of these cities, and I do not pretend to argue that is the case. Yet, making up for a varied sample of private and public decisionmakers, developers, experts, and opinion-setters whose voices have tangibly been at the heart of how these cities have been globalized, they still hint at these (changing) global horizons and their importance, beyond correlations and statistics, as an emerging worldview that embodies changing urban aspirations and reference points.

What this hints at, in the ranks of urban entrepreneurs narrowly but more likely across global city-speak generally, is perhaps some degree of generational change. New and fresh ideas might be afoot. New horizons emerge as relevant to shaping urban ambitions. New urban contexts uncommon just about a few years before now enter the lingo, imagination, and in some cases direct practice of these urban development elites—academics included. Yet this is not a seamless process. Interestingly, when measured against the degree of explicit global city discourse, two generations stand out in a way that does not suggest a shift proper, but perhaps a generational jump. If the older individuals among my interviewees (above sixty years) are the ones with the least explicit discourse, as measured by total average mention of the twenty concepts, it is in the forty-to-fifty-nine and the eighteen-to-twenty-five brackets (0.191 and 0.183, respectively) that the terminology of the global city tradition is most evident versus a more moderate result in the twenty-six-to-thirty-nine bracket (0.146). In the youngest of my interlocutors, the ideas of elites and premium connections are common enough that they feature in a third of interviews. In the forty-to-fifty-nine age bracket, this is the case with gateway functions only, but there is an overall higher salience for most of the other terms. I caution against broad generalizations emerging from these numbers, but I also point at the important power that these new urban horizons and possible correlations between aspirations and global city concepts might have when translated into an urban plan, policy, or real estate development.

Urban Entrepreneurs at Large

Few would dispute that the past decades have witnessed the globalization of architectural, planning, and more generally "urbanist" practices. This has taken place in many contexts around the planet via an internationalized professionalization as well as through a progressive appropriation of the international style of modernism by emerging global cities in the East and South.[21] Globalizing cities have of course been pivotal in this process. Architecture and architectural consulting firms, those that Australian historian Peter Rimmer first, and Kris Olds as well as Elizabeth Rapoport after, have called members of the "global intelligence corps" of (global) city builders, have thus become a progressively globalized industry that planners and local government officials in these cities need to attend to when tasked with shaping their metropolis in a global sense.[22] As Kevin Ward also highlighted, this practice has been pivotal throughout the twentieth century to "internationalize" the profession of the planner, as Kiara's Singaporean example above evidences, but the same can be applied to a variety of other urban practitioners. The way Rimmer, Olds, and Rapoport paint it, among many others, there is now a growing variety of urban entrepreneurs responsible for the burgeoning flows of urban development models, ideas, and practices. The ranks of the "world makers," to use a symbolic power expression, are growing and changing. Notable, of course, is the global urban imprint of consultants. This is no longer the "world's newest profession" as some professed, perhaps with little historical sense, at the outset of the millennium.[23] At the end of the first decade of the 2000s the management (or "corporate") consultancy industry was estimated to have reached a worth of $220 billion per year globally and has continued to do so quite successfully even through the increasingly troubled global waters of the 2010s.[24] This is a "knowledge industry" whose grip on urbanism is both manifest and yet little spoken about systematically.[25] It is, in turn, a critical piece of the puzzle of actors, institutions, and networks I have sought to illustrate here as essential in determining the urban governance of Sydney, Singapore, and Dubai, and how these places have been "globalized," especially when looking at these stories through the lenses of their urban developmental elites.[26]

The ranks of urban consultants and knowledge brokers have grown substantially. Equally, a clear expansion has also taken place in the international markets these actors rely on and travel through. This expansion networks urban developers and cities and also links cities and cities as well as cities and urban elites with a wide cast of actors ranging from knowledge institutions, multilateral organizations, and a wealth of investors, multinationals, and global urban "stakeholders," which are often hard to capture in a single unified list. This has much to do with the proliferation of urban innovations and buzzwords in the early 2000s. The popularity of the "smart city" in the early 2000s, for instance, ushered in a contingent of tech entrepreneurs and management experts capable of speaking of the digital transformation that our globalizing cities are poised to undergo, or in some cases have already been subject to. This burgeoning variety of urbanist expertise and global city "inputs" into localized urban imaginations and aspirations is then mixed with those who had for a long while been offering advice as to urban development elites. The same could likely apply to the realm of the arts and culture, whose entrepreneurs echo their renaissance counterparts, if not even earlier practices among empires of the East and West. Starchitects, designers, and planners are of course an evergreen reality in global cities, while health, sustainability, and wellbeing urban entrepreneurs (whom we could also argue have had a long history) have equally witnessed not just a sprawl of interest from city leaders but a number of fads and hit themes like the "happy city" or the "walkable city."[27] The list could go on and on. Yet more widely we could speak of the emergence of an increasingly explicit focus on "cities" as the focus of international investment, as an asset category, as a way of conducting urban development (if not development in general), as a cultural focus, which in itself has been tightly intertwined with the idea of the global city. The business of "cities" ideas, strategies and services, and of global cities advice in particular has become increasingly prominent throughout the first two decades of the twenty-first century. Consultancy companies themselves, like PwC, McKinsey, or EY, have recognized this through explicit "cities" strategies and senior firm roles, and major corporate actors have embraced it by appointing cities "leads" or rolling out flagship urban programs. If this is partly due to the wave of smart city interest in major tech companies, such as Siemens, SAP, and Cisco, we can now confidently argue the effect has spilled over into the wider market, with similar realities at the diverse but globally influential likes of British Petroleum (BP) or Mastercard. Even major banks have done so in the first decade of the 2000s—going from JP Morgan's major sponsorship of a Global Cities project at the Brookings Institution and Deutsche Bank's well-known grant that led to the establishment of the LSE Urban Age program, to Lloyd's, Citi Group, and HSCB more recently. International philanthropies too looked toward the "cities" business in the 2000s and 2010s, with sizable efforts from such large American foundations as Rockefeller, Bloomberg, Mellon, and Ford, along with mounting non-Western efforts from the Gulf riches (e.g., Qatar Foundation) to the Asian philanthropies (e.g., Li Ka Shing Foundation) via "old continent" European entities such as the Robert Bosch Stiftung, Wellcome Trust, or Realdania.

Chiefly, what this points out for our specific story here is the importance not just of individuals who have been casting and recasting global city-speak, aspirations, and imaginations internationally, but also the growing presence of a symbolic system underpinning these practices. In his 2017 (non-urbanist) book, American political scientist Daniel Drezner argues the "ideas industry" looms large behind our contemporary political system.[28] As Drezner puts it, the role of the "public intellectual" has a rich and colorful history in the early twentieth century, when the new mass media catapulted to semi-stardom those intellectuals who were able to write for the general public. Yet experts, in his concern, are also gradually being replaced by the emergence of "thought leaders." This has been happening at a time when—as another book published in 2017 by another American political scientist, Thomas Nichols, puts it—we might be facing the possible "death of expertise" by the hand of the increasingly democratic dissemination of information.[29] Rather than producing an educated public, Nichols speculates, this widening access to means of dissemination has instead created an army of ill-informed and angry citizens who denounce intellectual achievement and mount a campaign against "established knowledge of the previous centuries'" experts, from the academic to the certified professional. Symbolic power is in essence a "power of revelation": it is, as we have seen, the power to "constitute the given" by stating it.[30] Yet Drezner and Nichols point at concerning evidence that the legitimacy of those who have traditionally held some degree of control on what counts as "reality" is crumbling. If symbolic power relies on convening a vision rooted in reality, we are witnessing today in cities, states, and communities a changing field of worlding.

When Bourdieu first formulated his theory of symbolic power (the late 1970s and early 1980s), the French sociologist was able to argue a degree of difference between those symbolic systems produced and appropriated collectively by whole groups and those created by a relatively autonomous and closed group of specialists. Bourdieu uses the analogy of religion as moving from "shared myth" to a "specialized ideology" requiring specialized producers (like the church) of rites, interpretations, and practices, which are then performed and socialized across the wider society. In this reading, specialists and experts hold special prestige or status (i.e., symbolic capital) to, as we have seen, constitute the given by stating it with authority and legitimacy. Much of the story from the previous chapters, I would argue, testifies to the emergence, expansion, and rootedness of such system underneath the globalization of Sydney, Singapore, and Dubai.

Entrepreneurship, in turn, is at large in the practices, logics, and nature of much global city governance, becoming entrenched and institutionalized as the symbolic capital it wields allows cities and elites to grow, but not without problems. A critique of this comes from those who, for instance, have been pointing at the self-perpetuating nature of entrepreneurial jobs. In a series of skeptical commentaries in 2019, *Financial Times* editor Izabella Kaminska lamented the spread of "wishy-washy" roles in the knowledge economy, like "chief vision of-ficer," arguing that "companies need fewer mystics and more critical thinkers."[31] Cities, and perhaps global cities in particular, have seen a sprawl of similar roles, but so have the many businesses, international organizations, and even ac-ademia that have, as described above, embraced the world of cities. One could ascribe this to the expanding complexity of disciplines and skills. Some would also note this is very much a trend toward specialization at the heart of many knowledge-intensive industries that have critical clout in the making and situat-ing of global cities. Saskia Sassen called these the "intermediaries" of the global cities, whose roles do not fit neatly in the economic categories of the twentieth century and whose activity is increasingly central to our societies. Others, then, would treat this less gently, arguing we are also witnessing a heyday of what American anthropologist David Graeber less apologetically called "bullshit jobs."[32] The challenge here is understanding who makes their voices heard as global urbanists and whose interests those voices serve. So, if symbolic power depends on the degree to which "the vision proposed is founded in reality" but that reality is also a social construct, we could confidently argue that in the age of populist politics and "fake news" the degree of hold that experts have on the representation of what reality is might be relatively slipping away.[33] This is not to say that entrepreneurs do not matter. As Kaminska also underlined, these jobs do serve an important function. Knowledge mediators—whether in their man-agement form or indeed the many other facets of this type of entrepreneurship present today, including academics—perform an essential symbolic function. Organizational and innovation theorists have sought to advocate for the impor-tance of this function for the circulation of ideas.[34] In particular, when consid-ering the broader reality of corporate consulting, recent management studies point at a set of four key roles played to various degrees by private firms, indi-vidual experts, and indeed consulting academics, all of which apply to the case of cities and urban development: as sources of information, bringing new knowledge to the attention of those for whom they consult; as standard setters, driving the legitimation of new forms of common behavior; as "knowledge brokers," bridging knowledge from one industry to another and networking previously disconnected stakeholders; and as knowledge integrators, perform-ing translation functions needed to demystify and open up specialist informa-tion to those who would otherwise not be able to access it.[35] Importantly, brokering, by definition, implies the existence of divisions essential to all forms of symbolism. Symbolic entrepreneurs leverage here the particular symbolic power of making, or indeed revealing, groups by drawing global urban com-monalities and differences. Of course, as I have argued and as geography col-leagues have already detailed persuasively, not all entrepreneurialisms are the same.[36] Some are driven by new public management and neoliberal logics; others are spurred by a globalist ethos embedded in practices like "city diplomacy," city networking, and so forth. We are, as Phelps and Miao argued, confronted today by a spectrum of "varieties of entrepreneurialism" characterized by different economic logics, welfare stances and implications, stances on innovation, and scope of action.[37] The result, then, is not simply a totalizing and uniform symbolic system or a single "type" of symbolic entrepreneur, but a splintered and fragmented complexity that still might account to a loose system but cannot be reduced easily to a single element of it. Hence the picture I paint here is not one of a global conspiracy or a corporate grab that critics of the global city often tout. Yes, urban entrepreneurialism is indeed steeped in global market dynamics. Yet, it is also much more brittle and subject to more ebbs and flows than most global urbanists would care to admit, whereas some ideas, like those of the global city genre, have persisted through crises and fads for nearly a century.

POSTSCRIPT

Qantas lounge: Sydney airport, 4:00 p.m.

"I wonder what it will all look like in a decade." It is the middle of February 2020, and I am on my way back from Dubai a day after the end of the tenth World Urban Forum, nearly six years after the cooking-inspired conversation in the introduction of this book at the seventh edition of the Forum in Colombia. We are still, in a way, speaking about the recipe for global cities even if, for all intents and purposes, here we might be imagining more precisely how to *re*build them after yet another momentous (and very much "global") crisis. Back then, the chat with my illustrious counterpart in Medellin had been full of aspirations and imagined urban futures as he went in search of a recipe for how to build a global city. Now, after substantial jet lag and nearly a day of airport hopping from the UAE via Singapore to Australia, the discussion in the pristine Qantas first-class lounge at the Sydney airport is full of uncertainty and verging on the grim. "We will have to rethink it [the global city] in a different way if this all gets out of control," and to do that it would be "pretty convenient" to have a "guidebook" as to the essential pieces of what makes a city global. My opportunistic interlocutor perhaps unintentionally echoes the spirit of my introduction, giving me a perfect excuse for a themed postscript even though I am not about to rewrite this volume into an airport-style version of *How to Build a Global City . . . in 20 Easy Steps* (spoof title option that crosses my mind to give an even bigger headache to my University Press editor).

I am sitting at a table in the Qantas lounge with Lia, who works for a major multinational bank in Sydney that has quite the philanthropic profile in urban issues. We first met at a conference panel a couple of years earlier, and we have a close acquaintance in common downtown. We recognized each other among the midafternoon travel elites, and we are both killing time with small talk. Our brief discussion, fueled by a dire need for a few flat whites (essentially a steamed milk cappuccino ever popular in Australia), is perhaps more prophetic than we mean it to be. We are speaking of what will happen to global cities if we reach a global crisis in international connections as a novel virus outbreak is starting to fill the news. I am mainly speaking from my experience with the aftermath of SARS in the early 2000s, which was what led me to begin studying global cities in the first place. Neither of us can really imagine the shape of things to come, and yet a global urban imagination fueled by locked down cities from across all continents is to be at the very heart of the discussion and global pandemic reporting that is shortly to follow throughout the rest of 2020.

The deadly coronavirus is, unbeknownst to most global urban development elites, already sweeping across cities, jumping between airports just like the one we are in. In fact, Australia has already registered fifteen cases. China has passed fifty thousand infections and is now in the third week of a then astonishing lockdown, having quarantined the eleven million residents of Wuhan. My return trip was cut short from the mounting "viral storm," as a volume by Nathan Wolfe put it nearly a decade before, and I am heading back home from the summit in Abu Dhabi.[1] Instead of stopping over in Singapore for a workshop on global city futures and my usual visits across the island, my journey was fast-tracked (with but a flight change at Changi), and I am on an expedited route home to Melbourne. Singapore has just confirmed nine more cases, bringing its total to sixty-seven, with the National University restricting access on campus and starting remote teaching that will become the "new normal" for many of us in the months to come. Ministries, where I was expected to meet a few colleagues, are tightly surveyed, and visitors have to complete health declaration cards. It seems a far from apt moment to speak of the globalization of cities as the world retreats toward stricter and stricter quarantines, and yet this urban imagination of the crisis will rapidly become a common topic of discussion in the coming months as we witness images of major global centers emptied out, vacant streets, and global travel at a bare minimum.

Can global cities, as the turnstiles of globalization, withstand such a disruption? And for how long? What's next in a crisis hitting at the foundations of the global city? We exchange a few anecdotes of what the situation looks like in the UAE, Italy, and Hong Kong. In places like London, New York, and indeed my final destination of Melbourne, urban economies are seriously threatened by global connections put into question and slowly halting, with many of those world city gateway functions I wrote of in check and a spiraling world economy that does not seem to lend itself to be commanded and controlled from prime spots on the atlas that are also major gateways for global contagion.[2] In the following months, countless of the presumed global cities my many interlocutors made reference to in the book confronted a crisis perhaps deeper than anything they had witnessed since the two World Wars.

In spite of Dubai's status as the prime Middle East business hub, its reliance on real estate, global logistics, and tourism, compounded by an oil price freefall making its rich neighbor of Abu Dhabi less reliable in an expanding global recession, has set the Emirate in dangerous waters in the pandemic crisis. After a rapid response to the virus that was praised by the World Health Organization, Singapore has also repeatedly plunged back into lockdowns with little to no global connectivity and has closely scrutinized its port activities after the island experienced a spike of over nine thousand cases in its crowded low-wage migrant worker dormitories. Sydney's arts, education, and global livability appeal have all proved deeply fragile in the wake of international shutdowns, while the city's (and country's) reliance on China and Southeast Asian links had already been showing signs of trouble. The conversation is perhaps less inspirational than many I have had for the sake of this book and does not make it into the quantitative analysis depicted in previous chapters. It too often relies on tired tropes of the global city and comes too late to make it into my coded dataset, and yet it eventually touches on the heart of my investigation as did the many conversations that led to these pages. If the crisis worsens, speculates Lia, are we to see the "end of the global city model"? "You're the expert: what will global cities look like?" The demand for imagined urban futures, examples, or models from other continents is high. The role of urban expertise and entrepreneurial thinking is enhanced—if anything—by the global disruption. The conversation reminds me of a web clipping I had been saving for the pages of this book but that was long forgotten at that point in my laptop's memory. In a 2015 interview with design magazine *Dezeen*, Dutch architecture firm OMA partner Reinier de Graaf spelled out the role of what the elite saw as the urban expert in an article subtitled "10 Tips for Becoming a Successful Urban Consultant." He cited the capacity for comparative referencing, painting local diversity in global commonality, as essential in "becoming an authority." This "essential skill," as he saw it, is one that echoes loudly of symbolic power. For him, it was about making evident how city leaders (in local government) or the business of development can construct innovation by illuminating realities that are already existent somewhere. De Graaf spoke of networking through conferences and international mayoral forums as core to the business of the urban consultant, while "not insist[ing] on taking credit for your work" and "shield[ing] yourself by having your deliverables carry a brand other than your own."[3] Certainly, the debate on the pros and cons, downsides and benefits, or indeed morality and dangers of this brand of entrepreneurial practices could (and should) perhaps capture a whole volume behind the scope of my modest study. My goal here has been one of underscoring that urban entrepreneurship as well as the expertise necessary to shape urban imaginations and aspirations are deeply intertwined with the mechanics of symbolic power—something perhaps even more pertinent at the current historical junction. They play, as I hope to have shown in several occasions throughout the book, a prime role not just in speaking of cities globally but indeed in casting the boundaries of a global urban imagination that underpins the workings of developmental elites in the kinds of cities we have come across in this modest academic journey from Australia to the Emirates via Singapore. The demand for urban expertise in a time of rising turmoil deep across our cities is not receding and may in fact increase. It is also not just the business of for-profit external consultants and firms. Academia, in my view, sits at the very least in relation to these elites, and at a broader reading might in fact be somewhat part of them. Since February 2020 I have myself been called on by several of the kinds of media and elites depicted in the previous chapters to sketch my opinion on the future of global cities and what I imagine cities to be after the crisis. In that, I am but a drop in an ocean of expert opinions as to the post-pandemic future of cities, and even more so as to the future of cities in general. Major urban thinkers and experts have populated the pages of news outlets, blogs, research hubs, and city networks, to name but a few, since the outbreak of COVID-19. Yet they were already "there" in some form as pundits the world over proliferated through summits, op-eds, best sellers and TED Talks. The circuit shaping the direction of global urban imaginations and aspirations is alive and well, even though its elite conferences are at a standstill. This time the capacity to shape how people, elites or not, imagine and aspire to build "global" cities is perhaps even more important as many of the decisionmakers, just like most of the medium- and low-wage migrants and urban dwellers, are forced "in place" and unable to experience other urban realities firsthand.

Now more than ever those places, connections, and senses of the global nature of cities and urbanization, shared by people who are advised to stay distanced from each other, are imagined rather than experienced. The field, systems, and forms of symbolic power are rampant—a key arena where the shape of urban development will be cast and recast in the years to come. At the same time, global urbanism takes a twisted turn, and symbolic power becomes a very physical production of difference through quarantines and forced separations. Commonality and connection recede again in the back of lockdown mind-sets, even if the experience of COVID-19 is perhaps one of the most clearly "global" and globally-shared ones of the past half century. Lia's flight is called in one of the nearby gates, and we part ways midway through darker speculations of what

Sydney would look like if it were to be locked down like Wuhan. "Go figure," she utters as she heads toward her gate. Little did we know.

The Possibilities of a Global Urban Imagination

The cases in this book stress how the zone of scholarship-practice translation afforded by the working of a global urban imagination is much wider than critiques of the global city often make it. Importantly, some key ideas that have formed the backbone of the critical take on the global city, like that of splintering urbanism, are present at just about a degree of separation (read: synonyms) from literal scholarly mentions in the language and aspirations of many of the elites determining how cities globalize. The evidence as to the centrality and widespread presence in the global urban imagination of concepts like premium connections, elites, presence and absence "off the map," or world city hierarchy should be of some comfort for the engaged scholar. It speaks at least to the possibility that there is some common language upon which a more effective encounter between scholarship and practice could be built with the elites that shape urban development. Here is where more progressive global city imaginations by these elites could at least in some measure be constructed, not just as resistance, but as I note below, as better global urban aspirations. Of course, not all elites can be swayed—nor perhaps should they. Yet I would argue the evidence above speaks to a potential translation zone to be leveraged. Some of the results in previous chapters stress how this is not confined just to those practitioners and researchers with a "social" (sciences) sensibility in their backgrounds: STEM ("natural" scientific) backgrounds also seem relatively well attuned and conversant in some of the key concepts depicted here. The global city is a genre with much purchase across professional, disciplinary, and generational divides. At the same time, however, empirical material gathered for this book stresses once again the need for an even bigger effort to advocate for a better understanding, perhaps in some academe too, of the practice of core critical ideas (like those of metrocentricity or worlding) that a truly progressive urban imagination cannot do without. Across all cases, themes, and places described here, the unequal development of the global city is clearly displayed, as profits, competition, and particular interest often trump the concerns of many urban dwellers. A better, more responsibly and practically grounded global urban imagination needs to emerge from the current crisis.

This effort can, as I have attempted to demonstrate, build on the recognition of symbolic power that global city ideas wield. In doing so it of course has to appreciate the uneven power relations that underscore it. Essential to one's capacity to advocate for a better and more inclusive global city, in my mind, is the need to educate urban development elites, scholars included, as to the political underpinning of it all. The conversations across the book stress the still poorly understood dynamics of state rescaling and urban governance that, to name but one of many political (science) deficiencies of the global urban imagination, are so central in a power-laden reality like that of the global city. We should not take lightly the language of global city-speaking. This is because, as I have outlined, the global urban imagination has very material implications. It is also because symbolic power relations may be even harder to notice, grasp, and address than more violent forms of inequality across cities. The symbolism of many ideas about what a global city is and should be is in many of the cases depicted in this book a version of "gentle repression" posing as "free will"—a governance challenge I highlighted as early as chapter 1.[4] Building a city for users and not inhabitants, alienating an invisible working class, and creating an urban order based on limited and splintered liberties may prove to be a socially unsustainable strategy. The fragility of Dubai and the inequalities of Sydney, but also the oppressions of Singapore, stand as clear evidence of this. Leadership and elites have perhaps been accomplices to the construction of polarized ("dual") cities in an increasingly unequal urban age. This reminds us that, as Bunnell (and Arjun Appadurai before him) put it, within any given society "the 'capacity to aspire' is not evenly distributed"[5] and that the urban imagination of those who might come from worse conditions is often hardly captured in the visions and aspirations of the urban development elites. Here, the work of the responsible urban "expert" comes in a critical mission that should open up horizons of what counts as a "global" city, which cities count, and whose voices are afforded a capacity to portray urban aspirations and partake in global urban imaginations.

Yet, as I underline below, these well-meaning "global urbanists" in academia and across civil society, or indeed within major urban development institutions, cannot count themselves free from this political game. Exerting symbolic power, in Bourdieu's reading at least, implies exerting some degree of violence and domination. This form of power allows those who leverage it to do so in a far more subtle form than other means: it "makes it possible to obtain the equivalent of what is obtained by (physical or economic) force."[6] In that intrinsic quality, perhaps, it yields an even greater accountability. As we have seen throughout the book, this takes place because, in the workings of symbolic power, the normalized state of affairs (or *doxa*) is in fact not a form of explicit consent (to the divisions purported by those with power) but rather an implicit participation on the part of the audience, or even worse, the subjugated.[7] It rests on a taken-for-granted level of acceptance of "dispositions" (one's place in society) and divisions that are seen as natural and legitimized by those speaking with authority. Urban expertise and urban entrepreneurship, when applied internationally to shape the ways cities develop and urban projects are cast and recast, should not be treated lightly.

Rather, the entrepreneurialism of a "global" urbanist, as a practice of symbolic power, is inherently political (i.e., laden with power relations) irrespective of its purpose and moral allegiances. Claiming no higher moral ground and recognizing we are an accomplice to the production of at least some of today's urban imagination, scholars and "urbanists" need to account for the impact of their voices and turn it positively toward more inclusive global city futures. If scholars have historically been at the core of the "business of ideas," it is perhaps even more urgent that we reclaim more of that role as intermediaries ourselves in the translation zone depicted by the global urban imagination in this book. No doubt, in a time of abstraction and empirical dismantling of the metropolis as an aggregate of global ingredients for success, it should be a scholar's duty to unveil the "geographies of responsibility" that are intertwined with the politics of building global cities.[8]

Broadening the Activist Repertoire

In terms of "expert" status, international networks, and the capacity to unveil innovative knowledge, the academic is perhaps as poised to play a key role in the circulation and application of urban development ideas as the many other actors narrated in this book. Major academic institutions have understood this well for at least the past three decades. In fact, in much of the elite academia (but increasingly so in many other emerging contexts), universities themselves have been putting an increasing premium on consultancy roles for urban researchers, often at the expense of (as critics argue) the more "core" business of academia, such as teaching, fundamental research, and scientific peer review. A question of substantial responsibility is invested in these roles, whose advice is in many cases taken seriously and implemented through multimillion-dollar programs, initiatives that reach across millions of urban dwellers and, perhaps more narrowly but no less significantly, thousands of urban studies graduates across a vast multitude of disciplines each year.

It is indeed comforting to acknowledge that in some instances the case studies discussed in this book have allowed global city scholars to seriously engage with the processes of setting strategic direction and decision-making. This, to date, has mostly been the case of planning scholars. In Sydney, for instance, University of Queensland's planning professor Glen Searle, a well-established voice in the global city scholarship on the New South Wales capital, has taken various roles in strategic planning for the state government, authoring the relatively influential *Sydney as a Global City* discussion paper in the early days of the city's ascent in 1996. Likewise, it has been a constant of Singaporean scholarship that major scholarly figures from institutions like NUS have also taken roles as government advisers. Dubai's elite, while deeply affected by the work of GaWC and Sassen among others, still needs to develop more formal engagements with both a populace of indigenous researchers and the growing variety of international scholars currently investigating the Emirate, who are often ostracized from rather than welcomed into governing circles in favor of more ephemeral global urbanist consultants. Indeed, plenty of scholarship-practice bridges already exist in the field. It is imperative for global city scholars, especially from the more recent generations, neither to dismiss their capacity to impact policy nor to forger their literature's central normative purpose. In 1966 Hall's *The World Cities* was, after all, not just describing the centrality of certain metropolises but also aiming at informing planning in an urbanizing and interconnected world. In 1991 Sassen's *The Global City* equally pointed not just at the centralization of producer services in London, New York, and Tokyo but also at the need to act swiftly against the polarizing social structure of these cities. This story continues in many of the central texts of this scholarship and should not be trampled by the lure of the expanding market for global models, recipes, and effective growth strategies.

In this space the "global" urban scholar plays an essential role as a mediator of, and in between, ideas. This is a diplomatic role of sorts: a practice of engaged research that seeks to negotiate its complicity in and with the elite alongside its necessary societal mission. While much has rightly been written and advocated for scholarship to become "action research"[9] as participant in the struggle of the marginalized and oppressed in cities, there might also be a space for expanding the activist repertoire of urban studies to the realm of diplomatic skills to drive change within the workings of, rather than as a counterweight to, urban development elites. This is perhaps no less of a political stance than other forms of critique, resistance, and rejection. The act of translation of ideas between groups and places or indeed between global city imagination or aspirations and global city building, working as a "clearing house of possibility," can also be a profoundly political act.[10] It also does not, by default, negate the purpose or value of other activist tactics. Rather, it shows how symbolic power can be practiced for a social good. In this sense, the type of scholarly activism, even the argument that there could be some form progressive urban entrepreneurship, I advocate for here is blatantly a political stance, perhaps less radical than others but equally directed toward more inclusive and less extractive global city ideals.

Putting this symbolic capacity to work on the imaginations and aspirations of the elites would imply engaging with, developing greater legitimacy in, and shaping the global urban imagination of elites from within, or at the very least in dialogue with them. It would require allowing for time and effort to be spent in the practice of urban politics in the circles shaping the direction of cities like Singapore, Sydney, and Dubai, even though the incentive structures to do so are perhaps still not right in academia. As Keller Easterling fittingly put it in her *Extrastatecraft*, this stance might be about recognizing the value of urbanists (and urban researchers) in striving to reposition their skills in a more powerful place than at the margins of capital and market interests. As Easterling points out, we need to better understand the nature (or "code" as she puts it) of this symbolic system upon which urban development takes place, and take an active part in its (re)construction, even where it might be necessary to hack into this code to drive more inclusive purposes in the way we build cities.[11] The goal of this approach is not to deny the value of resistance and critique, as she suggests, but to expand (our) "activist repertoire" in the politics of city making.[12] This is, as she puts it, less of a "duel" against a Goliath empire of neoliberal actors and more of an altering of the "chemistry of the soil" that understands the modes of operation of the system that makes cities and strategically repurposes their components. This engaged approach might also underline that, in some cases, the tangible concerns of practitioners on the ground can be a reminder of societal needs to many academics who are perhaps a little too often divorced from the places they aim to study, or indeed pundits who pedal the global city genre with little appreciation for its scholarly roots.

The story presented in this book calls, at least in my view, for a new generation of urban scholars, students, and public intellectuals not to place themselves on a pedestal higher than the practitioner's. It also opens up avenues to explore the possibilities of a more progressive form of urban entrepreneurship. It is ultimately not a call for policing the territory of academia, but rather for considering the role of scholarship as expertise inherently embedded in the practice—a call for more applied global urban theorizing and speaking that claims a stake in and takes responsibility for building global cities. If, as we have seen, the symbolic power of global urbanism and the notions of the global city are centered on the possession of some degree of symbolic capital, scholars might be in many ways poised to leverage their status. While partly challenged by the proliferation of an "ideas industry,"[13] academic social recognition (if not prestige) can empower those in scholarly roles and allow them, like many of the other stakeholders depicted here, to exert influence. This positioning affords a critical opportunity to progressive scholars to practice at the heart of urban development "what they preach," shaping directly some of the foundational narratives, aspirations, and reference points that are shaping global city imaginations today.[14] If an essential part of symbolic systems and symbolic power is the "politics of group-making," casting differences among commonalities, it might be in the latter part of this symbolic dynamic that much scholarly value could be provided to a more inclusive global city genre.[15]

For Different Global Aspirations

Times, while ridden with crisis, might be poised for a change. Encouragingly, the research in the three cities of the book has pointed, at least to some degree, toward a generational change in the way urban development elites imagine the global city. This is still a highly political space, and one that demands action. The more recent cadres of urbanists depicted here display not only a broader comparative imagination of what counts as models of global cities but also a clear sense of the hierarchical differentiation between them: peripheries and cores remain at the heart of global urban thinking and speaking and are perhaps even better understood by the younger generations than they are by those educated in the 1980s or 1990s. Yet as this "map" of the world expands, the questions of splintering and unequal dwelling in our global(izing) cities become louder, and the attention for the academe is still solid in a time of pundits, symbolic entrepreneurs, and "urban solutionists" peddling miraculous innovations across the globe.[16]

This, at least to me, underscores the great promise of cosmopolitanism to promote a more progressive way of thinking and speaking of global cities. Cosmopolitan aspirations and imaginations might be a core ingredient in ensuring the rest of the global city imagination is not left to the whims of the market. As highlighted in previous chapters, this needs to be a sense of "cosmopolitan" that goes beyond the hijacked terminology of city branding experts. Specifically, a more progressive global urban imagination can benefit from a key trait of cosmopolitanism that is often absent in discussions of global cities: relationality. While competition and hierarchy were well captured by most of my interlocutors and the dominant global city discourse that rests on the search of distinction, the other side of this symbolic power coin is often forgotten. As Robinson put it, it is that commonality of "cities in a world of cities."[17] Inevitable ties bind global cities, and I argued here that they demand far better recognition and respect than they often get. Again, this is not a novelty for the global city genre and the imagination that emerges from its century-old scholarship. Relationality was already well understood in the heydays of modern global city thinking, as, for instance, by the world city hypothesis in the 1980s and Hall's notion of gateway functions in the 1960s—cities are not just dots on an atlas but connected dots whose networks form much of their fame, fortune, and collapse. Singapore's success has to do with Hong Kong and the links between the two city-states as much as it has to do with the Asian city's networks with London and, yes indeed, Sydney and Dubai, and vice versa. In a time of sweeping contagion and interrupted global mobility, this cosmopolitan lesson is perhaps more poignant than ever and something that symbolic power can be used to highlight, instead of competitively casting difference.

Entry points for this dialogue in the symbolic system I depicted here are not just conferences and the circuit of global city-speaking. There are very tangible and well-established tools and technologies of "building" and "planning" where global city elites can be engaged while constructing the future of cities like Sydney or Singapore. As shown in chapter 9, the processes of policymaking and strategic planning, for example, become more focused translation zones where the forging of the global imaginaries of cities and the input of entrepreneurs and experts (scholars included) can do much—good or bad. Strategic processes like the Dubai Strategic Plan or the London Plan act as performative devices that does not just represent these metropolises but rather conjugates them in the future tense. If strategy is not a response but a tool to convince the public of the feasibility of a long-term vision, the global city has provided in all these cases a widely accepted consensus machine: it appeals, as the previous chapter confirmed, across most social strata and governance stakeholders, while also offering a powerful statement on a city's location within the global economic and cultural geographies. Central in directing the developmental pathways charted by Dubai, Sydney, and Singapore, global city strategies represent a condensed version of these cities' (elites) view of the world. "Global city" has in fact been deployed in all of our cases as a catalyst to drive the transformative agency of these strategies, often in a globalist sense, but demonstrating that ideas about the "global" and the "urban" can be inscribed into the politics that are shaping urban development.

Reference to other cities, in these practices, tools, and aspirations, also becomes a central place in which to advocate for a more progressive view of the world from the (privileged) viewpoint of the global city and its elite. As we have seen, when it comes to thinking about cities other than one's own, the comparative drive embedded in both scholarship and practice offers some important possibilities. More precisely, conversations in Singapore, Sydney, and Dubai surface how, at least in these contexts, this variety of cities accounted for in the global urban imagination is wide and not limited to the usual (Northern) suspects. Singapore itself occupies a prime spot in urban development conversations, and regional reference points are as common as the classic New Yorks and Londons we think of when speaking of global cities. In a way, this broader imagination offers at least some degree of possibility to open up the dominant urban imagination to experiences and voices beyond the "metro" (to use one of the core concepts we explored) and ideally toward a more inclusively Southern global city sensibility. It is encouraging to spot Asian realities like Bangkok and Kuala Lumpur, or African and Latin American ones like Cape Town and Medellin, but indisputably much work remains to be done to cement and even broaden this global view of the "world" of cities.

This work will require a "geographical imagination," as Massey puts it, of the global city that is capable of looking "both within and beyond the city and hold[s] the two things in tension."[18] As Tim Bunnell reminds us, aspirations should not be spoken as "simply individual": they are shared in and across societies, and we should advocate for (and engage in the construction of, I would add) more "democratic" consideration of the imagination that underpins them toward an "ethics of possibility" for all, not just the few privileged to be part of the elite.[19] Therein lies the challenge. Often profit and particular interest have captured the popular field of urban imagination, as Asher Ghertner beautifully puts it in the case of Delhi, through a "normative self-imagery" that rules the present through preconstrued images of the future city.[20] Here, the mission of a progressive urban expert, be they a scholar or something else, is not only to lift the capacity to imagine and aspire of those who are not afforded that privilege, but also to widen the imaginary of those urban development elites who are all too often captured by circulating models and commonplace reference points.

Some of the lessons of a global city scholarship that dates back at least a century remain true. Some are questioned in their essence. Some become even more concerning. Globalization, of whichever kind the COVID-19 crisis will allow it to be, will likely still "hit the streets" of places around the planet. The capacity of agglomeration in a time of contagion, or the failures of leaders and promised innovations, might roll back talk of how the global city model might be in crisis. The splintering and deeply unequal nature of the workforce in these cities might become even starker if the global opportunities captured by great cities like Singapore or Sydney were to vanish. In a way, the stories collected in this book testify to the resilience of the global city in the face of manifold crises— something particularly poignant when writing in a time of pandemic threats. This, I would speculate, is because, as the study here has proved, "global city" is not a single idea that can be easily debunked by a particular crisis or critique. Rather, its complex global urban imagination, which my digest of twenty global city concepts might only have scraped the proverbial tip of the iceberg of ideas, wields far more symbolic power than we perhaps would like to acknowledge. In turn, the urban expert, academic or otherwise, is invested with a fundamental responsibility of, and toward, the ideas depicted in this book. Constructing translation zones as "a zone of critical engagement" opening to more progressive and inclusive aspirations is no easy task, and one that cannot be done if there is no dialogue between academia and practice.[21] Widening the imagination of what the global city is and who its "cityzens" are, especially in the wake of many of them lacking a clear voice among the elites depicted in this study, is key. It is essential to developing progressive urban imaginations of a "global" kind that remain respectful and conscious of localized viewpoints and grounded experiences. We should nurture cosmopolitan urban aspirations that can push for a more progressive sense of the "global city" portmanteau in practice and everyday-speak. The art of being "global," when centered on a symbolic act that broadens the practices of inter-referencing between cities, could support the creation of new and more nuanced cosmopolitan solidarities.[22] In a moment of historical crisis shared across continents and hitting at the heart of our most connected cities, the importance of this global urban imagination is anything but diminished.

Acknowledgments

This is a book that was written a fair few times. In the meantime, I lived in Sydney, Dubai, and Singapore, and as the vignettes of most chapters might give away, I did a lot of the groundwork for this in eateries of various sorts and social strata. That approach, taking perhaps the search for a "global city" recipe a little too seriously, continuously reminded me of the need for urban scholars to, at least at some point, plant their feet firmly onto the ground they aim to speak of. For more than I could possibly summarize here, a *grazie* of his very own (as ever) is very much due to the eclectic Luigi Tomba—a source of inspiration, the reason why I got into urban theory, and the voice of critical urban thinking that always reminded me there are livelihoods in the buildings and on the streets of these purportedly "global" cities.

As a near decade-long somewhat procrastinated effort, the book was sketched along the way across five institutions: the Australian National University, the National University of Singapore, the University of Oxford, University College London, and finally at the University of Melbourne. For this lengthy but perhaps necessary creative (if not creatively destructive) process, a few acknowledgements are de rigueur. That has to start with Cornell University Press, from Michael McGandy to Jim Lance, for bearing with just about four years of delays. I also thank Liz Schueler for patiently weeding through a first full manuscript and Mary Ribesky for help with production. My thanks to the Oxford Programme for the Future of Cities and Steve Rayner for betting on me in the first place, and for the many stimulating conversations with Oxford colleagues that convinced me that some more work was to be done. For that I am also indebted to Tim Bunnell for allowing me to spend some precious time in Singapore at the Cities Cluster and the Asia Research Institute at NUS, where the first cuts of this work were tested, redrafted, and rethought. A thanks for inspiration and input in my effort goes to Donald McNeill in Sydney for his pathbreaking work on this theme. Thanks also to the many colleagues at UCL's Department of Science, Technology, Engineering and Public Policy, especially the researchers I had the great luck to work with. From 2018, the University of Melbourne convinced me it was finally time to tell this story and offered some finally much-needed security and stability upon which I think a better book than it had been to date was finally hatched. That would have of course never happened without the support of Julie Willis in trusting my "global" project, and of the relentlessly collegial teammates of the Melbourne Centre for Cities who keep up my spirits at all times while delivering innovative research from the antipodes. In particular, much is owed to Brendan Gleeson for making me feel like I came back home down under and for remaining a source of support and advice in a time of great uncertainty.

Earlier versions of chapters have appeared in several journals, including *Urban Studies, Cities, Area* and *International Journal of Urban and Regional Research*. I would like to thank all of the editors for the chance to present some of the work in progress for this book to the wider public and to receive some feedback. For critical discussions and responses to some of this work, I am gladly indebted to JP Addie, Idalina Baptista, Neil Brenner, Greg Clark, Brian Collins, Ellie Cosgrave, Yasser Elsheshtawy, the GaWC gang (David Bassens, Ben Derudder, Michael Hoyler, John Harrison, and Michiel van Meeteren in particular), Maryam Karimi, Roger Keil, Michael Keith, Doreen Massey, Simon Marvin, Elizabeth Rapoport, Jenny Robinson, Ahmed and Rashid Bin Shabib, Emilia Smeds, Wendy Steele, and Vanessa Watson. Work with Daniel Pejic and Enora Robin over the last few years has been especially important in terms of framing where this project eventually ended up. Without their inputs, criticisms and comments, this would be little more than a pile of field notes.

Special gratitude, albeit perhaps too late, goes to (Sir) Peter Hall, who patiently talked me through the history of places, academic thinking, and the challenge of giving advice to global city elites. The same goes to Sue Parnell for getting me back on a purposeful path of urban inquiry without ditching the "global." Likewise, I owe more than just a glass of wine to Saskia Sassen, an always supportive and collegial voice, all too often reminding me the street is where the global city is really to be found. No acknowledgements would mean anything without ending with the countless patience with this neverending book from Becky, Adi, Rory, and Arrietty, who provided me with shelter, put up with my late nights and endless travels, and still find the spirit to take the mickey out of me at every possible chance. Same goes to Nini and Paolo for training me to travel and to realize the value of the "elsewhere" since well before I ever got into cities.

Of course, to none of the above should any of the mistakes made in these pages be attributed: shortcomings and miscalculations remain a flaw of my hopeful engagement with that unfinished project the global city is after all.

Notes

1. SPEAKING OF GLOBAL CITIES

1. Special mentions for the 2016 World City Prize were read at the event and are collated at https://www.lcckuanycwworldcityprize.gov.sg/laureates/2016/special-mentions (last accessed 19 March 2021).

2. In this chapter I use "world city" and "global city" interchangeably. More on the distinction of these terms from the world city scholarship to global city research is provided in chapter 2.

3. D. Madden, "City becoming World: Nancy, Lefebvre, and the Global-Urban Imagination," *Environment and Planning D: Society and Space* 30, no. 5 (2012): 772–87.

4. D. McNeill, *Global Cities and Urban Theory* (London: Sage, 2016).

5. B. Gleeson, *The Urban Condition* (London: Routledge, 2014).

6. Here I do not wish to take the military analogy lightly: the construction of today's global cities often confronts us with violent consequences, including the displacement of people, the occupation of land, the destruction of buildings, and clashes between many different actors in the city. Chapters 8 and 10 expand on this.

7. "Dubai Chosen to Host 2020 World Expo Trade Convention," *BBC News Middle East*, 28 November 2013.

8. Peter Shadbolt, "Will the World Be Wowed by Dubai's Futuristic Souk Built for Expo 2020?," *CNN*, 6 December 2013, https://edition.cnn.com/2013/12/05/business/dubai -world-expo-2020/index.html.

9. See, for instance, Edward L. Glaeser, "The Ascent, and Fall, of Dubai," *New York Times*, 1 December 2009.

10. Yasser Elsheshtawy noted, for instance, how this contrast extended into the public domain with the BBC and Qatar Foundation's *Doha Debate* "Is Dubai a Bad Idea?," https://archive.dohadebates.com/debates/item/indexb170.html?d=67&s=6&mode=transcript.

11. J. Robinson, *Ordinary Cities: Between Modernity and Development* (London: Routledge, 2013), 1.

12. On the value of the global city, see the exchange between Michiel Van Meeteren, Ben Derudder, and David Bassens, "Can the Straw Man Speak? An Engagement with Postcolonial Critiques of 'Global Cities Research,'" *Dialogues in Human Geography* 6, no. 3 (2016): 247–67; and Jennifer Robinson, "Theorizing the Global Urban with 'Global and World Cities Research' beyond Cities and Synecdoche," *Dialogues in Human Geography* 6, no. 3 (2016): 268–72.

13. S. Sassen, "Unsettling Master Categories: Notes on Studying the Global in CW Mills' Footsteps," *International Journal of Politics, Culture, and Society* 20, nos.1–4 (2008): 69–83; and A. Roy, "The 21st-Century Metropolis: New Geographies of Theory," *Regional Studies* 43, no. 6 (2009): 819–30.

14. Topical here is R. Burdett and D. Sudjic, eds., *The Endless City* (London: Phaidon Press, 2007).

15. The brand was first announced by Hong Kong's chief executive Tung Chee Hwa in his 1999 policy address that led to the Commission on Strategic Development and the launch of brand and collateral initiatives at a Fortune Global Forum in May 2001.

16. J. Robinson, "Cities in a World of Cities: The Comparative Gesture," *International Journal of Urban and Regional Research* 35, no. 1 (2011): 1–23.

17. P. Bourdieu, "The Forms of Capital," in *Handbook of Theory and Research for the Sociology of Education*, ed. J. Richardson (Westport, CT: Greenwood, 1986), 241–58; P. Bourdieu, "Symbolic Power," *Critique of Anthropology* 4, nos. 13–14 (1979): 77–85.

18. P. Bourdieu, "Social Space and Symbolic Power," *Sociological Theory* 7, no. 1 (1989): 14.

19. Bourdieu, "Symbolic Power," 79.

20. P. Bourdieu, *Language and Symbolic Power* (Cambridge, MA: Harvard University Press, 1991), 164.

21. P. Bourdieu, "The Market of Symbolic Goods," *Poetics* 14, nos. 1–2 (1985): 13–44.

22. P. Bourdieu, *Distinction: A Social Critique of the Judgement of Taste* (1984; London: Routledge, 2013).

23. City of Sydney, *Draft Corporate Plan 2006–2009* (Sydney: City of Sydney Council, 23 May 2005) p.12, https://meetings.cityofsydney.nsw.gov.au/Data/Council/20050523/Agenda/draftstrategicplan2006-2009sectionab.pdf.

2. THE IDEA(S)

An earlier version of this chapter was published in M. Acuto, "Finding the Global City: An Analytical Journey through the 'Invisible College,'" *Urban Studies* 48, no. 14 (2011): 2953–73.

1. Matthew Benns, "James Packer's $2b Barangaroo Development Vision to Help Make Sydney a Truly Global City," *Daily Telegraph*, Sydney, 28 February 2014. This is a development that would eventually come under fire long after the event described here, being deemed "not suitable" for operation in the early months of 2021. See, for instance, BBC News, "Crown Resorts: Australian Casino Firm 'Not Suitable' for Sydney Gaming Licence," London, February 10, 2021, https://www.bbc.com/news/world-australia-56005678.

2. J. Friedmann, "Where We Stand: A Decade of World City Research," in *World Cities in a World-System*, ed. P. Knox and P. J. Taylor (Cambridge: Cambridge University Press, 1995), 28.

3. M. Dear, *From Chicago to LA: Making Sense of Urban Theory* (New York: Sage, 2002).

4. W. Christaller, *Central Places in Southern Germany* (1933; Englewood Cliffs, NJ: Prentice-Hall, 1966).

5. P. Geddes, *Cities in Evolution: An Introduction to the Town Planning Movement and to the Study of Civics* (London: Williams, 1915).

6. R. D. McKenzie, "The Concept of Dominance and World-Organization," *American Journal of Sociology* 33, no. 1 (1927): 28.

7. N. Brenner and R. Keil, eds., *The Global Cities Reader* (London: Routledge, 2006), 57.

8. Friedmann, "Where We Stand," 317.

9. P. J. Taylor, "Hierarchical Tendencies amongst World Cities: A Global Research Proposal," *Cities* 14, no. 6 (1997): 32.

10. B. Derudder, M. Hoyler, P. Taylor, and F. Witlox, eds., *International Handbook of Globalization and World Cities* (Cheltenham: Edward Elgar, 2012), 2.

11. S. Sassen, foreword to *Relocating Global Cities: From the Center to the Margins*, ed. M. M. Amen, K. Archer, and M. M. Bosman (Lanham, MD: Rowman & Littlefield, 2006), ix.

12. S. Sassen, *Deciphering the Global: Its Scales, Spaces, and Subjects* (London: Routledge, 2007), 122.

13. Sassen, foreword, x.

14. Brenner and Keil, *Global Cities Reader*, 393.

15. R. Keil, "Global City Challenges: A Sympathetic Postscript," in *Global City Challenges*, ed. M. Acuto and W. Steele (London: Palgrave Macmillan, 2013), 232–36.

16. A. Maringanti, "Ordinary Entanglements in the World City," *Environment and Planning A: Economy and Space* 45, no. 10 (2013): 2314–17.

17. Donald McNeill, *Global Cities and Urban Theory* (London: Sage, 2017), 154.

18. Ibid., 138.

19. E. Apter, *The Translation Zone: A New Comparative Literature* (Princeton, NJ: Princeton University Press, 2006).

20. The methodological proxy for "authoritative" in my study, then, is that of citation: not just scholarly referencing but recognition in the pages of media, industry writing, and everyday conversations. This is not just taken as literal citation, as per academic canons, but also extended to the central role of synonyms to capture subtlety in translation.

21. While published near the final submission time for this manuscript, a special issue of *Urban Geography* was useful to direct my editorial and concluding considerations to questions of intra- and inter-elite boundary-spanning and the "urban belonging" of certain elites. See B. Van Heur and D. Bassens, "An Urban Studies Approach to Elites: Nurturing Conceptual Rigor and Methodological Pluralism," *Urban Geography* 40, no. 5 (2019): 591–603.

22. The correlation coefficient comes from the mathematical work of Auguste Bravais and Karl Pearson. See K. Pearson, "Notes on Regression and Inheritance in the Case of Two Parents," *Proceedings of the Royal Society of London*, no. 58 (1895): 240–42. Here I chose to perform a simple (as generally referred to) Pearson correlation assessment rather than a more complex statistical operation like multiple regressions or factor analysis with the explicit goal to simply organize systematically the discussion of the core concepts of the global urban imagination to offer comparative urban considerations as to my three case studies, rather than seeking more generalizable findings on "global cities" more widely as one might be tempted to do in front of the data set produced for this work.

23. This representation borrows logically and graphically from an idea presented by Stefan Zapf and Christopher Kraushaar in 2017 (https://www.oreilly.com/content/a-new-visualization-to-beautifully-explore-correlations) but simplifies it selectively to highlight correlations above 0.3 Pearson coefficient for ease of visualization for those readers not familiar with correlation analysis.

3. THE DEBATES

1. S. Mcinerney, "Guerrilla Dining Concept Goes Mainstream," *Sydney Morning Herald*, 6 July 2012.

2. S. Sassen, "Whose City Is It? Globalization and the Formation of New," *Public Culture*, no. 8 (1996): 205–23.

3. S. Sassen-Koob, "New York City: Economic Restructuring and Immigration," *Development and Change* 17, no. 1 (1986): 85–119; and L. Friedmann and G. Wolff, "World City Formation: An Agenda for Research and Action," *International Journal of Urban and Regional Research* 6, no. 3 (1982): 309–44.

4. D. Bell, *The Coming of Post-industrial Society* (1973; New York: Basic Books, 1978).

5. B. Bluestone and B. Harrison, *The Deindustrialization of America* (New York: Basic Books, 1982).

6. S. Sassen, *Cities in a World Economy: Sociology for a New Century* (Thousand Oaks, CA: Pine Forge Press, 1994), 102.

7. L. Sklair, "The Transnational Capitalist Class and Contemporary Architecture in Globalizing Cities," *International Journal of Urban and Regional Research* 29, no. 3 (2005): 485–500.

8. P. Eisinger, "The Politics of Bread and Circuses: Building the City for the Visitor Class," *Urban Affairs Review* 35, no. 3 (2000): 316–33.

9. J. H. Mollenkopf and M. Castells, eds., *Dual City: Restructuring New York* (New York: Russell Sage Foundation, 1991).

10. Ibid., 11.

11. See, for example, E. T. Van Kempen, "The Dual City and the Poor: Social Polarization, Social Segregation and Life Chances," *Urban Studies* 31, no. 7 (1994): 995–1015; S. Body-Gendrot, "Paris: A 'Soft' Global City?," *Journal of Ethnic and Migration Studies* 22, no. 4 (1996): 595–605.

12. P. Marcuse, "'Dual City': A Muddy Metaphor for a Quartered City," *International Journal of Urban and Regional Research* 13, no. 4 (1989): 697–708. Chris Hamnett, in particular, offered several rebuttals to Sassen's contention, rejecting to varying degrees the bifurcation of class structures as a too narrow perspective and pointing out how her original work lacked engagement with the effects of unemployment and nonindustrial restructuring. C. Hamnett, "Why Sassen Is Wrong: A Response to Burgers," *Urban Studies* 33, no. 1 (1996): 107–10.

13. M. Price and L. Benton-Short, *Migrants to the Metropolis: The Rise of Immigrant Gateway Cities* (Syracuse, NY: Syracuse University Press, 2008).

14. J. Binnie, J. Holloway, C. Young, and S. Millington, eds., *Cosmopolitan Urbanism* (London: Routledge 2006).

15. B. S. Yeoh, "Cosmopolitanism and Its Exclusions in Singapore," *Urban Studies* 41, no. 12 (2004): 2431–45.

16. R. Sennett, "Cosmopolitanism and the Social Experience of Cities," in *Conceiving Cosmopolitanism*, ed. S. Learmount (Oxford: Oxford University Press, 2002), 42–47.

17. See, for example, the work of Neil Smith on gentrification: N. Smith, *The New Urban Frontier: Gentrification and the Revanchist City* (London: Routledge, 2005).

18. S. Graham and S. Marvin, *Splintering Urbanism: Networked Infrastructures, Technological Mobilities and the Urban Condition* (London: Routledge, 2002). This, of course, applies to those processes of reconfiguration rooted in neoliberal forms of globalization.

19. Ibid., 33.

20. Ibid., 139.

21. As Graham defines them, these are "new or retrofitted transport, telecommunication, power or water infrastructures that are customized precisely to the needs of powerful users and spaces, while bypassing less powerful users and spaces." S. Graham, "Constructing Premium Network Spaces: Reflections on Infrastructure Networks and Contemporary Urban Development," *International Journal of Urban and Regional Research* 24, no. 1 (2000): 185.

22. Graham and Marvin, *Splintering Urbanism*, 349.

23. D. Harvey, "From Managerialism to Entrepreneurialism: The Transformation in Urban Governance in Late Capitalism," *Geografiska Annaler: Series B, Human Geography* 71, no. 1 (1989): 3–17.

24. As argued in Harvey, "From Managerialism to Entrepreneurialism", 8. See also B. S. Yeoh, "The Global Cultural City? Spatial Imagineering and Politics in the (Multi) Cultural Marketplaces of South-east Asia," *Urban Studies* 42, nos. 5–6 (2005): 945–58.

25. J. Lauermann, "Municipal Statecraft: Revisiting the Geographies of the Entrepreneurial City," *Progress in Human Geography* 42, no. 2 (2018): 205–24; and N. A. Phelps and J. T. Miao, "Varieties of Urban Entrepreneurialism," *Dialogues in Human Geography*, 2019, online first at https://doi.org/10.1177/2043820619890438 (to which I have provided a reply as M. Acuto, "Whatever Happened to Urban Governance?," *Dialogues in Human Geography*, 2020, online first at https://doi.org/10.1177%2F2043820620921029).

26. As noted in the useful primer by M. Dodgson and D. Gann, *Innovation: A Very Short Introduction* (Oxford: Oxford University Press, 2018).

27. R. Shearmur, "Are Cities the Font of Innovation? A Critical Review of the Literature on Cities and Innovation," *Cities* 29 (2012): S9–S18.

28. R. Florida, *The Rise of the Creative Class* (New York: Basic Books, 2004); and R. Florida, *Who's Your City?* (Toronto: Vintage Canada, 2010).

29. As advocated in, for instance, R. Florida, "The Flight of the Creative Class: The New Global Competition for Talent," *Liberal Education* 92, no. 3 (2006): 22–29; and R. Florida, "The Economic Geography of Talent," *Annals of the Association of American Geographers* 92, no. 4 (2002): 743–55.

30. R. Florida, *The New Urban Crisis* (New York: Basic Books, 2017). Interestingly the term was already used by a staple scholar of global city thinking, Manuel Castells, thirty years before to underline the systemic crisis urban development has been steeped in since at least the late-1980s, with likely little novelty as to Florida's depiction of deeply divided cities in the 2010s. See M. Castells, "The New Urban Crisis," in *Quality of Urban Life: Social, Psychological, and Physical Conditions,* ed. D. Frick, H. W. Hoefert, H. Legewie, R. Mackensen, and R. K. Silbereisen (Berlin: de Gruyter, 1986), 13–18.

31. Jeremy Kelly, "These Are the Most Innovative Cities in the World," World Economic Forum (blog), 24 May 2019, https://www.weforum.org/agenda/2019/05/these-are-the-most-innovative-cities-in-the-world/.

32. P. Bourdieu, "Social Space and Symbolic Power," *Sociological Theory* 7, no. 1 (1989): 23.

33. Clark, *Global Cities*, 48.

34. BCG has in fact a specifically designed consulting division, the Global Advantage Practice, building on this logic. See, for instance, a reiteration of this language in the recent *Unlocking Cities* (Boston: Boston Consulting Group for Uber, 2017), https://image-src.bcg.com/Images/BCG-unlocking-cities-2017_tcm93-178660.PDF

35. We tackled the theme of city leadership in a study of 202 cities, available in open access as E. Rapoport, M. Acuto, and L. Grcheva, *Leading Cities: A Global Review of City Leadership* (London: University College London Press, 2019).

36. M. Sotarauta, A. Beer, and J. Gibney, "Making Sense of Leadership in Urban and Regional Development," *Regional Studies* 51, no. 2 (2017): 187–93.

37. R. Hambleton and J. Howard, "Place-Based Leadership and Public Service Innovation," *Local Government Studies* 39, no. 1 (2013): 52.

38. T. Bunnell and A. Maringanti, "Practising Urban and Regional Research beyond Metrocentricity," *International Journal of Urban and Regional Research* 34, no. 2 (2010): 415.

39. J. Robinson, "Global and World Cities: A View from off the Map," *International Journal of Urban and Regional Research* 26, no. 3 (2002): 531–54.

40. T. Bunnell, D. Goh, C. K. Lai, and C. P. Pow, "Introduction: Global Urban Frontiers? Asian Cities in Theory, Practice and Imagination," *Urban Studies* 49, no. 13 (2012): 2785–93.

41. M. van Meeteren, B. Derudder, **and** D. Bassens**, "**Can the Straw Man Speak? An Engagement with Postcolonial Critiques of 'Global Cities Research,'" *Dialogues in Human Geography* 6, no. 3 (2016): 247.

42. S. Parnell, "Defining a Global Urban Development Agenda," *World Development* 78, no. 4 (2016): 529–40.

43. We summarize this turn in the report from our 2018–19 *Nature Sustainability* international expert panel on science and the future of cities in M. Acuto, S. Parnell, and K. C. Seto, "Building a Global Urban Science," *Nature Sustainability* 1, no. 1 (2018): 2.

44. Y. K. Heng, "A Global City in an Age of Global Risks: Singapore's Evolving Discourse on Vulnerability," *Contemporary Southeast Asia* 35, no. 3 (2013): 423.

45. T. Bunnell, "Conventionally Partial Critique," *Dialogues in Human Geography* 6, no. 3 (2016): 282–86.

4. THE RISE

1. T. Bunnell, "Inclusiveness in Urban Theory and Urban-Centred International Development Policy," *Journal of Regional and City Planning* 30, no. 2 (2019): 89–101.

2. K. Olds and H. Yeung, "Pathways to Global City Formation: A View from the Developmental City-State of Singapore," *Review of International Political Economy* 11, no. 3 (2004): 492.

3. S. Sassen, *Cities in a World Economy: Sociology for a New Century* (Thousand Oaks, CA: Pine Forge Press, 1994), 85.

4. P. Hall, "Towards a General Urban Theory," in *Cities in Competition: Productive and Sustainable Cities for the 21st Century*, ed. J. Brotchie (London: Longman 1995), 22; J. V. Beaverstock, R. G. Smith, and P. J. Taylor, "A Roster of World Cities," *Cities* 16, no. 6 (1999): 458. On the scarcity of scholarship, see K. Olds, "Sydney Boom, Sydney Bust?," *Urban Policy and Research* 18, no. 3 (2000): 287–89.

5. R. Fagan, "Industrial Change in the Global City: Sydney's New Spaces of Production," in *Sydney: The Emergence of a World City*, ed. J. Connell (Sydney: Oxford University Press, 2000), 144–66.

6. D. Elias, "Tell Melbourne It's Over, We Won," *Sydney Morning Herald*, 31 December 2003.

7. B. Derudder, M. Hoyler, and P. Taylor, "Goodbye Reykjavik: International Banking Centres and the Global Financial Crisis," *Area* 43, no. 2 (2011): 173–82.

8. M. Lennon, "The Revival of Metropolitan Planning," in *The Australian Metropolis: A Planning History*, ed. S. Hamnett and R. Freestone (Crows Nest: Allen & Unwin, 2000), 149–50.

9. F. Stilwell and P. Troy, "Multilevel Governance and Urban Development in Australia," *Urban Studies* 37, nos. 5–6 (2000): 909–30.

10. As summarized in D. McNeill, R. Dowling, and B. Fagan, "Sydney/Global/City: An Exploration," *International Journal of Urban and Regional Research* 29, no. 4 (2005): 935–44. Also see J. Connell, *Sydney: The Emergence of a World City* (New York: Oxford University Press, 2000).

11. S. Fainstein, L. M. Hoffman, and D. Judd, "Making Theoretical Sense of Tourism," in *Cities and Visitors: Regulating People, Markets, and City Space*, ed. S. Fainstein, L. M. Hoffman, and D. Judd (London: Blackwell, 2008): 239–53.

12. City of Sydney, *Chinatown Public Domain Study*, consultation draft (Sydney: City of Sydney Council, 2009), 3.

13. D. McNeill, "Fine Grain, Global City: Jan Gehl, Public Space and Commercial Culture in Central Sydney," *Journal of Urban Design* 16, no. 2 (2011): 178. An observation on the importance of culture is echoed in B. Yeoh, "The Global Cultural City? Spatial Imagineering and Politics in the (Multi)Cultural Marketplaces of South-East Asia," *Urban Studies* 42, nos. 5/6 (2005): 945–58.

14. McNeill, "Fine Grain, Global City," 165–66.

15. City of Sydney Design Advisory Panel, *Terms of Reference* (Sydney: City of Sydney, 2007), 1.

16. S. Bagaeen, "Brand Dubai: The Instant City; or the Instantly Recognizable City," *International Planning Studies* 12, no. 2 (2007): 174.

17. David Hirst, "Dubai, a Sheikdom Happy to Embrace Globalization," *Le Monde Diplomatique*, February 2001.

18. See, for instance, "Emirate Rebrands Itself as a Global Melting Pot," *Financial Times*, 12 July 2005.

19. Derudder, Hoyler, and Taylor, "Goodbye Reykjavik," 175.

20. D. Dudley, "Etihad Airways Pares Back Its Ambitions after Period of Turbulence and Losses," *Forbes*, 2 May 2019.

21. M. Hvidt, "The Dubai Model: An Outline of Key Development-Process Elements in Dubai," *International Journal of Middle East Studies* 41, no. 3 (2009): 397–418.

22. Y. Elsheshtawy, *Dubai: Behind an Urban Spectacle* (London: Routledge, 2009).

5. THE TRAJECTORIES

1. The museum was originally hosted by the Dubai Foundation for the Museum of the Future, which in April 2016 became, at the behest of Sheikh Mohammed bin Rashid, the Dubai Future Foundation, with the museum becoming a part of the broader foundation.

2. This Dubai Future Agenda is available at https://www.dubaifuture.gov.ae/mohammed -bin-rashid-approves-dubai-future-agenda/. At this time, little to no scholarly work is available on this facet of Dubai's governance.

3. As noted by Hala Badri, the then director general at Dubai Culture, at the 2019 We Are Museums Summit in Poland, https://www.eyeofdubai.ae/news/newsdetail.php?newsid =105391.

4. O. Söderström, *Cities in Relations: Trajectories of Urban Development in Hanoi and Ouagadougou* (London: John Wiley & Sons, 2014).

5. D. Massey, *For Space* (London: Sage, 2005), 155.

6. C. Davidson, *Dubai: The Vulnerability of Success* (New York: Columbia University Press, 2008); and K. Ulrichsen, *The United Arab Emirates: Power, Politics and Policy-Making* (London: Taylor & Francis, 2016).

7. M. Herb, "A Nation of Bureaucrats: Political Participation and Economic Diversification in Kuwait and the United Arab Emirates," *International Journal of Middle East Studies* 41, no. 3 (2009): 375–95.

8. Davidson, *Dubai*, 92.

9. A. Kanna, *Dubai: The City as Corporation* (Minneapolis: University of Minnesota Press, 2011).

10. M. Hvidt, "The Dubai Model: An Outline of Key Development-Process Elements in Dubai," *International Journal of Middle East Studies*, 41, no. 3 (2009): 397–418.

11. M. Hvidt, "Public–Private Ties and Their Contribution to Development: The Case of Dubai," *Middle Eastern Studies* 43, no. 4 (2007): 558.

12. M. F. Dulaimi, M. Alhashemi, F. Y. Y. Ling, and M. Kumaraswamy, "The Execution of Public–Private Partnership Projects in the UAE," *Construction Management and Economics* 28, no. 4 (2010): 393–402.

13. Kanna, *Dubai*, 161.

14. Y. Elsheshtawy, "Redrawing Boundaries: Dubai, an Emerging Global City," in *Planning Middle Eastern Cities*, ed. Y. Elsheshtawy (London: Routledge, 2004), 179.

15. On the second Harris plan, see S. J. Ramos, *Dubai Amplified: The Engineering of a Port Geography* (London: Routledge, 2016), 86–91.

16. M. Pacione, "Dubai," *Cities* 22, no. 3 (2005): 260.

17. For a discussion of these, see Y. Elsheshtawy, *Dubai: Behind an Urban Spectacle* (London: Routledge, 2009), 116–21.

18. "Landlords to Be Roped in for Renovating CBDs," *Khaleej Times*, 19 March 2006.

19. Raed Safadi, director of the strategic planning and policy section of the Department of Economic Development, declared, "Every single policy was being reviewed and scrutinised right now. . . . Otherwise we'd be in denial." Angela Giuffrida and Salam Hafez, "Dubai 2015 Strategy under Review," *The National*, 16 March 2009.

20. Lootah was appointed as acting director general of the Dubai Municipality in February 2006 and subsequently promoted to director general of the municipality on 7 January 2009.

21. On Abercrombie's legacy, see P. Hall, "Bringing Abercrombie Back from the Shades: A Look Forward and Back," *Town Planning Review* 66, no. 3 (1995): 227–42.

22. For more on the practice of the majlis, see Hava Lazarus-Yafeh et al., eds., *The Majlis: Interreligious Encounters in Medieval Islam* (Wiesbaden: Harrassowitz, 1999).

23. C. Davidson, *The United Arab Emirates: A Study in Survival* (Boulder, CO: Lynne Rienner 2005), 197–98.

24. As well described in J. Sampler and S. Eigner, *Sand to Silicon: Achieving Rapid Growth Lessons from Dubai* (London: Profile Books, 2003).

25. M. Hvidt, *Governance in Dubai: The Emergence of Political and Economic Ties between the Public and Private Sector* (Copenhagen: Centre for Contemporary Middle East Studies, University of Southern Denmark, 2007), 22.

26. J. Robinson, "Global and World Cities: A View from off the Map," *International Journal of Urban and Regional Research* 26, no. 3 (2002): 531.

27. J. Robinson, "Cities in a World of Cities: The Comparative Gesture," *International Journal of Urban and Regional Research* 35, no. 1 (2011).

28. Topical here is the narration of A. D. King, *Post-imperialism and the Internationalization of London* (London: Routledge, 1990).

29. P. Bourdieu, "Social Space and Symbolic Power," *Sociological Theory* 7, no. 1 (1989): 23.

30. E. Durkheim, *The Division of Labor in Society* (Basingstoke: Macmillan, 1984).

6. THE DISTINCTION

1. The text of the speech is available in C. G. Kwa, *S Rajaratnam on Singapore: From Ideas to Reality* (Singapore: World Scientific, 2006), 227–37.

2. A. J. Toynbee, *Cities on the Move* (Oxford: Oxford University Press, 1970).

3. The quotes are from a keynote address by Deputy Prime Minister of Singapore (2005–2011) Wong Kan Seng at the Singapore Perspectives 2011 Conference, January 17, 2011, https://www.strategygroup.gov.sg/media-centre/speeches/speech-by-dpm-wong-kan-seng-at-the-singapore-perspectives-2011-conference.

4. B. Katz and J. Wagner, *The Rise of Innovation Districts: A New Geography of Innovation in America* (Washington, DC: Brookings Institution, 2014).

5. On the 1970s boom, see M. T. Daly and R. J. Stimson, "Sydney: Australia's Gateway and Financial Capital," in *New Cities of the Pacific Rim*, ed. E. J. Blakely and R. Stimson (Berkeley: University of California at Berkeley, 1992), 1–42.

6. P. Murphy and S. Watson, *Surface City: Sydney at the Millennium* (London: Pluto Press, 1997).

7. P. Spearrit, "Consuming Sydney," in *Talking about Sydney: Population, Community and Culture in Contemporary Sydney*, ed. E. Freestone, B. Randolph, and C. Butler-Bowdon (Sydney: University of New South Wales Press, 2006), 199–212.

8. P. McGuirk, "The Political Construction of the City-Region: Notes from Sydney," *International Journal of Urban and Regional Research* 31, no. 1 (2007): 179–87.

9. P. Christoff and N. Low, "Recent Australian Urban Policy and the Environment: Green or Mean?," in *Consuming Cities*, ed. N. Low (London: Routledge, 2000), 246–49.

10. T. Hundloe and G. McDonald, "Ecologically Sustainable Development and the Better Cities Program," *Australian Journal of Environmental Management* 4, no. 2 (1997): 88–111.

11. P. Dean, "The Construction of Sydney's Global Image," in *Future City*, ed. S. Read, J. Rosemann, and J. van Eldijk (New York: Spon Press, 2005), 52.

12. The plan is available at https://catalogue.nla.gov.au/Record/3795053.

13. City of Sydney Council, *Sustainable Sydney 2030: The Vision* (Sydney: City of Sydney Council, 2008), 7.

14. S. Zukin, "Changing Landscapes of Power: Opulence and the Urge for Authenticity," *International Journal of Urban and Regional Research* 33, no. 2 (2009): 543.

15. *Dubai Dreams*, episode 3, "Alabbar," first aired November 1, 2005, on BBC 2, dir. By Ann Lalic.

16. M. Davis, "Sand, Money and Fear in Dubai," in *Evil Paradises: Dreamworlds of Neoliberalism*, ed. M. Davis and D. Monk (New York: New Press, 2007), 57.

17. On hypermodernity, see G. Lipovetsky and S. Charles, *Hypermodern Times* (London: Polity, 2005).

18. M. A. E. Saleh, "The Changing Image of Arriyadh City: The Role of Socio-cultural and Religious Traditions in Image Transformation," *Cities* 18, no. 5 (2001): 328.

19. S. Zukin, "Cultural Strategies of Economic Development and the Hegemony of a Vision," in *Urbanization of Injustice*, ed. A. Merrifield and E. Swyngedouw (New York: New York University Press, 1997), 223.

20. G. Debord, *The Society of Spectacle*, trans. D. Nicholson-Smith (New York: Zone Books, 1994).

21. D. Sudjic, "Height of Madness," *Guardian*, 15 March 1996.

22. The "Bilbao effect" has since become a shorthand for when iconic urban developments contribute to uplifting the fortunes of a city within which they are placed. See W. Rybczynski, "The Bilbao Effect," *Atlantic Monthly* 290, no. 2 (September 2002): 138–42.

23. See, for instance, M. Hvidt, "The Dubai Model: An Outline of Key Development-Process Elements in Dubai," *International Journal of Middle East Studies* 41, no. 3 (2009): 418.

24. *Dubai Dreams*, "Alabbar."

25. A. D. King, "Worlds in the City: From Wonders of Modern Design to Weapons of Mass Destruction," in *Spaces of Global Cultures*, ed. A. D. King (London: Routledge, 2004), 3; and D. McNeill, "Skyscraper Geography," *Progress in Human Geography* 29, no. 1 (2005): 43.

26. Author's notes from the Media e-Session with Prime Minister al Maktoum, ruler of Dubai, 18 April 2009.

27. The firm itself, along with the developer (Emaar), has repeatedly stretched the comparison. Curiously, Wright's project was never seen as financially viable.

28. As indicated by Emaar chairman Mohammed Alabbar at the Council on Tall Buildings and Urban Habitat earlier last year. Cf. "Burj Dubai Offices to Top US$4,000 per Sq Ft," *Zawya*, 5 March 2008.

29. See, for example, the special issue "Burj Dubai" in *Arabian Business* 4–9 January 2010.

30. T. Bunnell, "Views from Above and Below: The Petronas Twin Towers and/in Contesting Visions of Development in Contemporary Malaysia," *Singapore Journal of Tropical Geography* 20, no. 1 (1999): 1.

31. Ibid., 4.

32. A. L. Huxtable, "The Tall Building Artistically Reconsidered: The Search for a Skyscraper Style," *Architectural Record* 172, no. 1 (1984): 11.

33. Bunnell, "Views from Above and Below," 18.

34. L. Sklair, "Iconic Architecture and Capitalist Globalization," *City* 10, no. 1 (2006): 21.

35. The expression is from B. Latour, "Where Are the Missing Masses? The Sociology of a Few Mundane Artifacts," in *Shaping Technology / Building Society*, ed. W. Bijker and J. Law (Cambridge: MIT Press, 1992), 225–58.

36. Interview with Sheik Mohammed bin Rashid al Maktoum in the CBS documentary *Dubai Inc.*, first aired in the program *60 Minutes*, 14 October 2007.

37. D. Sudjic, *The Edifice Complex: How the Rich and Powerful (and Their Architects) Shape the World* (London: Penguin, 2006), 317.

7. THE LEADERSHIP

1. "World's Tallest Building Opens in Dubai," *BBC Online News*, 4 January 2010.

2. M. Sotoudehnia and R. Rose-Redwood, "'I Am Burj Khalifa': Entrepreneurial Urbanism, Toponymic Commodification and the Worlding of Dubai," *International Journal of Urban and Regional Research* 43, no. 6 (2019): 5.

3. See, among others, G. Wearden, "Dubai Receives a $10bn Bailout from Abu Dhabi," *Guardian*, 14 December 2009.

4. With necessary apologies for the gendered nature of this Anglophone expression and the further empowering of male leaders, who sadly, as E. Rapoport, L. Grcheva, and I showed in *Leading Cities: A Global Review of City Leadership* (London: University College London Press, 2019), still account for more than 85 percent of city leaders internationally.

5. See J. D. Sidaway, "Globalising the Geohistory of City/State Relations: On 'Problematizing City/State Relations: Towards a Geohistorical Understanding of Contemporary Globalization' by Peter J. Taylor," *Transactions of the Institute of British Geographers* 33, no. 1 (2008): 150.

6. C. Davidson, *Dubai: The Vulnerability of Success* (New York: Columbia University Press, 2008), 158.

7. A. Kanna, *Dubai: The City as Corporation* (Minneapolis: University of Minnesota Press, 2011), 141–43.

8. B. Jessop, "Entrepreneurial City," in *The Wiley-Blackwell Encyclopedia of Urban and Regional Studies*, ed. A. M. Orum, M. García, D. R. Judd, C. P. Pow, and B. R. Roberts (Oxford: Wiley Blackwell 2019), 28–41.

9. B. Jessop and N. L. Sum, "An Entrepreneurial City in Action: Hong Kong's Emerging Strategies in and for (Inter) urban Competition," *Urban Studies* 37, no. 12 (2000): 2289.

10. M.b.R. al Maktoum, *My Vision: Challenges in the Race for Excellence* (Dubai: Motivate Publishing, 2006).

11. R. Florida, *Cities and the Rise of the Creative Class* (London: Routledge, 2005), 67–85.

12. Interview with City of Sydney planning officer, Sydney, 8 July 2009.

13. In this case the expression is used by Florida in *Cities and the Rise of the Creative Class*, 283.

14. J. Peck, "Struggling with the Creative Class," *International Journal of Urban and Regional Research* 29, no. 4 (2005): 767.

15. Glaeser often underscores the returns of geographic proximity as "human beings get smart by hanging around other smart people." E. L. Glaeser, "Cities Do It Better," *New York Times*, 27 April 2010. Also see E. Glaeser, ed., *Agglomeration Economics* (Chicago: University of Chicago Press, 2010).

16. The importance of cities for the flows of information and ideas is of course not a novelty: ever since the pioneering nineteenth-century work of English economist Alfred Marshall, these considerations have progressively occupied center stage in economic analysis. See E. V. Knight and G. Gappert, eds., *Cities in a Global Society* (London: Sage, 1989).

17. D. Sudjic, *The Edifice Complex: How the Rich and Powerful (and Their Architects) Shape the World* (London: Penguin 2006), 376.

18. P. Hall and M. Tewdwr-Jones, *Urban and Regional Planning* (London: Routledge, 2019), 251.

19. R. D. Putnam, "Diplomacy and Domestic Politics: The Logic of Two-Level Fames," *International Organization* 42, no. 3 (1988): 427–60.

20. K. P. Tan, *Governing Global-City Singapore: Legacies and Futures after Lee Kuan Yew* (London: Taylor & Francis, 2016).

21. P. Bourdieu, "Authorized Language: The Social Conditions for the Effectiveness of Ritual Discourse," in *Language and Symbolic Power*, ed. P. Bourdieu (1975; Cambridge, MA: Harvard University Press, 1991), 110.

8. THE GOVERNANCE

1. S. Gerathy, "Former Lord Mayor Lucy Turnbull Appointed to Head Greater Sydney Commission," ABC News Sydney, December 3, 2015, https://www.abc.net.au/news/2015-12-03/lucy-turnbull-appointed-to-head-up-greater-sydney-commission/6998596.

2. D. Cornwall, "Gladys Berejiklian Usurps Lucy Turnbull's Planning Powers," *Australian* (Melbourne), 19 July 2018.

3. M. Bleby, "Lucy Turnbull-led Greater Sydney Commission Gets Direct Line to Premier," *Financial Review*, 26 July 2018.

4. New South Wales Premier press release, "New Focus for the Greater Sydney Commission," Sydney, NSW, June 26, 2018, https://www.nsw.gov.au/media-releases/new-focus-for-greater-sydney-commission.

5. M. Painter, "Reshaping the Public Sector," in *New Developments in Australian Politics*, ed. B. Galligan, I. McAllister, and J. Ravenhill (Melbourne: Macmillan, 1997), 148.

6. D. McNeill, R. Dowling, and B. Fagan, "Sydney/Global/City: An Exploration," *International Journal of Urban and Regional Research* 29, no. 4 (2005): 942.

7. G. Searle and M. Bounds, "State Powers, State Land and Competition for Global Entertainment: The Case of Sydney," *International Journal of Urban and Regional Research* 23, no. 1 (1999): 165–72.

8. J. Allison and J. Keane, "Positioning Planning in the New Economic Landscape," in *Renewing Australian Planning?*, ed. B. Gleeson and P. Hanley (Canberra: Urban Research Program, RSSS, Australian National University, 1998), 23–44.

9. See J. Hillier and S. Searle, "Rien Ne Va Plus: Fast Track Development and Public Participation in Pyrmont-Ultimo, Sydney," in *Sydney Vision: UTS Papers in Planning* (Sydney: Planning Program, Faculty of Design, Architecture and Building, University of Technology Sydney, 1995).

10. P. McGuirk, "State, Strategy and Scale in the Competitive City: A Neo-Gramscian Analysis of the Governance of Global Sydney," *Environment and Planning A* 36, no. 2 (2004): 1020.

11. C. Aulich, "Australia: Still a Tale of Cinderella?," in *Comparing Local Governance: Trends and Developments*, ed. B. Denters and L. Rose (Basingstoke: Palgrave, 2005), 194.

12. McGuirk, "State, Strategy and Scale in the Competitive City," 1026.

13. As opposed to, for instance, the broad national involvement in the industrial "long boom" of the 1950s and 1960s.

14. P. McGuirk, "Producing the Capacity to Govern in Global Sydney: A Multiscaled Account," *Journal of Urban Affairs* 25, no. 2 (2003): 219.

15. NSW Planning, *City of Cities: A Plan for Sydney's Future* (Sydney: New South Wales Department of Planning, 2005), 6.

16. L. Visentin, "Premier Consolidates Control over Big-Picture Vision of Sydney," *Sydney Morning Herald*, 25 June 2018.

17. J. Tovey, "Booming City Needs Another Heart," *Sydney Morning Herald*, 21 July 2010; B. Fagan and R. Dowling, "Neoliberalism and Suburban Employment: Western Sydney in the 1990s," *Geographical Research* 43, no. 1 (2005): 76.

18. R. Bunker and G. Searle, "Seeking Certainty: Recent Planning for Sydney and Melbourne," *Town Planning Review* 78, no. 5 (2007): 633.

19. G. Searle, "Is the City of Cities Metropolitan Strategy the Answer for Sydney?," *Urban Policy and Research* 24, no. 4 (2006): 553.

20. As noted in R. Bunker, D. Holloway, and B. Randolph, "The Expansion of Urban Consolidation in Sydney: Social Impacts and Implications," *Australian Planner* 42, no.3 (2005): 16–25.

21. P. McGuirk, "Neoliberalist Planning? Re-thinking and Re-casting Sydney's Metropolitan Planning," *Geographical Research* 43, no. 1 (2005): 64.

22. As in the case of the Australian federal government's *State of Australian Cities 2010* report's reliance on global city rankings as key indicators for the study carried out by the Major Cities Unit of Infrastructure Australia.

23. Interview with NSW director of metropolitan and regional strategies, 26 February 2011.

24. P. McGuirk, "The Political Construction of the City-Region: Notes from Sydney," *International Journal of Urban and Regional Research* 31, no. 1 (2007): 184.

25. P. McGuirk, "Producing the Capacity to Govern in Global Sydney," 206.

26. P. Dean, "Sydney, a City Gone Global," *Archis* 8, no. 176 (2000): 1–11.

27. The expression is from J. Punter, "Urban Design in Central Sydney, 1945–2002: Laissez-Faire and Discretionary Traditions in the Accidental City," *Progress in Planning* 63, no. 1 (2005): 11–160.

28. City of Sydney Act of 1988. The boundaries of the City of Sydney were changed several times throughout the 1900s, and the current zoning was reestablished only in 2004 with the merger of South Sydney in the City of Sydney Council.

29. Committee for Sydney, *Sydney 2020* (Sydney: PricewaterhouseCoopers, 1998), 21–22.

30. Committee for Sydney, *Global Sydney: Challenges and Opportunities for a Competitive Global City* (Sydney: SGS Economics and Planning Pti, 2009), 43.

31. City of Sydney, *Annual Review 2007/08*, (Sydney: City of Sydney Council), p.11 (emphasis added).

32. "Campaign against Yellow Culture Is Launched," History SG, http://eresources .nlb.gov.sg/history/events/47129576-377a-44fe-a05f-fefddf0cb765 (accessed 26 March 26, 2021).

33. D. K. Emmerson, "Singapore and the Asian Values Debate," *Journal of Democracy* 6, no. 4 (1995): 95–105.

34. Lee Hsien Loong, "National Day Rally 2004," speech, 22 August 2004, https://www .pmo.gov.sg/newsroom/prime-minister-lee-hsien-loongs-national-day-rally-2004 -english.

35. Quoted in G. Rodan, "Singapore in 2005: 'Vibrant and Cosmopolitan' without Political Pluralism," *Asian Survey* 46, no. 1 (2006): 180–86.

36. Y. K. Heng, *Managing Global Risks in the Urban Age: Singapore and the Making of a Global City* (London: Routledge, 2016), 45.

37. A., Thornley, Y. Rydin, K. Scanlon, K. West, "Business Privilege and the Strategic Planning Agenda of the Greater London Authority," *Urban Studies* 42, no. 11 (2005.): 1947–68.

38. P. Bourdieu and J. C. Passeron, *Reproduction in Education, Society and Culture* (1977; London: Sage, 1990).

39. D. L. Swartz, "Drawing Inspiration from Bourdieu's Sociology of Symbolic Power," *Theory and Society* 32, nos. 5–6 (2003): 519–28.

9. THE STRATEGIES

1. S. R. Clegg, C. Carter, M. Kornberger, and J. Schweitzer, *Strategy: Theory and Practice* (London: Sage, 2011).

2. C. McFarlane, "The Comparative City: Knowledge, Learning, Urbanism," *International Journal of Urban and Regional Research* 34, no. 4 (2010): 725.

3. Ibid., 726.

4. P. Dean, "Sydney, a City Gone Global," *Archis* 8, no. 176 (2000): 8.

5. See, among others, M. Bounds and A. Morris, "Second Wave Gentrification in Inner-City Sydney," *Cities* 23, no. 2 (2006): 99–108.

6. Interview with Dubai government officer, Abu Dhabi, 30 November 2010.

7. B. Pritchard and G. Searle, "Planning for Creativity and Innovation in a Global City: Sydney's Information Technology Clusters in the Context of the 2005 Metropolitan Strategy," *International Journal of Foresight and Innovation Policy* 5, nos.1–3 (2009): 205–13.

8. City of Sydney, *Positioning Sydney as the Clever City* (Sydney: Council of the City of Sydney, 1999), 11–12. As also noted in P. McGuirk, "State, Strategy and Scale in the Competitive City: A Neo-Gramscian Analysis of the Governance of Global Sydney," *Environment and Planning A* 36, no. 2 (2004): 1030.

9. This was noted already in P. Murphy and C. T. Wu, "The Case of Sydney," in *Globalization and the Sustainability of Cities in the Asia Pacific Region*, ed. F. C. Lo and P. Marcotullio (Tokyo: United Nations University Press, 2001), 399–427.

10. T. Reisz, "Making Dubai: A Process in Crisis," *Architectural Design* 80, no. 5 (2010): 43.

11. Dubai Plan 2021, https://u.ae/en/about-the-uae/strategies-initiatives-and-awards /local-governments-strategies-and-plans/dubai-plan-2021 last accessed 26 March 2021.

12. Marcuse, "Globalization and the Form of Cities," in M. Jenks, D. Kozak, and P. Takkanon, eds., *World Cities and Urban Form: Fragmented, Polycentric, Sustainable?* (London, Routledge, 2013), 26.

13. Ibid., 33.

14. City of Sydney Council, *Review of International Strategies*, Sydney, NSW: City of Sydney Council, May 2007), 4.

15. A. Ferguson, "Melbourne Judged World's Most Liveable City," *Sydney Morning Herald*, 30 August 2011.

16. Committee for Sydney, *Global Sydney: Challenges and Opportunities for a Competitive Global City* (Sydney: SGS Economics and Planning Pti, 2009), 2–3.

17. See, for instance, T. Brody, "False Creek, Dubai," *BCBusiness Online*, 1 September 2006.

18. A. Kumar, "Dubai Rents Looking Up," *Gulf News*, 3 March 2012.

19. For a summary of the tower's building history and the substantial problems the project encountered after a structural failure and subsequent flooding of the site in February 2007, see C. McElroy, "The Twisting Tale of Infinity," *Construction Week Online*, 12 April 2012. On the analogous Canadian project, see "Dubai-Style Tower Planned for Vancouver," *Construction Week Online*, 15 April 2012.

20. For a review of habitus as sense of "one's place" see J. Hillier and E. Rooksby, eds., *Habitus: A Sense of Place,* 2nd ed.(London: Routledge, 2017).

10. THE CITYZENS

1. L. Khong (@LawrenceKhong), "Taking a #selfie with more than 6000 members in just one service, all #wearwhite to defend marriage," Twitter, June 29, 2014, 10:45 p.m. (https://twitter.com/fcbcsg/status/483214770355449856?lang=en).

2. D. Ley, "Transnational Spaces of Everyday Lives," *Transactions of the Institute of British Geographers* 29, no. 2 (2004): 151.

3. See ABC Fact Check, "Without a Home," Australian Broadcasting Corporation, https://www.abc.net.au/interactives/homeless/ last accessed 26 March 2021.

4. See more information at https://everybodyshome.com.au

5. Committee for Sydney, *The Golden Egg* (Sydney, NSW: The Committee for Sydney, 2001).

6. D. Massey, *World City* (London: Polity 2007), 97–113.

7. D. Jopson, "The Savvy Sliver of Sydney That Puts It among the World's Heavyweights," *Sydney Morning Herald*, 4 March 2002.

8. Compare S. Baum, "Sydney, Australia: A Global City? Testing the Social Polarisation Thesis," *Urban Studies* 34, no. 11 (1997): 1881, with S. Baum, "Suburban Scars: Australian Cities and Socioeconomic Deprivation," in *Urban Research Program Research Paper* (Brisbane: Griffith University & URP, 2008), 16. A trend similar to that of Hong Kong is illustrated in R. Forrest, A. La Grange, and N. M. Yip, "Hong Kong as a Global City? Social Distance and Spatial Differentiation," *Urban Studies* 41, no. 1 (2004): 20727.

9. Baum, "Suburban Scars," 10.

10. T. Bunnell and A. Maringanti, "Practising Urban and Regional Research beyond Metrocentricity," *International Journal of Urban and Regional Research* 34, no. 2 (2010): 415.

11. J. Go, *Postcolonial Thought and Social Theory* (Oxford: Oxford University Press, 2016).

12. T. Bunnell, "Conventionally Partial Critique," *Dialogues in Human Geography* 6, no. 3 (2016): 282.

13. R. Keil, *Suburban Planet: Making the World Urban from the Outside In* (London: Wiley & Sons, 2017).

14. G. Hugo, *Sydney: The Globalization of an Established Immigrant Gateway* (Syracuse, NY: Syracuse University Press, 2008), 94–95; and E. Healy and B. Birrell, "Metropolis Divided: The Dynamic of Spatial Inequality and Migrant Settlement in Sydney," *People and Place* 11, no. 2 (2003): 65–85.

15. The term is from P. Marcuse, "Dual City: A Muddy Metaphor for a Quartered City," *International Journal of Urban and Regional Research* 13, no. 4 (1989): 697.

16. R. Bunker, D. Holloway, and B. Randolph, "The Expansion of Urban Consolidation in Sydney: Social Impacts and Implications," *Australian Planner* 42, no. 3 (2005): 53.

17. J. Dodson and N. Sipe, "Unsettling Suburbia: The New Landscape of Oil and Mortgage Vulnerability in Australian Cities," in *URP Research Paper* (Brisbane: Griffith University Urban Research Program, 2008), 30.

18. See D. Pumain, "Alternative Explanations of Hierarchical Differentiation in Urban System," in *Hierarchy in Natural and Social Sciences*, ed. D. Pumain (The Hague: Springer, 2006), 169–222.

19. J. Parsons, "Sydney: We Need to Talk about Our Postcode Prejudice," *Guardian*, 23 August 2016.

20. S. Graham, "The Spectre of the Splintering Metropolis," *Cities* 18, no. 6 (2001): 365.

21. Respectively in Y. Elsheshtawy, "Transitory Sites: Mapping Dubai's Forgotten Urban Space," *International Journal of Urban and Regional Research* 32, no. 4 (2008): 968; and M. Davis, "Fear and Money in Dubai," *New Left Review* 41 (2006): 60.

22. For an analysis of the Chinatown phenomenon, see K. Anderson, "The Idea of Chinatown: The Power of Place and Institutional Practice in the Making of a Racial Category," *Annals of the Association of American Geographers* 77, no. 4 (1987): 580–98.

23. D. Westley, "Is Dubai Still Good Value?," *Gulf News*, 13 March 2006.

24. The expression is from Graham, "Spectre of the Splintering Metropolis," 368.

25. P. Bourdieu, "Symbolic Power," *Critique of Anthropology* 4, nos. 13–14 (1979): 80.

26. L. Wacquant, "Pointers on Pierre Bourdieu and Democratic Politics," *Constellations* 11, no. 1 (2004): 3–15.

27. P. Eisinger, "The Politics of Bread and Circuses: Building the City for the Visitor Class," *Urban Affairs Review* 35, no. 3 (2000): 316–33.

28. D. L. Swartz, *Symbolic Power, Politics, and Intellectuals: The Political Sociology of Pierre Bourdieu* (Chicago: University of Chicago Press, 2013), 83.

29. P. Bourdieu, *The Logic of Practice*, (Stanford, CA: Stanford University Press, 1990), 133.

30. Quoted in R. Lipschutz, "Reconstructing World Politics: The Emergence of a Global Civil Society," *Millennium* 21, no. 3 (1992): 396.

31. D. Harvey, *Justice, Nature and the Geography of Difference* (Oxford: Blackwell, 1996), 309. Also see D. Massey, "Power-Geometry and a Progressive Sense of Place," in *Mapping the Futures*, ed. J. Bird (London: Routledge, 1993), 67.

32. Massey, *World City*, 215.

33. Z. Bauman, *Community: Seeking Safety in an Insecure World* (Cambridge: Polity, 2001), 57.

34. G. P. Zachary, *The Global Me* (New York: Public Affairs, 2000).

35. R. J. Shiller, "The New Cosmopolitans," *Project Syndicate*, 15 December 2006.

36. Ibid.

37. W. Vrasti and S. Dayal, "Cityzenship: Rightful Presence and the Urban Commons," *Citizenship Studies* 20, no. 8 (2016): 994–1011.

38. R. Baubock, "Reinventing Urban Citizenship," *Citizenship Studies* 7, no. 2 (2003): 139–60.

39. T. Blokland, C. Hentschel, A. Holm, H. Lebuhn, and T. Margalit, "Urban Citizenship and Right to the City: The Fragmentation of Claims," *International Journal of Urban and Regional Research* 39, no. 4 (2015): 655–65.

40. S. Ali, *Dubai: Gilded Cage* (New Haven, CT: Yale University Press, 2010), 64.

41. See *As If I Am Not Human: Abuses against Asian Domestic Workers in Saudi Arabia* (New York: Human Rights Watch, 2008).

42. *Building Towers, Cheating Workers* (New York: Human Rights Watch, 2006).

43. R. Kasolowsky, "NASDAQ OMX to List in Dubai, DIFX Rebrands," *Reuters*, 18 November 2008.

44. T. P. Caldeira and J. Holston, "Democracy and Violence in Brazil," *Comparative Studies in Society and History* 41, no. 4 (1999): 691–729.

45. S. Sassen, "Locating Cities on Global Circuits," *Environment and Urbanization* 14, no. 1 (2002): 13–30.

11. THE COMPARISONS

1. L. Kong, "Ambitions of a Global City: Arts, Culture and Creative Economy in 'Post-Crisis' Singapore," *International Journal of Cultural Policy* 18, no. 3 (2012): 279–94.

2. As per the national *Research, Innovation and Enterprise Plan 2020* (RIE2020), subtitled "winning the future through science and technology," issued by the Ministry of Trade and Industry (MTI), https://www.mti.gov.sg/-/media/MTI/Resources/Publications/Research-Innovation-and-Enterprise-RIE-2020/RIE2020.pdf (accessed March 29, 2021).

3. M. H., Lee and S. Gopinathan, "University Restructuring in Singapore: Amazing or a Maze?," *Policy Futures in Education* 6, no. 5 (2008): 569–88.

4. J. Tan, "Singapore: Small Nation Big Plans," in *Asian Universities: Historical Perspectives and Contemporary Challenges,* ed. P. G. Altbach and T. Umakoshi (Baltimore: Johns Hopkins University Press 2004).

5. K. Olds, "Global Assemblage: Singapore, Western Universities, and the Construction of a Global Education Hub," *World Development* 36, no.6 (2007): 959–75; R. Sidhu, K. C. Ho, and B. Yeoh, "Emerging Education Hubs: The Case of Singapore," *Higher Education* 61, no.1 (2011): 23–40.

6. Speech by Prime Minister Lee Hsien Loong at the opening of Campus for Research Excellence and Technological Enterprise (CREATE), November 16, 2012, https://www.pmo.gov.sg/Newsroom/speech-prime-minister-lee-hsien-loong-opening-campus-research-excellence-and.

7. See the intervention forum on this theme in the January 2021 issue of *IJURR* for more on this: M. Acuto, D. Pejic, and J. Briggs, "Taking City Rankings Seriously: Engaging with Benchmarking Practices in Global Urbanism," *International Journal of Urban and Regional Research* 45, no. 2 (2021): 363–77.

8. M. Acuto, D. Pejic, J. Nunley, and T. Moonen, "Why City Rankings Matter," *Scientific American*, July 2, 2019.

9. P. J. Taylor, G. Catalano, and D. R. Walker, "Measurement of the World City Network," *Urban Studies* 39, no. 13 (2002): 2367–76.

10. A good summary of this rationale is found in P. Taylor, "The Interlocking Network Model," in *International Handbook of Globalization and World Cities*, ed. B. Derudder. M. Hoyler, P.J. Taylor and F. Witlox (Cheltenham: Edward Elgar, 2011), 51–63.

11. J. V. Beaverstock, R. G. Smith, and P. J. Taylor, "A Roster of World Cities," *Cities* 16, no. 6 (1999): 445–58.

12. B. Derudder and C. Parnreiter, "Introduction: The Interlocking Network Model for Studying Urban Networks: Outline, Potential, Critiques, and Ways Forward," *Tijdschrift voor economische en sociale geografie* 105, no. 4 (2014): 373–86.

13. The expression is from an interview with a junior planning officer in the City of Sydney, Sydney, 9 July 2010.

14. New South Wales Department of Planning (NSW Planning), *City of Cities: A Plan for Sydney's Future* (Sydney: New South Wales Department of Planning, 2005), 27.

15. New South Wales Planning, *Metropolitan Plan for Sydney 2036* (Sydney: New South Wales Government, 2010), p. 47, https://catalogue.nla.gov.au/Record/5159032.

16. New South Wales Government, *Sydney over the Next 20 Years: A Discussion Paper* (Sydney: NSW Department of Planning and Infrastructure, 2012), p. 11, https://catalogue.nla.gov.au/Record/5980840.

17. We highlight this more in depth in M. Acuto and D. Pejic, "Shaping a Global Comparative Imagination? Assessing the Role of City Rankings in the 'Global City' Discourse," *Area* (2021), https://rgs-ibg.onlinelibrary.wiley.com/doi/10.1111/area.12710.

18. P. Bourdieu, *The Logic of Practice* (Stanford, CA: Stanford University Press 1990), 127–28.

19. P. J. Taylor and B. Derudder, *World City Network: A Global Urban Analysis* (London: Routledge, 2015), 33.

20. Taylor, "Interlocking Network Model," 63. Taylor has often pointed to J. Jacobs, *The Economy of Cities* (New York: Vintage, 1969) as key inspiration for this understanding.

21. P. M. McGuirk, "State, Strategy, and Scale in the Competitive City: A Neo-Gramscian Analysis of the Governance of 'Global Sydney,'" *Environment and Planning A* 36, no. 6 (2004): 1019.

22. D. McNeill, R. Dowling, and B. Fagan, "Sydney/Global/City: An Exploration," *International Journal of Urban and Regional Research* 29, no. 4 (2005): 937.

23. Mike Bloomberg (@MikeBloomberg), "If you can't measure it, you can't manage it and you can't fix it," Twitter, 21 January 2014, 9:15 p.m., http://bit.ly/1f43OrV cc: @BloombergDotOrg #philanthropy.

24. For instance: A. M. Townsend, *Smart Cities: Big Data, Civic Hackers, and the Quest for a New Utopia* (New York: W. W. Norton, 2013); and L. Bettencourt and G. West, "A Unified Theory of Urban Living," *Nature* 467, no. 7318 (2010): 912.

25. R. Kitchin, *The Data Revolution: Big Data, Open Data, Data Infrastructures and Their Consequences* (London: Sage, 2014).

26. NSW Planning, *City of Cities*, 26–27.

27. P. Dean, "The Construction of Sydney's Global Image," in *Future City*, ed. S. Read, J. Rosemann, and J. van Eldijk (New York: Spon Press, 2005), 48.

28. J. Punter, "Urban Design in Central Sydney, 1945–2002: Laissez-Faire and Discretionary Traditions in the Accidental City," *Progress in Planning* 63, no. 1 (2005): 11.

29. City of Sydney Council, "Sustainable Sydney 2030: One Year On," media release, 12 August 2009.

30. Property Council of Australia, *Initiatives for Sydney* (Sydney: Property Council of Australia, 2002).

12. SYMBOLIC ENTREPRENEURS

1. D. Bell and A. De-Shalit, *The Spirit of Cities: Why the Identity of a City Matters in a Global Age* (Princeton, NJ: Princeton University Press, 2013).

2. L. A. Eng, "The Kopitiam in Singapore: An Evolving Story," in *Migration and Diversity in Asian Contexts*, ed. A. E. Lai, F. L. Collins and B. S. Yeoh (Singapore: Institute of Southeast Asian Studies, 2013), 228.

3. The expression comes from the global recruitment circuit and discussions of innovation, where companies such as McKinsey and IDEO have popularized the search for individuals with a breadth of interdisciplinary engagement coexisting with a depth of particular expertise.

4. "NTUC Enterprise to Buy Kopitiam by Year-End," *Channel NewsAsia*, 17 October 2018.

5. P. Knox, "Starchitects, Starchitecture and the Symbolic Capital of World Cities," *International Handbook of Globalization and World Cities*, ed. B. Derudder, M. Hoyler, P. J. Taylor, and F. Witlox (Cheltenham, UK: Edward Elgar); D. Ponzin, and M. Nastasi, *Starchitecture: Scenes, Actors and Spectacles in Contemporary Cities* (Milan: Monacelli Press, 2016); D. McNeill, *The Global Architect: Firms, Fame and Urban Form* (London: Routledge, 2009).

6. Despite the partly "green" and "environmentalist" planning for the building, the tower allows parking for more than 2,400 cars.

7. L. Sklair, "Iconic Architecture and Capitalist Globalization," *City* 10, no. 1 (2006): 21.

8. P. M. O'Neill and P. McGuirk, "Reconfiguring the CBD: Work and Discourses of Design in Sydney's Office Space," *Urban Studies* 40, no. 9 (2003): 1764.

9. D. McNeill, "Fine Grain, Global City: Jan Gehl, Public Space and Commercial Culture in Central Sydney," *Journal of Urban Design* 16, no. 2 (2011): 166.

10. Interview with former City of Sydney senior officer, London, 10 December 2010.

11. D. McNeill, "Office Buildings and the Signature Architect: Piano and Foster in Sydney," *Environment and Planning A*, 39, no. 2 (2007): 487.

12. K. Olds and D. Edginton, "Globalization and Urban Change: Capital, Culture and Pacific Rim Mega-projects," *Canadian Journal of Urban Research* 10, no. 2 (2001): 330.

13. E. Rapoport, "Globalising Sustainable Urbanism: The Role of International Masterplanners," *Area* 47, no. 2 (2015): 110–15.

14. J. Rykwert, *The Seduction of Place: The History and Future of the City* (New York: Oxford University Press, 2004).

15. A. Bryman, "The Disneyization of Society," *Sociological Review* 47, no. 1 (1999): 25–47.

16. M. Acuto, D. Pejic, and J. Briggs, "Taking City Rankings Seriously: Engaging with Benchmarking Practices in Global Urbanism," *International Journal of Urban and Regional Research* 45, no. 2 (2021): 363–77.

17. City of Sydney Council, *Sustainable Sydney 2030: The Vision* (Sydney, NSW: City of Sydney Council, 2008), 179.

18. See, for instance, City of Sydney Council, *Affordable Housing Research Paper*, September 2008, 1115.

19. William McKell Institute, *Homes for All* (Sydney: McKell Institute, 2012).

20. Committee for Sydney, *Global Sydney: Challenges and Opportunities for a Competitive Global City* (Sydney: SGS Economics and Planning Pti, 2009), 20.

21. T. J. Misa, "Appropriating the International Style," in *Urban Machinery*, ed. M. Hård and T. J. Misa (Cambridge, MA: MIT Press 2008), 77–98.

22. P. Rimmer, "The Global Intelligence Corps and World Cities: Engineering Consultancies on the Move," in *Services and Metropolitan Development: International Perspectives*, ed. E. Daniels (London: Routledge, 1991).

23. C. McKenna, *The World's Newest Profession* (Cambridge: Cambridge University Press, 2006).

24. M. Law, "Managing Consultants," *Business Strategy Review*, no. 20 (2006): 62–66.

25. M. Kipping and L. Engwall, *Management Consulting: Emergence and Dynamics of a Knowledge Industry* (Oxford: Oxford University Press, 2002).

26. Critically, once again, this story can also be told very effectively (and necessarily) from a multitude of other points of view beyond these developmental elites. See, for instance, great work on this in E. Robin and L. Nkula-Wenz, " Beyond the Success/Failure of Travelling Urban Models: Exploring the Politics of Time and Performance in Cape Town's East City," *Environment and Planning C: Politics and Space* (2020), https://doi .org/10.1177%2F2399654420970963.

27. A useful summary can be found in N. Dunn, "Urban Imaginaries and the Palimpsest of the Future," in *The Routledge Companion to Urban Imaginaries,* ed. C. Lindner and M. Meissner (London: Routledge, 2018), 375–86.

28. D. W. Drezner, *The Ideas Industry* (New York: Oxford University Press, 2017).

29. T. Nichols, *The Death of Expertise: The Campaign against Established Knowledge and Why It Matters* (Oxford: Oxford University Press, 2017).

30. P. Bourdieu, "Social Space and Symbolic Power," *Sociological Theory* 7, no. 1 (1989): 23.

31. I. Kaminska, "The Entire Economy Is Fyre Festival," *Financial Times*, 21 February 2019.

32. D. Graeber, *Bullshit Jobs: A Theory* (London: Allen Lane, 2018).

33. Bourdieu, "Social Space and Symbolic Power," 23.

34. E. Pellegrin-Boucher, "Symbolic Functions of Consultants," *Journal of General Management* 32, no. 1 (2006): 1–16.

35. I draw this typology from A. Canato and A. Giangreco, "Gurus or Wizards? A Review of the Role of Management Consultants," *European Management Review* 8, no. 4 (2011): 231–44.

36. D. McNeill, "Start-ups and the Entrepreneurial City," *City* 21, no. 2 (2017): 232–39.

37. N. Phelps and J. T. Miao, "Varieties of Urban Entrepreneurialism," *Dialogues in Human Geography* 10, no. 3 (2020): 304–21.

POSTSCRIPT

1. N. Wolfe, *The Viral Storm: The Dawn of a New Pandemic Age* (New York: Macmillan, 2011).

2. The intersection of global cities and infectious disease had already been made apparent a decade before SARS-COV-2 by S. H. Ali and R. Keil, eds. *Networked disease: Emerging Infections in the Global City* (London: John Wiley & Sons, 2011). I pick up the necessity of not forgetting these lessons with several of the same colleagues in M. Acuto, S. Larcom, R. Keil, M. Ghojeh, T. Lindsay, C. Camponeschi, and S. Parnell, "Seeing COVID-19 through an Urban Lens," *Nature Sustainability* 3, no.12 (2020): 977–978.

3. R. de Graaf, "At Your Service: 10 Tips for Becoming a Successful Urban Consultant. Interview with Reinier de Graaf," *Dezeen*, 5 February 2015.

4. N. Klein, *The Vatican to Vegas: A History of Special Effects* (New York: New Press, 2004), 11. I owe a note of gratitude to Leslie Sklair for pointing out this excellent work to me.

5. T. Bunnell, "Urban Aspirations," *The Wiley-Blackwell Encyclopedia of Urban and Regional Studies*, ed. A. M Orum, D. R. Judd, M. García Cabeza, Pow C. P., and B. R. Roberts (London: Wiley Blackwell, 2019). Bunnell draws here on A. Appadurai, "The Capacity to Aspire: Culture and the Terms of Recognition," in *Culture and Public Action*, ed. V. Rao and M. Walton (Stanford, CA: Stanford University Press, 2004), 59–84.

6. P. Bourdieu, "Symbolic Power," *Critique of Anthropology* 4, no. 13–14 (1979): 83.

7. In many ways, subjugation can be far less conspicuous than what our common imaginary of the term gives away: as Bourdieu notes, a "captive" audience of listeners is also subject to the symbolic power of a speaker, and the production of distinction (or commonality) applies to many mundane activities of our everyday lives. P. Bourdieu, *Masculine Domination* (1998; Stanford, CA: Stanford University Press, 2001), 41.

8. D. Massey, "Geographies of Responsibility," *Geografiska Annaler. Series B, Human Geography* 86, no. 1 (2004): 5–18.

9. C. Cahill, "Including Excluded Perspectives in Participatory Action Research," *Design Studies* 28, no. 3 (2007): 325–40.

10. M. Cronin and S. Simon, "Introduction: The City as Translation Zone," *Translation Studies* 7, no. 2 (2014): 131.

11. K. Easterling, *Extrastatecraft: The Power of Infrastructure Space* (London: Verso, 2014).

12. Ibid., 213.

13. D. Drezner, *The Ideas Industry* (New York: Oxford University Press, 2017).

14. I. Docherty and D. Smith, "Practising What We Preach? Academic Consultancy in a Multi-disciplinary Environment," *Public Money and Management* 27, no. 4 (2007): 273–80.

15. L. Wacquant, "Symbolic Power and Group-Making: On Pierre Bourdieu's Reframing of Class," *Journal of Classical Sociology* 13, no. 2 (2013): 274–91. Bourdieu is particularly concerned here with highlighting the ways in which certain social classes, through the division of labor but also via media such as television and other cultural artifacts, maintain their grip on society. He puts much emphasis on the violence and domination embedded in symbolic power as the pursuit of distinction. Yet the overall logic of symbolic power asks us, more generally, not to underplay the power relations embedded in the production of difference and commonality.

16. S. Montero, "Leveraging Bogotá: Sustainable Development, Global Philanthropy and the Rise of Urban Solutionism," *Urban Studies* (2018): 1–23, online first, https://doi .org/10.1177/0042098018798555.

17. J. Robinson, "Cities in a World of Cities: The Comparative Gesture," *International Journal of Urban and Regional Research* 35, no. 1 (2011): 1–23.

18. D. Massey, "On Space and the City," in *City Worlds*, ed. D. Massey, J. Allen, and S. Pile (London: Routledge/Open University, 1999), 158.

19. T. Bunnell and D. PS Goh, "Urban Aspirations and Asian Cosmopolitanisms," *Geoforum* 1, no. 43 (2012): 1–3. See also: A. Appadurai, *The Future as Cultural Fact: Essays on the Global Condition* (London: Verso, 2013).

20. D. A. Ghertner, *Rule by Aesthetics: World-Class City Making in Delhi* (New York: Oxford University Press, 2015).

21. E. Apter, *The Translation Zone: A New Comparative Literature* (Princeton, NJ: Princeton University Press, 2006), 5.

22. A. H. Ong, "Introduction: Worlding Cities, or the Art of Being Global," in *Worlding Cities*, ed. A. Roy and A. Ong (New York: Wiley & Sons, 2011).

Index

www.ingramcontent.com/pod-product-compliance
Lightning Source LLC
Chambersburg PA
CBHW031127270326
41929CB00011B/1528